PIAGET
SYSTEMATIZED

The author with Jean Piaget

PIAGET
SYSTEMATIZED

Gilbert E. Voyat

The City College of
The City University of New York

With a Foreword by Jean Piaget

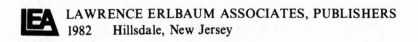
LAWRENCE ERLBAUM ASSOCIATES, PUBLISHERS
1982   Hillsdale, New Jersey

Lawrence Erlbaum Associates, Inc., Publishers
365 Broadway
Hillsdale, New Jersey 07642

Library of Congress Cataloging in Publication Data

Voyat, Gilbert:
  Piaget systematized .

  Bibliography: p.
  Includes index.
  1. Child development. 2. Cognition in children.
3. Piaget, Jean, 1896–   . I. Title.
LB117.V69   155.4′13′0924   81-17283
ISBN 0-89859-026-4   AACR2

Printed in the United States of America
10   9   8   7   6   5   4   3   2   1

In Memoriam of Jean Piaget with my deepest gratitude. To my wife Mary, with all my love.

Contents

Foreword by Jean Piaget   xi
Preface   xv

INTRODUCTION   1

TASKS

    Geometry   31
    Space   51
    Number   79
    Time   103
    The Development of Movement and Speed   113
    The Development of Physical Causality   131
    The Development of Early Logic   149
    The Development of Formal Logic   175
    The Determination of Cognitive Maps   191

EPILOGUE   197

REFERENCES   201

SUMMARY INDEX OF STAGES   203

Préface

Cet ouvrage n'a rien d'un guide pour s'orienter dans nos trop nombreux ouvrages, ni d'un aperçu théorique de l'ensemble de la théorie opératoire du développement cognitif : son objectif est essentiellement de faire comprendre la signification et l'importance de la notion de stade par opposition à la simple succession des âges, en cherchant à dégager les patterns typiques de développement qui caractérisent chacun de ces stades.

Pour atteindre ce but, l'auteur s'est livré à l'analyse détaillée de 150 épreuves couvrant les différents domaines de (plus de) la pensée opératoire, infra-logique aussi bien que logique, ce qui lui permet de montrer l'étendue des stades pour des âges donnés aussi bien que les conduites typiques correspondant à ces stades.

Quant au plan de l'ouvrage, une première partie porte sur l'analyse des critères utilisés de la détermination des stades et la manière dont les difficultés ont été résolues à cet égard. Une seconde partie décrit les 150 épreuves utilisées et la troisième, en dégageant les patterns déjà mentionnés, en montre la concordance de la théorie opératoire des (chercheur) stades.

Au total, cet ouvrage est un bon instrument d'~~effort~~ analyse montrant les avantages d'un examen opératoire pour l'appréciation des avances et des retards d'un sujet donné. Il faut féliciter G. Vosal d'avoir réussi cette entreprise ~~difficile~~ difficile et fournit un si bon instrument d'utilisation pratique.

Jean Piaget

Foreword

Jean Piaget

Let me say first what this book does not do. It does not present or explain my writings, nor clarify my operational theory, nor recapitulate my view of cognitive development. Its basic purpose is to bring out the meaning and importance of the *stages,* showing that they are not a mere sequence of operational forms of behavior and clearly describing the typical development and behavioral patterns characteristic of each one.

The work is a contribution of major importance in that it gives a detailed account of over one hundred and fifty of our experiments concerning the logical and infralogical aspects of operational development. This approach enables the author to define the stages, which are so often misunderstood, quite clearly, and to illustrate the reactions that characterize them. Not only is a considerable portion of our experimental work carefully described, but the relationships between the different experiments are pointed out also, so that the differences and similarities between distinct areas of cognitive thinking become plain. More particularly, a vital distinction is drawn between *age* and *stage,* so dispelling the confusion embodied in so many interpretations. For the essential thing about the stages is their sequence: The age at which a given stage is reached may vary from one social environment to the next.

We should remember that aside from the various activities of followers of the Geneva school and the spread of our ideas in the United States, the mainstream of American experimental psychology is still largely in thrall to a behaviorist ideology that continues to put up vigorous and sophisticated resistance to any aspect of my theory based on a constructivist epistemology—and indeed to any theory founded on the idea of overall structure. To the idea of successive synthesis, attained by means of dynamic equilibrations between horizontal and vertical extensions of thought within a context of sequential structural reconstructions, the average American psychologist or educational theorist responds by dismissing the whole thing as a reflection of what he calls the "Genevan enigma." This attitude is compounded by the constraints imposed by the pragmatic and quasi-utilitarian approach that dominates American psychology and educational theory, an approach founded on the notion of the acceleration of development within the context of the individual, constant and rapid progress. The fact that this perspective remains basic to the concerns of so many American educators and psychologists gives rise to what we call the "American question."

Within such a context this book by my friend and colleague Gilbert Voyat should serve to clear up a good many problems. The child must have the chance to carry out structured operations, for what is indeed involved in our view is the construction, control and assimilation of reality by the subject himself. We do not think in terms of a subject whose activity is defined as a sequence of mimetisms and external determinations. For us reality is an original construction, not a "copy." In this connection it is worth noting two spheres in which the behaviorist influence makes itself felt in the United States. On the one hand we find an educational practice which, though doubtless open to a broad range of experiments in teaching methods, remains completely circumscribed by the imperative need to accelerate development at all costs. And on the other hand we find a theoretical psychology confined by a framework whose sole function, in reality, is to justify these pedagogical assumptions. In the eyes of many American educational theorists the period during which the child constructs an operational universe is inconceivable without thinking in terms of the earliest possible introduction of reading, writing, and arithmetic—these "three R's" being the sacred cows of U.S. pedagogy.

Ideologically speaking, operational theory has carved out an important place for itself in North America, yet it continues to exist in parallel with the dominant behaviorist school of thought, apart from it, and at odds with it. The success of behaviorism lies in the fact that it appears to answer those needs which are perceived as the most immediate ones of education. One of the problems with the operational view, from the behaviorist perspective, is the stress it puts on the individual's own activity, as well as the essential function of factors of assimilation and of equilibrium in cognitive development. For a majority of American educators, imbued as they are with the behaviorist precepts, the main contradiction in our theory derives from the fact that we set out to discover, analyse and explain how the child constructs reality, whereas the American "common-sense" approach proceeds in the firm belief that specific external manipulations and constant programming can successfully stimulate and shape individual development.

This amounts to treating development as an accumulation of successive specific forms of behavior and completely ignoring both overall structures and the autonomous activity of the subject.

One kind of interaction between operational theory and the predominant tendency of American experimental psychology is worth mentioning. This might reasonably be described as the "systematic operationalization" of our experimental procedures (to use the term in Bridgman's sense, which is very different from ours). This trend is clearly an attempt to integrate our theory. It has found expression in two areas. The first is the conceptual and theoretical sphere, where the work of Berlyne and that of Beilin best exemplify it. Interestingly enough, Berlyne dubs me a neo-behaviorist whereas Beilin prefers the label "neo-maturationist": here is a clear indication of how difficult it is for Americans to understand not only the notion of interaction but also that of new constructions as the outcome of internal regulations. The second area in which this tendency has made itself felt is the experimental and empirical one, where our work is operationalized, repeated or, modified according to the dictates of a methodology oriented, more often than not, toward statistical results rather than to the less quantifiable results obtainable by means of direct observation of the child's thought processes.

This last pitfall has been effectively avoided by Gilbert Voyat in the present work: Far from placing our efforts in some statistical setting, he lucidly portrays the structural context that is paradigmatic to our approach.

With regard to the two levels of interaction between behaviorism and operational theory, we should say that we are not excluding the possibility of areas of common ground between the two approaches: Indeed the discovery of such areas has indisputably given rise to many useful contributions and findings. A basic difficulty remains, however—one stemming from the epistemological foundations of our approach and not from problems of methodological or conceptual adaptation. The antagonism we come up against here reflects a confrontation between two methodological conceptions. For our part we have always sought to adapt our conceptual and experimental tactics to the questions we are asking. Behaviorism, on the other hand, defines its problems by the methods it has at hand. In the first approach the problem posed determines the method followed; in the second the methodological or statistical framework determines the formulation of hypotheses and the way in which problems are tackled.

Generally speaking attempts at integration along such lines tend to *confuse* the concept of operational evaluation with that of psychological testing, if not to *substitute* the latter for the former. Such confusion or substitution boils down to a subtel but real enough reversal of our viewpoint: We have never treated the development of intelligence as a steady accretion of specific reactions. Rather, we have sought to analyse intelligence as an overall structure and as a creative process.

xiv

Happily, this is the view of things taken by Gilbert Voyat in what follows. He is to be congratulated for successfully completing so daunting a task, and for supplying the American reader with a tool of great theoretical and practical utility.

Preface

The major purpose of "Piaget Systematized" is to provide the educator, the child psychiatrist, the clinical, developmental and school psychologist with a clinical tool that can help a cognitive evaluation and diagnosis of children and adolescents. The systematic presentation of more than 150 Piagetian tasks could easily lead to misunderstandings. In order to avoid this it may be useful to offer some clarification.

To describe the principal behavioral features of cognitive stages for each task provides the opportunity for repeating Piagetian experiments with a minimal effort and convenient materials (to the extent that it is possible). In addition this description clarifies which behaviors are characteristic of a particular age-range. This information allows for a comprehensive analysis of a child's cognitive structure and for a developmental diagnosis. However the book is more than a diagnostic tool. It can also help in deciding which types of cognitive interventions would be appropriate as well as how they can be devised and planned.

"Piaget Systematized" does not have a statistical basis. Piaget has often stressed that the clinical method and its results principally involve a comprehensive description of cognition. Piaget's descriptions cannot be taken from a statistical point of view. He is mainly interested in the manner by which intellectual operations are constructed, how they form, are stabilized in a child's mind and from where they derive.

Furthermore "Piaget Systematized" provides a fair characterization of some of the main contributions of the Genevan School of Psychology. The book presents in details eight essential domains of intellectual development, namely, space, number, time, movement and speed, elementary and formal logic, geometry and physical causality. Piaget's contributions are of course not limited to these domains. They cover the important areas of logical and infralogical thinking which constitute essential aspects of all knowledge. The structural features characterizing these domains can be discovered in specific cognitive skills, basic to school activities, such as the three R's. The tasks should be useful to assess actual and potential school performances

As a clinical tool "Piaget Systematized" provides an overview of cognitive behavior relevant to specific stages. Those stages reflect different levels of thought and have various criteria of organization. In this connection remember that cognitive stages involve an integration, a reorganization and an anticipation: each new stage integrates the previous one, contains its own laws of organization and anticipates the succeeding one. From a structural point of view, each stage has a developmental relation to both the preceeding and the succeeding one. This explains the overlap observed between stages: for instance, a first stage will cover an age-range of 4 to 6 years of age; a second can begin at 5 years and last until 7 years of age whereas a third one can begin at 6 years and last until 8 years of age. Bear in mind that each cognitive stage embodies a particular cognitive organization. This organization is reflected in the concept of stages and in the relevant behavioral patterns described here.

In short "Piaget Systematized" is a dictionary or perhaps a lexicon of typical cognitive developmental behaviors in the normal child and adolescent. Norms are given in terms of age-range and abnormal development is discussed from the point of view of delays (or sometimes advances) observed in various cognitive domains. It seems particularly important to have a development perspective, when confronted with behaviors that appear unusual or atypical.

Finally Piaget's greatness is his ability to enter into the minds of the children and describe the world as it appears to, and is lived by them. The perusal of this book should make it easier for the reader to enter into the child's mind and discover there an unlimited richness that these tasks by no means exhaust.

ACKNOWLEDGMENTS

The experiments on which this book is based were originally prepared by the Developmental Curriculum Project of the Eastern Home Office of the Prudential Insurance Company, Newark, New Jersey. Dr. Robert Hall is the Project Director. I would like to thank him here. He was one of the first to realize the necessity of such a study. I would also like to thank the collaborator of this book, Ms. Judith Auricchio Pope, who with a great deal of dedication, prepared the presentation of the tasks. Many colleagues and friends showed support for and interest in this project. To all of them I say thank you. Deserving perhaps special mention are those individuals whose help whether they are aware of it or not, was particuarly appreciated. Among them are Dr. Howard Gruber of Rutgers University, Dr. Jacques Voneche and Dr. Bärbel Inhelder of the University of Geneva, Dr. Bernard Kaplan of Clark University and Dr. Barbaba Wilson.

Finally I wish to thank by wife Mary for her constant and lasting support in my effort.

Gilbert Voyat

PIAGET
SYSTEMATIZED

INTRODUCTION

The title of this study calls for clarification. After all, what does it mean to "systematize" Piaget?

Surely the title is given explanation through the content of the study and the idea behind the presentation in these pages of more than 150 experiments conducted by Piaget and his Geneva colleagues.

Yet, the concept of "explanation" itself gives me pause. Do I want to explain Piaget? Do I want to explain children? Do I want to show what children think, do, and believe at different moments of their lives? Do I wish to "map" the world children construct? Is this enterprise a pragmatic attempt to lay bare developmental intellectual processes? Is this book about understanding Piaget through the minds of children, or comprehending children through the mind of Piaget?

This last question alone poses a difficult and interesting experimental problem. Piaget, following Binet's tradition of careful behavioral descriptions, has promoted a genuine revolution in our understanding of human development; but on a theoretical level one can still ask the following important question: To what extent is this understanding biased by the particular philosophical position Piaget takes when observing children? It is by now commonly acknowledged that what is observed is transformed by the observer himself, and that an interpretation is inherently part of the theoretical framework from which it originates.

In thinking about the problems of explanation, I have found myself in various states of mind whose polarity is of some interest. At one extreme, I thought it crucial to explain the underlying theoretical concepts—the epistemological considerations and the abstract constructs—that Piaget had

1

come to use in his writing. However, from that point of view, it felt strange, if not paradoxical, that in order to present various aspects of a child's world, one would first have to approach by way of a thorough and comprehensive, theoretical and abstract prelude that would in effect clarify Piaget's own world. At the other extreme, I felt that to expose what children actually do and say when presented with a Piagetian experiment should be explanation enough: that a simple summary of the behaviors that had been observed in Geneva would reveal the child's world to us clearly enough that we might dispense with complex theoretical considerations.

I am aware that this polarity symbolizes a problem likely to be encountered by anyone seriously studying the intellectual development of children through dealing with Piaget's writings. It leads one to ask: Is Piaget difficult to understand because children are? Or is it because Piaget's writings are difficult to read that children seem difficult to understand? I will not answer directly, except to say that I suspect both propositions are in some sense true.

Having pondered these problems for quite a while, I came to the conclusion that I should first state simply how this book could be put to practical use. After all, pragmatic, down-to-earth considerations are not alien to the psychologist! As a matter of fact, this book is useful not only for psychologists but for the daily work of a great many people who deal with children. It is meant to be an effective tool; an instrument to be used for uncovering and understanding children's intellectual activities.

Let us consider some examples. Suppose you are a clinical or developmental or a school psychologist facing a child who presents a number of problems. You would like to know not only what the child's scores are on standardized tests but also the specific nature and area of the child's problems. You open this book and find it divided into three main sections: In the first there is a presentation of the conceptual framework; in the second you find 152 experiments; and in the third part there is, among other things, a chart of expected occurrence of behaviors at different ages. Should you want to explore some aspects of the child's conceptions of space, you can choose from 25 experiments those that seem most relevant to your goal. For instance, perhaps the child has problems with spatial orientation and with reversals, and you would like to determine whether this difficulty is broad or limited, whether it exists within a particular context, whether it reflects a developmental gap. There are, of course, other questions of the same nature that can be asked, but my point is this: The psychologist is, with this book, in a position to explore in depth the way the concept of space is organized in a given child. In other words, the book is like a file from which to choose according to one's immediate needs. This particular example of space concepts can, of course, be applied to each of the other cognitive domains treated in this book. It illustrates one type of cognitive exploration the book makes possible: exploration within a specific domain of cognitive functioning—an "intra-area" inquiry.

Consider another kind of use. The psychologist might want to explore aspects of the child's intellectual functioning in several different cognitive domains. It might be important, for instance, to determine whether there is a gap, and if so what type of gap, in a child's functioning in logic as compared with his performance in geometry. The psychologist can make such comparisons using some or all of the many experiments in any of the various domains. Indeed, he can eventually come up with a broad detailed picture of a child's intellectual functioning. Such a "cognitive map" allows one to assess the extent to which observed advances and delays can be considered normal, partially normal, or abnormal. Furthermore, the chart of expected occurrences of behaviors at given ages (Part III) can be used as a table of reference for making these decisions.

The examples I have given refer specifically to clinical and developmental psychologists, but they are relevant for a variety of other people who share an interest in children's intellectual functioning and its clarification, or for anyone seeking to identify cognitive structures within an individual child. Thus, although this book is a diagnostic tool, it is equally an educational one that can serve researchers as well as clinicians or teachers.

Let me now proceed with some remarks about Piaget's style and ways of presenting his findings.

THE CONCEPTUAL FRAMEWORK

"Operands" and "Structures"

One may distinguish two types of difficulties in reading a text of Piaget. The first is perhaps syntactical—or perhaps it is merely the style of the man himself. ("Le style est l'homme même," said the Comte de Buffon.) Piaget writes while thinking, thinks as he writes; and one is forced to follow that unique pathway of thinking.

But his mode of thinking is also reflected in the choice of words that are perfectly clear to him and not necessarily to us. Many Piagetian words are borrowed from other fields of science, and many do not have a meaning specific to psychology alone. Sometimes both aspects prevail in his choice of a particular term. This does not imply that his reasons are superficial ones or only the function of a very eclectic mind. His justifications are clearly related to his concern for understanding the nature of knowledge in a broad sense.

Let me give an important example. The word *operation* is basic to understanding Piaget. In *Six Psychological Studies,* it appears with a frequency of approximately once per page, as if this term must underlie the whole theory. As a matter of fact, it almost does. But what does it mean and what notions does it cover? What is its precise definition?

One definition, from the book just mentioned, is:

> An operation is in effect an internalized action which has become reversible and coordinated with other operations in a grouping governed by the laws of the system as a whole. To say that an operation is reversible is to say that every operation corresponds to an inverse operation as is true, for example, for logical or arithmetic addition and substraction (p. 121).

This definition itself poses numerous problems. One is related to the fact that the term *operation* has not only the general sense given here but also specific meanings. Piaget speaks of various types of operations: combinatory or formal, concrete, multiplicative, and others. What we have here is a generic term that has not only psychological connotations but also logico-mathematical ones.

As a matter of fact, in order to speak of an "operation," in Piaget's terms, four conditions should be fulfilled.

First, an operation is an *action,* an action performed either mentally or concretely. For instance, to unite two classes of objects into a new set (e.g., women + men = human adults) is an action that adults can perform mentally but that the child first performs with concrete objects before internalizing it in the form of a mental or symbolic operation.

The second condition is that an operation is an internalized action. In learning arithmetical operations the child may only understand them when manipulating objects. Later these arithmetical operations will interiorize themselves under generalized and abstract forms that can be applied to all objects. At the last stage of development, the child will be able to abstract any kind of object, as it is done in pure matematics. When that time comes, the child is no longer called child but adult or adolescent.

In this context, the development of mathematical notions can be conceived along three distinct levels, separated in time but functionally related. On the first level (preoperational) the child simply manipulates, acts with real concrete objects. They may be stones that he arranges. On the second level (concrete generalization), he will be able to use with any object a relationship that he has abstracted from a particular experience. This form of abstraction remains concrete because it is still related to a given content. Piaget, in fact, calls this second level of intelligence (concrete operational), concrete because it is based on experience with real objects, and operational because it involves abstractions from that experience. On the third level, the child can abstract any kind of object and use it in any form within a logico-mathematical framework. That is to say, he will use the abstraction itself as a new property and a new operation. This form of abstraction Piaget calls "formal," because it dissociates the form from any given content, the possible from the necessary.

Do these descriptions imply that any abstraction will be an operation? The answer is no. We still have to mention two other conditions that are necessary in order to speak of an operation.

The third condition of an operation is that an action not only *has* to be internalizable, it also has to be *reversible,* that is, that it can be performed in either direction. For instance, we can add but we can also subtract; we can unite but also dissociate. Obviously not every action is reversible. Smoking a cigarette is not a reversible action because we cannot unsmoke it. But if we pour water from cup A into cup B, we can pour it back; in this case our action is reversible.

This notion of reversibility is a fundamental one. It allows us to think operationally as a necessary condition for relating an initial state to a final one. Moroever it is directly related to the idea of "invariance" or "conservation." Without reversibility we would have no conservation or reciprocity. We would be unable to distinguish between a transformation and a state. Hence we have to understand what has remained constant during a transformation in order to understand not simply the transformation but even the initial and final states. Since a transformation is really an operation in itself, and since the states are related to each other by the transformation, it follows that the states are dependent upon the transformation. This point has many consequences and implications.

For example, if we present to a child a glass (A) of particular width and height, half-filled with water, and another glass (B), narrower but taller than A, and empty, we will call state S1 the situation in which A is half-filled and B is empty, and S2 the subsequent state in which B is almost filled but A is empty. We will call the transformation T the pathway from one state to another, that is to say in this case, the pouring from A to B, as well as the change of the water level in S2 since B is narrower than A. For the child to understand these two aspects of the transformation, he must be able to understand the operation of conservation, because this operation is precisely what has transformed S1 and S2. Furthermore, a correct description of the states themselves does not imply knowledge of the transformation.

This is how and why Piaget distinguishes between these two aspects of thinking: The figurative aspect deals with the description of states, concerns perception, and entails schemata; the operative aspect, on the other hand, provides understanding of pathways from one state to another, referred to as schemes of action and abstraction.

Before he has built adequate logical operations, the child thinks only in terms of the states; he thinks in an essentially figurative, preoperational, or intuitive way. When water is poured from glass A into glass B, the 4-year-old child will say that we have "more to drink" in B because the water level is higher. He does not yet grasp conservation. He merely compares the initial configuration to the final one. It is not that the child fails to note the pouring from A to B. The action itself is very well perceived, but the child does not use it to relate the states to each other. For him each state exists independently. He observes that the water level has changed and concludes that the quantity itself must have changed. In other words, he relies on perceptual features that though relevant, are not sufficient as evidence of conservation.

Such a child is called "preoperational" because he does not have the ability to use true reversibility. Yet his answer is not purely perceptual either; it represents partial understanding of the situation. When he has understood the meaning of the reversible action, he will use it to establish conservation. He will say, "The quantity does not change; we can pour it back; it is taller but it is also thinner, "thus rising two of the three possible justifications that appear at this level: identity, compensation, and reversibility. He will think in an operational manner in terms of the transformation.

The fourth and last important condition for existence of an operation is that it never be an isolated operation; an operation is always *interdependent with other operations*. Together they constitute a structured totality. Here we arrive at the notion of *structure*.

If we combine different operations and try to find their relations, we come upon another problem of formalization. On the one hand, there is no such a thing as an isolated operation, since an operation is always interdependent with other operations. Therefore it is essential to keep in mind that a structure concerns the relationship between operations that are separable as well as integrated. On the other hand, each operation has its own structure.

For instance, seriation has a logical structure that is apprehended in a different manner by the preoperational, the transitional, or the concrete operational child. Seriation is but one of the operations that a concrete operational child comes to understand. It has its own structure and also maintains a close relationship with the total realm of concrete operation to which it belongs.

In *Six Psychological Studies*, Piaget defines the word *structure* as follows:

> We shall define structure in the broadest possible sense as a system which presents the laws of properties of a totality seen as a system. These laws of totality are different from the laws of properties of the elements which comprise the system (p. 143).

This definition again poses problems. The essential idea involved in the notion of structures is that a particular moment of the development of the intelligence can be formalized or represented in a logico-mathematical way. In this sense, a structure is an abstraction but an astraction with a psychological meaning. Thus, when it is said that a child masters an operation (e.g., conservation), what is emphasized is the idea that this specific operation can be used by him as a general rule and will be manifest in many different instances of his behavior. It has become a "heuristic of behavior."

This study furnishes an extensive and organized framework of behaviors in which various theoretical concepts may be explored; it is the framework on which Piaget's theory of operations and structures has been built.

APPLICATIONS AND EXTENSIONS OF
THE THEORY

This consistent and well-built theory of Piaget's has given rise to many extensions. Some of these consist of systematic replications of the experiments among various cultures. This is extremely useful and constitutes what could be considered horizontal extension; it tests the theory under different and often much better controlled circumstances.

Other extensions are various theoretical and experimental studies referring to a Piagetian framework. These can be useful too, in clarifying concepts and contributing to development of the field itself.

In this context there is another tendency that need to be mentioned: a tendency to talk more and more about Piaget's concepts (e.g., notably, "conservation") while forgetting (or even neglecting to study) the initial materials, experimental conditions, and observed behaviors that gave birth to the concepts. This happens, paradoxically, partly because certain classic experiments have been so much discussed, so often and so widely replicated or adapted, that some people know them "by heart" and others think they do—and some must have the impression that Piaget has spent half of his life pouring water from one beaker to another and the other half developing a genetic-epistemological "theory of conservation"! Discussion that does not tie Piaget's concepts to his procedures and observations of behavior creates a tendency to stereotype, to simplifying the real, which can lead to stultification of the theory itself.

The fact is that understanding or testing a Piagetian concept requires knowing how Piaget's experimental exploration of it was performed. In the famous conservation experiment already alluded to, for instance, it is essential that the child perceive all the transformations, and this means returning to an initial configuration after one transformation before proceeding to the next; otherwise the logical analysis of the *concept* is *not* possible from the point of view of a process oriented approach. If the experimenter, having poured from one of two identical wide beakers to a narrow one, does not pour back from the narrow to the wide beaker before going to the next transformation, the intent and meaning of the experiment are lost. In this connection, the present study can serve a very useful purpose as a source book that describes a great number of Piaget's original experiments, as they should be administered.

An interesting phenomenon, then, is this dual, in some ways contradictory, evolution of Piaget's influence: On one hand there are theoretical, if not philosophical, reflections; on the other hand, experimental extensions. All this opens the possibility of polarizations, tensions, new contradictions, new findings—sources of development of the theory itself. But there is also the clear and present danger of theoretical rigidification and stagnation, through neglect of Piaget's specific procedures and oversimplification and premature "applications" of his findings.

Since Piaget is concerned with epistemology, the study of the nature and grounds of knowledge, it is not without good reason that he has chosen to work with children to understand the emergence of knowledge. Unlike his predecessor Kant, he attempts exerimentally to demonstrate how cognitive categories are constructed. Yet he has insisted on an experimental background broad enough that its results allow interpretations such as to serve the theory of knowledge and its development.

A comment of Seymour Papert (McCulloch, 1965), reminds us of the conceptual and experimental necessities to which Piaget has constantly obligated himself:

> The advantages of this genetic approach are obvious. The structure of thinking of children is simple enough for simple experiments to lay bare its epistemological architectonics and show operations . . . processes similar in nature to those postulated by philosophers . . . (p. xv).

By his observations of children, Piaget is guided to formulate more precise theoretical tools for the conceptualization of the mechanisms of knowing than any classical epistemologist ever possessed.

Veritably, Piaget is the prototype of the experimental philosopher who is also a philosophical experimenter!

SCOPE AND FORMAT OF THE SYSTEMATIZATION

One of the first decisions I had to make in this enterprise was how to choose from among so many original and very creative experiments those which would best serve the purposes and intents my study reflects. This first and fundamental decision was not easy to reach. It was based finally, in the main, on recognition of the importance and widespread influence of the work published since 1940 on various specific cognitive areas—logic, space, time,and so forth. I also included the area of physical causality as originally conceived in 1927, for reasons that will become clear later. As to the other considerations, it is essential—and must suffice—for the moment to note that the cognitive areas chosen constitute fundamental aspects of intellectual development and are relevant to developmental, clinical, and educational psychology. In Part II, I will present a short introduction to each area systematized, discussing characteristics and significance from psychological and epistemological points of view.

The 152 experiments cover eight areas of cognitive function that were explored and studied in Geneva for many years. More precisely, they were investigated at different periods of the Geneva history, and this fact underlies another implicit intention of this study. There has been virtually no study of the overall epistemological development the Piagetian school has undergone. I felt it could be of interest to represent—making sectional cuts, so to speak— various and rather widely separated moments in the experimental life of Piaget's Geneva. It is in fact the main focus of a recent study with J. Glick (Glick & Voyat) Piaget Reexamined (in preparation)

Technology itself has of course very much changed our lives during the time span of the Geneva experience. It is not my intent to analyze the effects of these and other developments on Piaget's work, since that would constitute an entirely different study. Yet in attempting to understand the coherence of the theory, the notion of stages and structures, the modifications of experimental goals over the years and their impact upon presentation and results, surely it would be helpful to proceed through sectional cuts in time. The material presented here represents, after all, the work of more than 30 years!

Let me now outline the general scheme of the presentation of the experiment.

The experiments are grouped in eight cognitive areas or domains. They are numbered consecutively throughout and also by code and number within areas. The domains are as follows (listed here to show their ordering, the number system, and the number of experiments in each domain): *Geometry* (1:G1-19:G19); *Space* (20:S1-44:S25); *Number* (45:N1-69:N25); *Time* (70:T1-76:T7); *Movement and Speed* (77:M1-91:M15); *Physical Causality* (92:C1-13:C22); *Early Logic* (114:E1-137:E24); *Formal Logic* (138:F1-152:F15).

Within the domains, the experiments are ordered as they appear in the books in which Piaget and his colleagues have reported them. (In almost all cases, all experiments in a given domain are from a single book.) These various sources are identified, and the location of each experiment is further cited by chapter. The bibliographical references are to the original French-language editions. All of these have been translated into English in editions still in print. However, the translations have come out in quite haphazard sequence, and often many years after the original publications. The references to the French editions provide the real time sequence, which is as follows (in terms of the area designations listed above): Physical Causality (1927); Number (1941); Time (1946); Movement and Speed (1946); Geometry (1948); Space (1948); Formal Logic (1955); Early Logic (1959).

Each experiment has as headline the "principle" designating the particular concept or cognitive function it explores. This is followed by a description of the task itself. I have tried to make these descriptions complete enough to facilitate replication, and to allow an easy demonstration to the child particularly by teachers, without violating the essence and intent of the naturalistic clinical method for which Piaget has been both credited and criticized.

Following the task, the reader will find brief descriptions of the behaviors characterizing developmental stages, relative to that task, and the age-ranges those behaviors cover. All this of course is based on Piaget's own descriptions, protocols, and discussions.

In addition to this basic presentation (sometimes referred to hereafter as the "index of behaviors"), I supply in the chart in Part III, on page 000-00, a "summary index of stages," a graphic summary of the age-ranges of all stages, for all the experiments, which also provides a quasi-quantitative index of "expected occurrences"—indications of how likely it is that a child of a given age will be at a given stage.

Thus the systematization as a whole comprises two main sets of information. The first names the principles explored and describes the tasks, specifying and often illustrating the materials to be used. It is also an index of *tasks* used to explore concepts and cognitive functions. The second defines *stages* in terms of observed behavior, age-range, and expected occurrence at a given age.

LOGIC OF THE SYSTEMATIZATION

My treatment of stages, in the presentation of the experiments, is of course meant to report briefly what behaviors Piaget found, at what ages, and how he classified them in stages. However, I wanted to simplify matters somewhat. Moreover, I encountered certain other problems requiring decisions about the presentation of stages and age-ranges.

Before discussing these in detail, I should remind the reader of two general aspects of the stage theory.

The experiments are of two kinds. Some require, for successful completion of the task (achievement of the principle involved) the use of formal thinking; for these, stage 4 is the last stage indicated. The other experiments do not require the formal level of thought but are successfully completed at the concrete operational level; for these stage 3 is the last stage. Stages 1 and 2 are always characterized by preoperational behaviors, stage 3 by concrete operations, stage 4 by formal thinking.

The reader should know that according to the general theoretical framework the preoperational level of development lasts from 2 till 6 or 7 years of age, the concrete operational period starts at about 7 and ends at about 9–11, and the formal level begins at about 9–11. Piaget especially cautions against the ridigity of assigning an upper limit of 15 years for the mastery of the formal level of thinking. Although our age-range specifications do not go beyond 15 years of age, the reader should keep in mind that this upper limit can be in many instances stretched to a much later age (Piaget, 1972).

Criteria for Presentation of Stages

Piaget in his presentations usually describes not only stages but also substages. For example, in experiment 20 S1, in which he reports three stages, the first two are subdivided: 1a, 1b; and 2a, 2b. Although there are many differences between the substages, they do not constitute separate stages. I have provided a one-stage treatment for all such cases, because it was my intent to present a summary of global stages with their most crucial behavioral features. However, the reader will often find ways to identify intrastage changes in the behavioral descriptions of stages: references to "initial" or "beginning" phases and to "later" development, indications that the child "increasingly" or "progressively" or "gradually" exhibits certain behaviors, and so forth.

There are some cases in which Piaget's presentation begins with stage 2 because stage 1 is characterized by the inability of the child to comprehend the problem itself. This is the case, for instance, in experiment 35 S16, dealing with understanding of the conic sections. Stage 2, the first described by Piaget, covers the age-range 4 to 8, and stage 3, also described, begins at 6 and ends at 9 years of age. Piaget's treatment implies that this task addresses itself to older children, even though the stage 2 age-range begins at 4. In such cases I have indicated an age-range of 4–5 for stage 1. What this means in practice is that very few young children can be expected to understand the task. When stage 1 is shown as having an age-range of 4–5, this generally means that children 3–4 years old or younger could not profitably be questioned on the given task.

There are similar cases in which four stages are mentioned by Piaget but only three are described. In experiment 36 S17, for instance, stage 2 covers the age-range 5 to 7; stages 3, 7 to 11; and stage 4, 11 to 12. In such cases also I assign to stage 1 the age-range 4–5, with the meaning defined above.

Sometimes, as in a whole series of geometry experiments beginning with 5 G5, Piaget describes and illustrates stage 1 and substage 2a together in terms of one set of behaviors, and treats substage 2b separately. In all such cases, the first stage in my presentation is labeled 1–2a, the second is 2b, and the third is 3. Usually the examples given by Piaget do not specify which children are at stage 1 and which at substage 2a. In 8 G8, however, the youngest child described, between 4 and 5 years of age, is assigned to stage 1, and the next youngest, between 5 and 6, to substage 2a. In this case, as in the others, I give the total age-range for stage 1–2a as determined by the ages of all the children described (including, in this case, the 4-year-old).

Similarly, when my first stage is labeled 1–2, this means that Piaget reports one set of preoperational behaviors typically starting at stage 1 (and with the youngest child described usually 4 or 5 years of age) and lasting through stage 2 (till 7 or 8 years of age), as in experiments 1 G1 and 25 S6.

The reader will see a very few other special situations in which my presentation of stages reflects Piaget's grouping of two or more stages (e.g., 125E12) or his failure to exemplify one or more stages (123E10).

My main intent in the labeling and grouping of stages and substages was to provide an easily accessible file that reports Piaget's own usages systematically but without introducing complications having more to do with theoretical than with practical considerations.

The same intent guided my resolution of a related but somewhat more difficult problem: determining criteria for representing the lower and upper age limits (i.e., the age-ranges) for stages, given Piaget's various kinds of indications.

Criteria for Age-Ranges

In describing behavioral stages for a given experiment, Piaget sometimes provides one kind of information, sometimes several kinds, about the ages associated with the observed behaviors. The underlying logic of his mode of presentation has probably to do with the evolution of the notion of stages over the years—an epistemological problem not dealt with in this study.

He almost invariably presents a number of examples (protocols) reporting individual children's actual responses, verbal and othewise, to illustrate each stage. These examples are usually identified by the children's names (in abbreviated form) and their exact ages (in years and months), and presented in order of increasing age. (In his notation, 7;3 means 7 years and 3 months. In my discussions I shall use, the notation 7.3.)

Sometimes Piaget defines an age-range generally, perhaps in a heading or in the course of discussion, by referring to the beginning and/or ending ages of a stage. Most often such a reference says or implies that these lower and upper limits are approximate. (For example, he may define an age-range as being from 4–5 to 7–8 years, or as lasting till "about 4;6 years," or as beginning "on the average" at 7 years.) Some caution is required in interpreting such references (often parenthetical), since it is not always clear whether they refer to observed behaviors in the given experiment or to Piaget's general theoretical age hierarchy of stages.

Sometimes Piaget includes among the descriptions of individual children a case explicitly noted as being exceptional (e.g., "advanced" or "very precocious"). And sometimes he mentions specific ages of children whose behavior belonged to a given stage but is not described; my inference usually is that some or all of these cases are exceptional.

In general, I have used the following rationale in determining age-ranges for my presentation: When examples of individual children are given, I have used them as will be explained to define the range, excepting only cases that seemed clearly exceptional. In the absence of such examples, I have taken the general definition as valid. Some variations on this system have been required, for practical or theoretical reasons; but in general they represent no more than ones year's difference between alternative indications. My intention always is to use and represent the clearest possible evidence of Piaget's own judgments about what ages were most *typically* associated with the kinds of behavior being described.

In using individual examples to define an age-range, I use the age of the youngest child described to define the lower limit and that of the oldest child for the upper limit. But I simplify the presentation by changing the given year-and-month ages to integral year levels. For the lower limit I take the *lower* level of the year span in which the *youngest* child's exact age (e.g., if the age is anywhere from 4.0 to 4.11, then I use age 4 as the lower limit of the range). For the upper limit I take the *upper* level of the *oldest* child's year span (e.g., if the age is anywhere from 7.0 to 7.11, then the upper limit is age 8). Obviously this slight extension downward and upward is entirely justified by Piaget's own usage, and most especially by his basic conception of one age-range of a stage.

To illustrate some of the situations that arise in determining age-ranges, I will describe my treatment of the various stages for experiment 41 S22.

Of stage 1 Piaget says only that it is "omitted as outside the possibilities of experimentation." In such cases, as explained in the previous section, I present stage 1 with the age-range 4–5, meaning that few children aged 4 or younger can be expected to handle the task.

For stage 2 Piaget gives several age indications. In a heading he defines the age-range as being from 4–5 to 7–8. In the examples given, the age of the youngest child is 5.1 and that of the oldest is 6.6. Following the examples, he adds that many similar examples were found between the ages of 5 and 7, "and even up to 8;2 and 8;6 (one case even of 9;1)." I treat these ages (8.2 and older) as exceptional; but because Piaget defines the upper limit as 7–8, I use age 8 as the upper limit rather than age 7 (which would be indicated by the last example given: age 6.6). For the lower limit, however, I use age 5 (indicated by the first example given: age 5.1) rather than age 4 (from Piaget's lower limit definition: 4–5).

Of stage 3 Piaget says that it appears (begins) "about the age of 7 or 8"; and examples are given for substages 3a (ages ranging from 7.3 to 10.6) and 3b (7.6 to 10.5). No decision is required here. I combine the substages, as explained in the previous section, and use the ages 7.3 and 10.6 to define the range: 7–11.

For stage 4 the only information given is the examples (ages ranging from 10.11 to 12.1). Thus the range is 10–13. Generally, I have acted according to the following principle: When ages and age-span were clearly indicated, I have taken them as valid information. When only individual examples were offered, I have used them to define the age-span provided that no other information was given.

Now let us examine some implications of these age-range indications. In experiment 41 S22, as we have seen, stage 4 (stage of achievement) covers the age-range 10 to 13. This means that mastery of the principle involved can be attained by some children by age 10. We do *not* know what proportions of subjects at stage 4 were at ages 10, 11, 12, and 13. (We do not even know for sure that a subject who at stage 4 when tested at age 13 had not already achieved that stage when he was 9). We also observe that stage 3 behavior occurs at least until 11 years of age for some children. In other words, the age-ranges of these stages overlap at ages 10 and 11. In this case, what we are *not* in a position to determine is what proportion of subjects aged 10 or 11 were at stage 3 and what proportion at stage 4.

The reader will understand why this is so. To provide such proportions would require controlled replication of each experiment—duplication of a substantial amount of Piaget's original work—an enterprise totally beyond my aims and possibilities. (Such work is actually being done in Geneva by Dr. Vinh Bang.) My intent is to systematize some of Piaget's work, not to provide statistical norms.

Yet my presentation is not simply a qualitative systematization. In the age-range chart I supply an index of expected occurrence of behaviors at given ages, which I will explain later. Moreover, the basis stage age-range presentation permits a considerable degree of accuracy and contains all the information required to discuss Piaget's theory of development in terms of stages. For instance, referring again to experiment 41 S22: since stage 3 covers the age-range 7 to 11, we can certainly assume *theoretically* that it is normal for a 9-year-old child, in the middle of that range, to be at stage 3, that a 9-year-old who is at stage 4 (age-range 10-13) is advanced one year, and that a 9-year-old at stage 2 (age-range 5-8) is delayed one year.

GUIDELINES FOR CLINICAL JUDGMENT

To use this study as a clinical tool, one needs criteria by which to judge the stage achieved by a child not from a theoretical point of view but from a practical one. The following general guidelines can help the clinician to establish such criteria. The reader should keep in mind that criteria should not be rigidly applied but clinically weighted. The reader should also keep in mind that Piaget's experiments are not *tests*. They are tasks that help to elaborate a "cognitive map," a unique cognitive organization: the real child as opposed to the theoretical one.

If in comparison to a theoretical age-span a real child presents a one-year advance or delay on one or a few tasks, this is not in itself a sign of abnormality. A delay of more than one year (even if it is less than two years) might require attention and should be investigated further, using a number of tasks in each of several areas of intellectual functioning. The mere presence of a delay on one task or a set of similar tasks is certainly not sufficient to make a definitive judgment about the case. *Any* child will show *some* advance or delay. *What matters is overall cognitive organization, not the result in a specific experiment.*

In fact, although the question of the determination of the criteria of stages is still open to experimental investigation, it is nevertheless valid to assert that the typical normal cognitive organization of a child necessarily entails heterogeneous global organization. For example, a normal child might be at stage 2 for one experiment in space, at stage 1 for another in the same area, and at stage 3 for an experiment in early logic.

In order to determine a global picture of a child's cognitive functioning it is necessary to determine the general level of functioning within each cognitive area. Each principle explored is part of, and serves for the determination of a stage within an area of cognitive functioning. The cumulation of several principles within a given area allows a global determination of intellectual functioning in this area, and comparison of such determinations among the different areas offers the possibility of an overall cognitive assessment.

In short, both types of investigation can be pertinent; the choice of one or the other (or both) will depend upon the clinician's needs, which in turn must be concerned with the needs of the child. Comparison within an area (e.g., space) will place the clinician in a position to localize, define, and detail the child's potentialities and deficiencies in the given domain. Comparisons between areas (e.g., space and early logic) will provide a broader clinical picture of these potentialities and deficiencies. One cannot insist enough on the simple criterion that the child's needs, and not merely the clinician's more general goals and hypotheses, should at all times be a primary consideration. This leads me to emphasize now the clinical method of observation.

THE CLINICAL METHOD

The Genevan method of inquiry is properly part of the psychological tradition of naturalistic observation. My systematization respects the intent of such a mode of investigation, and some of its salient characteristics will be discussed here.

Piaget's experiments are not standardized tests, and they should not be thought of or treated as such. They are conceptual explorations that do not call for a static, rigid presentation. The task descriptions supplied are meant to allow freedom in exploring the concept with the child and at the same time to provide a coherent structure for its investigation. Each experiment calls for logical organized actions of child and experimenter in a situation of collaborative effort between them. The Genevan method contrasts with standardized test procedures inasmuch as the latter take a predetermined approach to dynamic mental problems.

With the Piagetian method, for instance, there are no "right" or "wrong" answers, and no time limits, because the technique consists in continually adapting the exchange to the spontaneous reactions of the child. In exploring each concept, the examiner tries to follow the child's thought processes within a logically well-structured situation. The essence of the task description is to respect and capture this logic—in effect to define the concept—without crystallizing it into one unique way of administering the task.

Let me describe the modus operandi in some detail.

For each task, the child is first presented not with a question but with the materials he will be using. This moment, when the materials are presented, suitably arranged, should be considered as one that gives the child an opportunity to anticipate the logic required to fulfill the task. The initial presentation also allows the examiner an opportunity to motivate the child favorably. It should put the child in contact with the materials and with the examiner; it should help to develop rapport. The child might even be asked to make up a story. This technique can also serve to exhibit the child's own language usages, so that the examiner can follow suit in the questioning that will follow.

At the beginning, as throughout the task, the focus is on eliciting the spontaneous thoughts and actions of the child. What is to be ascertained is the child's own understanding, however that understanding is expressed— verbally or behaviorally. The experimenter does not distort the child's views by imposing his own order; rather he tries to follow the child's lead, as given by words and actions, to discover the child's intent. Thus (it cannot be too often emphasized), a particular task description gives only a general framework to follow. The *details* of the task must surely depend on the logic of the concept; but they *must also depend on the child.*

In the first place, plans for specific materials to be used, and for the wording of questions related to them, will sometimes need to be determined by the local situation or by what is already known about a particular child. In the second place, the experimenter needs to be ready at every moment to introduce variations suggested by the child's reactions at that moment to arrangements of materials and to questions asked. Questions already asked may need to be asked again using different wording. Materials already used one way may need to be used another way, or augmented by use of different but related representations.

By such variations of factors specified or implied in the task description, new information about a set of results may be obtained. For example, if there is uncertainty as to whether a child has offered a conceptual or perceptual solution to a problem, varying the perceptual factors might yield further and perhaps definitive results. Varying the way or the order in which questions are asked enables the examiner to double-check the child's understanding of what he was asked—to determine, for example, whether a child really understood a question the first time, or was merely repeating some part of it as his answer.

If it becomes clear that the child does not understand the task at hand, then the experiment should not proceed; some understanding of the initial question and the problem is a prerequisite of participating in the task.

Each time the child gives an answer, either verbally or through an action, he should be asked for a justification ("Why?" "How do you know?" "What would you do to show that's correct?"...). The justification is central, as it tells about the processes involved in the child's problem-solving and the stage of thinking he has attained. Non-verbal justifications are often obtained from non-talkative children. It is important not to interrupt the child, behaviorally or verbally, if a spontaneous result rather than a provoked response is to be obtained.

As another means of establishing the validity of an obtained result, the method known as counter-suggestion or contra-proof is sometimes useful. Using this technique, the examiner responds to a child's answer by saying something like this: "Well, but [somebody else] said just the opposite. Was he wrong? Are you wrong?" Such questioning can make clear how strongly the child is convinced of his expressed beliefs (right or wrong) as to the solution of the problem. A function of the contra-proof, then, is to aid in differentiation between operational, transitional, or preoperational behaviors, in borderline cases. It is generally used when there is a question about the strength of the child's response.

Observe that the contra-proof is not presented as a solution (even if it is one), but in the manner of a challenge. In fact, in Piagetian experiments there is no intent to present solutions to the child. The goal is to observe the child's own mode of operating.

The protocol should contain a precise recording of the verbal exchange between the experimenter and the child, along with precise descriptions of all activities and constructions. In short, it records everything the child does and says.

The information thus gathered and recorded allows the psychologist to determine what stage of cognitive development the child has attained.

It should be noted again that these stages are defined in terms of structured whole, not isolated pieces of behavior. Thinking that is characterized as "concrete," for instance, encompass a structure allowing the resolution of the concrete problems embodied in elementary classifications and logical relationships. This structure also implies that the child is able to grasp the nature of logical necessities as they are represented, for example, in an operation such as conservation of matter. The emergence of a structured whole allows generalization from one particular piece of behavior to others of the same type. The appearance of an operational group allows, as standardized test results generally do not, identification of a mental structure.

Structured wholes go beyond operations actually carried out and are the base for a whole system of possible operations. The pathway from a lower stage to a higher stage is equivalent to an integration, the lower becoming part of the higher mode. Concrete operations serve as a base for the formal operations of which they become part. The combinatorial method, for instance, is based on changes of order that are possible during childhood and later develop into combinatorial operations, as Inhelder (1970) explains in this comment:

> The structure of combined groups and lattices of formal thought marks the peak of adolescence. The structure develops between the ages of eleven and fourteen and reaches an equilibrium at about fifteen years.
>
> The group of formal operations integrates the partial groups in a structured whole. The adolescent carries out a group of formal operations of the lattice type when he makes a combinatorial analysis. For example, the adolescent can make up a mixture of a number of chemical solutions not merely by chance but through combinations associating each of the elements with all the others of the system. This reveals a new structure and shows an unlimited degree of reversibility and mobility (p. 341).

The hierarchy of structures, as well as the status of their coexistence at different levels of development, is still an open experimental question, and this study is in part an attempted toward its solution.

Piaget has argued that the succession of stages of cognitive development is constant but that the age at which the structures appear can be expected to vary. The age of achievement cannot be fixed. The age-range descriptions I have provided constitute an attempt to solve the problem of age-stage without violating Piaget's expressed characterization of his stages. They are based on structured wholes which follow one another in a constant order according to a law of integration. The phases of integration govern dynamic processes in what Piaget calls "equilibrium" and are in fact at the source of the problem of the mechanisms of development. This study, which is in a sense an attempt to pose the problem itself, provides and offers some suggestions for solving it. I hope to clarify this crucial issue in developmental psychology: Cognitive development is both continuous and marked by moments of discontinuity when a new stage is achieved that signifies a qualitative change in the child's apprehension of the real.

When it comes to deciding what stage an individual child has attained with respect to a cognitive function or area, the child's global cognitive organization and his holistic nature become particularly crucial. The Piagetian model of intellectual development describes stages that are defined in terms of cognitive structures, and it represents the cognitive evolution of an abstract child—an epistemic subject. Whereas one is confronted with real children, the model's representations of stages and structures are not descriptions and interpretations of an individual subject but are part of an attempt at formal analysis of cognitive behavior.

The model derives from the observation of individual behaviors and becomes an epistemological abstraction. Construction of the model proceeds through conceptual steps at three levels:

1. The first level involves unstructured, intuitive observation of various behaviors which are broadly characterized. For instance, to state that a child is preoperational is to imply that this kind of intelligence is mediated through symbolic forms whose main meanings are, and, for quite a while, will remain a essentially egocentric, idiosyncratic, private, and largely unsocialized. This general and global connotation does not, in principle, leave room for heterogeneity among children so classified, since "preoperational thinking" refers to a global mode of apprehension of the real.

2. The second level involves the observation and description of individual behaviors that are then interpreted within the previous conceptual framework. Thus, when one infers from or interprets individual behaviors one proceeds, actually, from the first framework: from a reflection of an abstract model constituted by a summary of behaviors extracted among a population of children, whose conceptual similarities constitute a stage.

3. The third level involves the organizing of behaviors in a comprehensive abstract view of the epistemic subject.

Considered at this most abstract level, one of the impressive facts about Piaget's theory is the manner in which it is possible to differentiate between preoperational and operational behaviors through the relatively simple criterion of the subject's ability in coordinating several observations or relationships or cues among each other. The theoretical expression of the same fact can be found in the idea of "grouping" that Piaget used first in connection with the child's development of number and quantity and later in relation to time, movement, and speed.

It should be helpful here to describe the general form of almost all the experiments we possess concerning the genesis of the intelligence.

A child is confronted with a situation (concrete or abstract), realized by physical apparatus, or described by words, or both. Given this situation, a problem is posed and the child is invited to find the actions, directly or verbally that will answer the problem.

The general task of the psychologist will be to find a representation of the child's pathway—the child's solution—through a set of steps that may be of two kinds: operations of encoding of information, and operations of transformation of information (operations of composition).

One might suppose that operations of the first type do not go beyond the domain of perception. In a sense this is true, but what is actually more important than the action of encoding information is the selection of the information encoded.

One example will illustrate the problem, as well as the error of some psychologists who want to explain preoperational thinking through a simple formula such as, "The child is dominated by perception." Let me take the experiment (conservation of matter) in which one of two similar balls of clay (A and B) is later transformed into a long sausage shape (C). Consider the subject who judges that A and B are equal but then estimates that C is "more to eat" than A, even though the transformation of B into C has been made before his eyes. It is quite evident that the preoperational child judges quantity of matter according to the elongation of C. Yet it is not completely correct to state that his judgment is either entirely perceptual or solely dominated by perception. As a matter of fact, in order to estimate that C has "more" than A, one has to annul the global perception of the quantities of A and B, to the benefit of one *selected* aspect of the new configuration: the length of C.

Thus even in preoperational behaviors there are always strictly cognitive elements in the child's thinking. The act of annulling one dimension to the profit of another is not simply a perceptual judgment but entails cognitive factors too. The investigator must also be on guard to distinguish between the situation described or perceived by the experimenter and the situation represented or perceived by the child. Between these two realitites, sometimes referred to as subjective and objective, there is room for several kinds of misconception.

One kind of misunderstanding arises when the child's description and the experimenter's perception do not coincide, or promote the same interpretation. This is one of the reasons why the use of justifications by the child is so fundamental in the clinical method of investigation. It allows us as much as possible to relate to the child's own understanding of the situation presented to him.

Another failure of understanding occurs when the adult (teacher, psychologist, parent....) imposes or tries to impose his own description and interpretation of a situation upon the child. The role of "teacher" that most of us assume in front of children is not always inappropriate; but the purpose of Piaget's experiments is to conduct not a teaching enterprise but a learning one—a learning one for the experimenter as well as for the child. The experiments require of the experimenter a real decentration from the adult's world—something it is easy to talk about but not necessarily easy to do. The experiments all have the explicit goal of extracting the child's spontaneous thinking. They should never imply a judgment of the child by the adult.

The psychological distance between the child and the adult implies finally the necessity of a reciprocal interaction with its own dialectic and assimilative/accommodative connotations. The Piagetian model of experimenting cannot be autocratic.

This and other aspects of Piaget's clinical method have important relevance to factors in children's development, further analyzed in our next section.

FACTORS OF DEVELOPMENT

From Concrete to Formal Logic

Interesting questions about the pathway from concrete to formal reasoning are related to the factors of development. This pathway is very much marked by intervention of the social millieu, and a number of cross-cultural studies have shown that substantial delays occur in some milieus. This situations has led to serious questioning as to whether everyone needs to take this pathway. Whereas concrete operational thinking is cross-culturally observed—with advances and delays, to be sure, but everywhere observed—such is not the case with formal logic.

Concrete operations are clearly necessary for the intellectual adaptation of a majority of individuals, regardless of cultural background or sociological organization. Concrete operations involve the systematic manipulation, physical or mental, of concrete objects. To use Piaget's own frame of reference, such operations use an "intrapropositional" logic, since the child is concerned in deducing abstractions from the objects themselves. Concrete operations thus belong to the period of the child's life wherein he learns properties of classes, relations, number, and so forth, within a concrete context.

With the advent of the formal level of thought, a new evolution occurs: It is the acquisition of a combinatorial or "interpropositional" logic that deals with the construction of possible rather than necessary realities. At this level we construct abstractions of abstractions: logical operations to the second power. Perhaps the activity most characteristic of this thought is that of the mathematician, who constantly exercises formal operations in his work, dealing and playing with logical thinking—with possible realities rather than necessary ones. He proceeds in his method of thinking through exact deduction and induction.

Formal logic encompasses all possibilities and defines the last stage of development. It is in this sense that Piaget should be understood when he states that the formal level of thinking is the highest stage of cognitive development. It is the highest and also the ultimate stage of development, since one cannot logically conceive of a higher formalized stage, at a psychological level of functioning. This is a consequence of the theorem of Gödel (1931) that can be interpreted as follows: In order to find contradictions within a structure S1, one needs a structure S2 that encompasses S1 and permits a reflection from S2 upon S1. In the case of formal operations, this possibility is not real, since formal logic entails generalizations ad infinitum. This last stage is closed from the point of view of its structure (combinatorial nature or INRC grouping) and functionally capable of dealing with virtually an infinite number of problems and situations. It is in this sense that comparisons with "intelligent automata" can be made using the Turing machine, for instance, as a reference. Its paradox comes from the fact that a machine with finite states can generate and solve any conceivable problem, provided infinite space and time.

In short, the formal level of thought encompasses all possible worlds. Furthermore it is at this level of development that one might find the greatest gap between a cognitive structure and performance in its applications: Since the formal level of thought implies the greatest possibility of generalization and also entails complete dissociation between the form of an intellectual operation and its content, there is a psychological distance between the structure and its actualization.

This gap has two dimensions. In the first place, formal operations may be available and developed but not needed or wanted in all of our activities. In the second place, this structure may exist potentially, with concrete operations ready to be integrated, but not yet integrated and reorganized, into the higher order of generalization possible with formal thought.

Actually, all stages of development have this dual nature and meaning. On the one hand, they encompass characteristic abilities available to all appropriate moments; on the other hand, they deal with new possibilities offered at each new moment. Thus we have intelligence conceived simultaneously as a state (equilibrium, in Piaget's terms) and as a process (equilibration).

To return to formal logic. Suppose one does not see the necessity for everyone to travel the pathway from concrete to formal thought. Certainly one cannot claim that all people in a given population can be or need to be "walking mathematicians." Does this mean that formal logic could be the exclusive property of mathematicians or scientists whereas the rest of us could get along at a concrete operational level of thought? The answer is clearly no, but its justification cannot necessarily be found in a simple structural analysis taking into account psychological factors alone.

Let us consider further the first aspect of the dual nature of stages. Observe that even a mathematician will not be thinking formally in every sector of his activities. He might behave in quite preoperational ways in many instances. For instance, it is not doubtful that champion chess player Bobby Fischer can operate at a formal level of thought; as everyone knows, playing chess implies the use of combinatorial hypothetico-deductive thought, and in Fischer's case of course such use represents exceptional mastery. Yet as chess followers have come to realize, in reading about Fischer's erratic, apparently capricious behavior during the Icelandic championship match, many instances of his behavior could be considered childish, preoperational, instinctive, or impulsive, depending upon the school of psychology to which one belongs. The point is that Fischer presented contrasting types of behavior during the match. I am not denying that the total spectrum of behaviors displayed could have been in fact part of a strategy used by Fischer to "break" his adversary Spassky. Even if that is true, it does not mean that the contrast did not exist. It is also interesting to note that in this case emotions were used quite correlatively with cognition. It is also conceivable that this case is not an isolated one and that all human beings make use of heterogeneous levels of affectivity and cognition at all times—even though contrasts as marked as those of the example would not normally be observed in an experimental sample population. Yet it is an interesting case because the contrast between two types of behaviors, preoperational and formal, has been much publicized and has come to generate what could be called a "Fischer personality style."

The fact that the formal level of thought is conceived as the last and highest level of intellectual development does not mean that a real subject who has reached it should or could be consistently operating at that level. The real human being is not and probably should never be totally logical. What characterizes a human subject is probably his very heterogeneity; the coexistence of different levels of thinking is probably a source of continuous development. The epistemic subject is at a formal level of thought all the time! But the epistemic subject is the subject in abstraction and not an individual in particular!

Along with the formal level of thought per se, which allows maximum generalization, develops formal thinking which is more specialized. This form of thought will be used by an individual only in certain selected situations rather than continuously. Although always available, it is not always applicable. To quote Piaget (1970):

> The more development progresses and the more a subject advances in development, the more a diversity is found in given tasks and in individual abilities.... I daresay that I reason logically in the field of psychology or epistemology; but if you ask me questions in areas not known to me, say physics, I may well reason like an infant; my reasoning would be at an altogether inferior level as compared to that in my professional specialty. As a consequence I see no contradiction in observing individuals of any age who function quite logically in the limited area of their specialty but are quite retarded and on an inferior level in those fields that are outside their specialty.

This suggests that diverse behaviors comprise the normal situation; normality is essentially a situation of heterogeneity. And this underlines the necessity of studying a large number of cognitive areas in order to understand any given individual.

The role of specialization in the acquisition of the formal level of thought is related to certain questions concerning the role of social factors in the pathway from concrete to formal thought. In fact, social factors intervene in a dual manner. (*a*) Social factors intervene to determine the extent to which formal thought is needed in terms of the level of organization of a given society. (*b*) Social factors interevene to determine the proportions of children who will or can accede to the formal levelof thinking. Moreover, social factors are related to the socio-economic distrubition of a population, so this distribution itself determines in part which children will reach a given level of cognitive achievement.

A problem one faces in American education, for example, comes from the fact that the so-called low socio-economic groups (in simpler language, the poor) represent a quarter of the total population and that only a few of these children receive sufficient educational support to develop mastery in formal thought. It is one thing for an individual to have the formal level of thinking at his disposal and to choose to actualize it or not in different situations; it is another thing to be denied this choice as a result of an educational system. The existence of these two situations reflects a de facto educational unfairness.

It is of course obvious that highly technological societies have a greater need of formal thinkers than so-called more primitive societies. Technology stems from formal models (mathematical, architectural, ...) made into realities. This implies the necessity of an educational system correlative with the level of technology a society has achieved. And related to this fact are questions to be asked about the connections between the structure of a stage such as the formal level of thought, its presence or absence within an individual, and its relative distribution within a society or culture.

In cnsidering the results of comparative studies it seems to me essential to attend to three main issues.

1. In the first place, it is always most important to remember that it is individual children, with their own various needs and potentialities, that we must be concerned to understand.

2. Then there is the problem of the absence or the presence of a given stage of intellectual development for a given society as a whole. The relationship between levels of technological development and underlying types of cognitive levels is quite evident. A society comes to be called "primitive" because the level of its technology has not yet come to imply the extensive use of formal thinking. This is still open to experimental investigation. The expression "primitive society" makes sense only to the extent that one wants to determine the types of needs a "primitive" organization tends to fulfill. It does not imply the absence of formal thinking per se; it means only that in terms of logico-mathematical development most individuals have not achieved mastery of formal thinking. Primary needs, on the other hand, tend

to be of a concrete nature and as such imply universal use of a concrete operational form of thought. In this connection one should recall that Piaget's work is a reflection upon intellectual development taking place in a highly developed technological society.

Piaget has sometimes been accused of promoting the notion of an "ideal logico-mathematical thinker." I believe this is unfair because his observations are the results of a focus on necessarily stated relationships between individuals and on technological outcomes of those relationships in a particular society; they reflect a belief in a necessary relationship between a form of thinking and its use within a culture. Even in terms of this belief the accusation is not well founded, since Piaget is an observer of psychological and epistemological realities, not a would-be determiner of them.

3. Finally there is the problem concerning the number and distribution of individuals within a developed technological society who have achieved a formal level of thinking. If a greater proportion of individuals of low socio-economic status fail to achieve mastery of formal thought, we cannot assume it is the consequence of widespread lack of individual potential among the groups affected. We must uneasily suspect that a large segment of the population is prevented from achieving proficiency in formal thinking as a result of educational, that is to say environmental, circumstances not related to the general level of technological development. The fact is that both low and high socio-economic groups belong (I did not say adhere) to the same culture.

Our uneasiness derives in part from the belief that, given a high level of technology, formal thought should in principle exist in fair proportion among all segments of a population as a potentiality. A truly democratic system of education, then—that is to say a system which would in fact give equal chances of development—could be defined in terms of equal proportions of people acceding to the formal level of thought from their various socio-economic backgrounds. This surely sound utopian, but I cannot help thinking that it could be realized. Presumably it means changes in social and political priorities which would benefit society as a whole.

FROM PREOPERATIONAL TO CONCRETE LOGIC

We have considered in some depth the intervention of socio-cultural factors of development in the pathway from concrete to formal logic. When we come to analyze the earlier pathway from preoperational thinking to concrete operational thought, we find a different situation. This transition entails a more restricted permeability to social factors. The preoperational child as an intuitive and egocentric thinker sees a reality and constructs it essentially from one point of view. He has not yet mastered a coherent system for co-ordinating the points of view and perspectives which will allow him later to go beyond the directly perceptible. In a profound sense the appearance is the real, and abstract cognitive operations are not yet part of his world.

One of the main problems of the preoperational child is his dependence upon perceptual features. For him, conservation is only at best a possibility which has to be checked in each case, in each concrete situation. For him reality consists in a succession of perceptual configurations, in a decoding of static situations. Emotionally and cognitively he is plainly dependent upon an adult's reality; yet his own reality is qualitatively different from the adult's. Initially, he does not differentiate between his fantasy world—the product of his imagination—and the objective world.

His problems are indeed difficult at best. I am always astonished at our tendency, as adults, to add to those problems by overinsistence on imposing our own realities and standards. Some preoperational children have the burden of facing up to the high expectancies of teachers and parents who implicitly penalize children by trying to force their development, focusing on performance and competition. One preoperational children have to live down to the low expectancies that educational systems or personnel impose on them. These are quite effective burdens. Only later, if ever, will an individual realize what their impact on him has been.

When a child is learning how classify objects, he has not only the task of understanding that objects can be grouped in terms of their similarities ("comprehension" or "intension" of a set); he has also to coordinate the comprehension of a set with the number of objects in it (its "extension"). For a long time, during his preoperational period of thought, the child tends to confuse the number of objects he sees with the logical properties determining how these objects are grouped. Such problems in coordination can be readily observed in simple tasks of class inclusion. When a 5-year-old child is shown representations of 12 horses and 2 cows and is asked if horses and cows are both animals, he can adequately name the set: he knows that horses and cows are both animals. Yet when asked whether in front of him there are more horses or more animals, he says there are more horses than animals, confusing the extension of the number of elements in the set with their comprehension (the feature under which they are grouped). In effect, the extension of the set dominates his thinking; he displays a lack of equilibrium between compre-hension and extension of sets. This is only one of the types of difficulties that occur in constructing "logical" operations—only one of the kinds of problems a child must solve to achieve fundamental mastery of "elementary logic."

Classifications, seriations, and all other operations of the kind Piaget calls "logical" (as distinct from "infralogical") have three essential characteristics. First, logical operations involve entire objects or properties that can be isolated; to state similarities is to isolate features and group them abstractly.

Secondly, the position of the objects in space is irrelevant with respect to classification; in other words, where the objects are has nothing to do with the act of classifying them. Thirdly, logical operations deal with a discontinuous world.

One way to understand what logical operations accomplish is to be aware that they introduce continuity into a discrete world. When a child constructs operations dealing with space, time, or speed, he faces what Piaget calls "infralogical" operations. To construct an operation dealing with spatial measure, for example, is to understand how a continuous entity (a dimension of space) can be subdivided into units involving a metrical component. An operation dealing with speed may require measuring in at least two such continua (one in space, one in time). In such cases (involving measurement), as in all other kinds of infralogical operations, the child deals with parts of objects or entities, with a reality that has to be understood as a continuous one and where location within a continuum is of fundamental importance.

In a profound sense logical and infralogical operations are antithetical yet constructed simultaneously. This implies a real dialectic within the cognitive realm of thought—a dialectic that is probably sufficient in itself as a source of conflict to promote intellectual development. It is its own source of equilibrium and disequilibrium.

To sum up: The concrete operational period of thought is characterized by the acquisition of the notion of conversation, by the appearance of reversibility, and by the possibility of concrete operations inherent in manipulation of objects. There is an intrapropositional logic built that will be the basis for the interpropositional logic that characterizes the formal level of thought.

---

*In order not to make this kind of writing unduly distracting, I used throughout this study *he* rather than *he* and *she* and ask for the reader's indulgence.

TASKS

Geometry

INTRODUCTION

Almost all of us have some intuitive concept of geometry and have had some experience with it in school. Retrospectively, "geometry" comes to represent a school subject dealing with "rectangles, triangles, circles, ..." One also remembers that, in using geometry, one "proves" things, constructs "proofs"; one "deduces" relationships between figures and parts of figures. If asked to provide an overall definition, one might be most likely to come up with "the study of shapes."

Our school experience of geometry has involved us in a relationship with an ancient Greek: Rectangles, triangles, and circles are Euclidean figures. Originally concerned with measurement of and relations among such figures and with practical applications to early problems of building and land management, geometry received in Euclid's *Elements* an axiomatic treatment that became the historical model for the development of abstract deductive mathematical disciplines. This development has eventually involved algebra and other disciplines, as well as geometry. The history of geometry itself, since Euclid's time, was first marked by a pathway from the synthetic geometry of Euclid to the analytic geometry of Descartes, who introduced number coordinates into Euclidean geometry. Later, geometry was invested with non-Euclidean aspects, explored in the 19th century by Rieman and others, systematized in the 20th Century by Klein.

Non-Euclidean geometry involves the study of "topological properties and relationships of shape and position: open, closed; in front of, behind; inside, outside; and so forth. In child development, some of these topological relationships are understood *first*. They are new extentions of sensorimotor coordinations achieved when the infant's own body is the referent— coordinations of his own actions and changes of position.

This situation constitutes a paradox. Historically, the first type of geometry to appear, and until very recently, the only type studied in school, was Euclidean. Only later in the 20th Century has geometry come to deal formally with topological properties. Yet developmentally, topological relationships are first to appear, followed considerably later by Euclidean ones.

At 3 or 4 year sof age, the child has assimilated various topological relationships. He knows when an object is in front of another, whether it is closed or open, and when a rectangle is on top of or inside a circle. But to him a circle and a rectangle are *alike,* because both are closed figures; copying a circle, a square, and a triangle, he will draw more-or-less similar closed plane figures with no sharp corners, and copying an open figure he will draw an open figure. He spontaneously classifies the figures in terms of a topological property.

At 5 years of age most children have begun to differentiate between a circle and a rectangle (and a triangle) on the basis of new properties they have abstracted by comparing such figures. Circles, rectangles, and triangles are now assimilated as *different* in significant ways while still sharing properties representing an earlier level of abstraction. The new properties are Euclidean (e.g., straight, curved; three sides, four sides; long, short). The child gradually assimilates such properties and makes increasingly fine discriminations involving them.

However, not until much later, when the formal level of thought is attained in adolescence, are students able to deal withe interplay of proportions involved in the Euclidean geometry of traditional school experience.

Thus, the development of geometry presents a strange reversal: in its ontogenetic formation it proceeds from topology to Euclidean geometry; historically, it is just the opposite. According to Piaget, the reason for the ontogenetic sequence lies in the greater number of conservations involved in dealing with Euclidean figures. In topological relationships, only correspondences between whole objects are involved, and it is only correspondences not involving measurement that need to be conserved to compare two figures. In an Euclidean frame of reference, proportions within figures must be compared, not merely the general configuration of two objects. Thus, Euclidean relationships are more abstract and involve more conservations. The point is that Piaget provides a psychological interpretation of the development of geometry. Observe that his goal can be clearly defined: Having noted the historical evolution of geometry, Piaget uses developmental concepts to explain its observed reversal in child learning. His primary concern is an epistemological one that actualizes itself in cognitive experiments with children. The results in turn affect our interpretation of the historical development of geometry as a science.

REPRODUCING RELATIONS BETWEEN OBJECTS

Tasks 1 G1

Given: A sand tray, and small objects to represent buildings and other features of the child's school neighborhood. The "school building" should have a "front" and a "back." (With older children the experiment can be carried out with pencil and paper.)

The child is asked to: (*a*) create a "map" of the area around his school; (*b*) draw and describe a path to a specified familiar place, for example, to show the route he takes on the way home from school; and (*c*) recreate the map when the "school building" is rotated 180°.

Stages

1–2 [AR 3–7]: (Task is not possible for children under 4. They relate locations and distances only to their own body orientation, are confused when they turn around, and do not even use distant landmarks such as a mountain range as permanent points of reference. These difficulties persist to some extent through Stage 2.) The child exhibits three kinds of interrelated behaviors: (1) Relations between landmark objects on his map are distorted by subjective interest (e.g., valued places are juxtaposed) or motor association (habitual journeys), and relations (always between two objects at a time), are not coordinated; (2) the child describes paths in terms of recollected turnings, identifying landmarks only secondarily and by reference to such actions, not relating stages of journey to an objective space; and (3) he cannot recreate the map when the school building is rotated 180° (turns objects around on their own axes, leaving most other relations intransformed). [Lack of coordinated reference points; inability to represent displacements (positional changes, changes of position)]

3 [AR 7–10]: Initially, the child's map consists of two or three well organized but uncoordinated subsystems; parts of paths are described correctly in terms of landmarks, but the parts are not properly integrated; some subsystems of the map are correctly rotated, but not all. Later, (3b) all parts of the task are mastered. [Initially, partial objective coordinations of space; finally, complete spatial coordination (coordinate system)]

SPONTANEOUS DEVELOPMENT
OF MEASUREMENT

Task   *2 G2*

Given: A model tower (about 80 cm high) built of about 12 blocks of various sizes and shapes; a collection of many similar blocks, about 2 meters away from the model and separated from it by a movable cardboard partition; sticks and paper strips of various lengths that could be used for measuring.

The child is asked to build a tower "just as tall as" the model. The model tower is on a bench or table, and the child is asked to build his on a lower bench, table or on the floor, so that the bases of the two towers are at perceptibly different levels.

Stages

1 [AR 3–4]: Some children rely only on memory after visual inspection of the model; others move the partition and look back and forth from one tower to the other as they build, analyzing the shape of the model and duplicating some of its elements in their towers. [Perception, with or without visual transfer, is the only means of comparison used]

2 [AR 5–9]: Children use positional changes (i.e., they move things) in making comparisons, but without coordination of relationships (e.g., different base levels). First, things to be compared are moved close together (e.g., elements of towers) or physically linked (as by a long stick bridging the tops of the towers). Gradually, the child begins to use an intermediary term, which is first his own body, using hands or fingers to enclose and transfer a length, or using some part of the body to imitate and transfer a length) and then an independent third object (e.g., a stick, or a third tower build and moved from model to copy; but the child succeeds in "measuring" only when the common term is already the same length as the thing it stands for, and some children fail to compare it with both towers. [Manual transfer and body transfer supplement visual inspection; an imitative middle term is introduced for comparison]

3 [AR 7–9]: Initially, the child can measure the towers qualitatively with any "ruler" as long as or longer than the towers (he can mark a height exactly and transfer it properly), but fails when the ruler is shorter (he may try to ad something, like his hand or a block or stick, to make up the difference, but transfer is then problematical, and he cannot use a short ruler to subdivide a longer remainder); he understands the roles of parallel placement in measuring and of transitivity in the use of a middle term (if

A = B and B = C, then A = C). Gradually, the child learns to measure quantitatively, using a block or a short stick, which he systematically steps along the length measures, while counting, and transferring any small remainder properly; transitivity now relates successive changes in position of a unit part (A + A = 2A, 2A + A = 3A, and so on). [Operational comparison of total lengths, using a common measure; later, subdivision of length, with iteration of a unit of measure]

RECONSTRUCTING DISTANCE RELATIONS

Task 3 *G3*

Given: Two objects ("trees"), A and B, identical in height, placed about 50 cm apart on a table; and objects to be placed successively between the trees (e.g., a card partition taller than the trees, a large cube, many small cubes).

The questioner should carefully avoid any verbal reference to motion (e.g., walking, travelling), but will sometimes indicate by gesture the distances AB and BA.

Before anything is inserted between A and B, the child is asked: "Are the trees close together or far apart?" After each interposition: "Are the trees as close together (far apart) now as they were before I put the wall (house, bricks) in?"

With the same two trees (nothing inbetween), and later after one of them is raised to a much higher level, the child is asked: "Is it far from here to here (B to A)?"

Stages

1 [AR 4–5]: Distance relation between A and B is recognized only when nothing is interposed between them; otherwise the child deals only with two separate intervals defined by soemthing "closer" to A and also to B. Distances AB and BA are often judged unequal. [Distance relation is negated by partition (lack of composition); distance is not symmetrical (AB ≠ BA)]

2 [AR 4–7]: Overall distance between A and B is judged as depending on the width of interposed objects; the bigger the filled interval, the smaller the distance. Other children judge that the distance AB is not affected by the partition, but do not equate distances AB and BA. [Nonconservation of distance, with or without symmetry; conservation of distance, without symmetry]

3 [AR 5–8]: The child recognizes that distances AB and BA are the same regardless of interposed objects and different heights. [Sustained conservation and symmetry of distance; integration of filled and empty intervals; implied spatial field]

CONSERVATION OF LENGTH: SHAPES

Task   4 G4

Given: A straight rod (AB) of wood or clay, and a longer, curved strand (CD) of plasticine, arranged side by side.

These figures are shown to the child, who traces both with his finger. "Which is longer?" (If necessary, "Which path would make an ant walk farther?")

The experimenter straightens out the curved figures, and then returns it to its original shape. At each step the child traces the figures and the questioning is repeated.

Stages

1 [AR 4–5]: Because the imaginary lines AC and BD are parallel, the child judges the two lengths AB and CD to be equal, even after CD has been straightened out and then returned to its original shape. [Length is judged perceptually in terms of endpoints]

2 [AR 4–7]: When traced, the curved line is judged longer (CD AB), but some children revert to their earlier judgment (AB = CD). Gradually, the child learns to evaluate length in terms of configuration and not merely of endpoints. [Intuitions are organized; length is sometimes conserved]

3 [AR 5–8]: The child makes correct judgments with little or no trial and error, and applies unit measures consistently.

CONSERVATION OF LENGTH: DISPLACEMENTS

Task   5 G5

Given: Two small, straight sticks, A and B, of equal length (5–10cm), arranged horizontally parallel with end points aligned.

The child is asked: "Is one longer, or are they both the same length?" The experimenter then executes a series of displacements, while the child watches, and questions the child at each step. After each transformation and before the next, A and B are returned to their initial position. The child may be asked to make some transformations himself.

Basic displacements, which may be added to and varied: (1) A is moved to the right, about a third of its length. (2) B is moved to the left. (3) A and B are moved simultaneously, A right and B left.

Stages

1–2a [AR 4–7]: After displacement, one line (usually the one moved) is judged longer; the child focuses on a projecting end point. [Length is not conserved]

2b [AR 4–8]: The child still focuses sometimes on motion and end points, but not always. When only one stick is moved, it is usually judged longer, but equality may be conserved when A and B are moved simultaneously. When displacement is very slight, the child may affirm equality of A and B; when larger, not. Some children, after some displacements, spontaneously restore A and B to the initial pattern, using reversibility to establish equality. [Progressive perceptual regulations; conservation is possible but not consistent]

3 [AR 6–8]: The child affirms the equal length of A and B regardless of displacements. [Conservation affirmed and justified as logical necessity]

CONSERVATION OF LENGTH: DISTORTION OF SHAPE

Task   6 G6

Given: Matches lined up end-to-end in two parallel rows with end points aligned; same number of matches in each row, 5 or more.

After equality of the length of rows is noted, the experimenter will rearrange one row in various ways, introducing angles or curves, with match tips still touching, so that the endpoints of the rows no longer coincide (unless more matches are added). One or more matches may be broken in half at times, so length is not definable by number of pices. After each change, the child is questioned about the length of the rows. (If necessary: "Will two ants walking along the roads have the same distance to cover?")

Variation: Two narrow strips of paper, both 30 cm long, are laid side by side. One of these will be cut up by the experimenter into two parts (later subdivided further) and the pieces arranged in various shapes for comparison with the intact strip.

Stages

1–2a [AR 4–6]: The child fails to affirm equality even when he can count the same number of matches in the rows; with matches and also with paper strips, his judgments are dominated by perceptual factors—rectilinear distance between endpoints, degree and kind of shape change, and so on. [Absence of conservation]

2b [AR 6–8]: Children oscillate between conservation and nonconservation, displaying variable and nondefinitive reactions like those for Experiment 5 G5; some children establish equality by trial and error. [Intermediate reactions and progressive regulations; conservation conceived as a possibility]

3 [AR 6–9]: The child recognizes equality through coordinating subdivision and displacement operations. [Conservation conceived as logical necessity]

CONSERVATION: SUBDIVIDING A STRAIGHT LINE

Task   *7 G7*

Given: Pairs of horizontally parallel stretched wires or strings threaded each with a single bead; most pairs are of equal length, about 30cm. Several rods of various lengths are at hand to measure with.

With beads A and B in place at starting positions at ends of one pair of strings, the experimenter moves bead A a certain distance and asks the child to move bead B the same distance ("just as far"). The exercise is repeated, using various moves of bead A and different starting points.

Stages

1–2a [AR 4–7]: The child succeeds only when starting points are vertically aligned, since he concentrates only on aligning the arrival points and disregards resulting gross inequities of length traveled in other cases. [Ordinal solution; no attempt at measure]

2b [AR 6–8]: Children begin to coordinate points of arrival with points of departure, solving some problems intuitively if only approximately: some use only visual inspection as justification; others may try to "measure," but without understanding how to go about it. [Intermediate reactions; intuitive solutions by visual inspections]

3 [AR 7–9]: Children use measurement as the principal means of determining the positions of the beads. They all understand the transitivity

of equal length and can use a measuring rod that reaches as far as A to transfer the length to the B string. Some have learned to use a short rod as a unit to subdivide and transfer a longer length. [Operational qualitative measure; later, systematic compositions of measures]

LOCATING A POINT IN A PLANE

Task   8 G8

Given: Two identical rectangular sheets of paper, one of which has a dot on it (off-center in both dimensions), and a rod that can be used for measuring. The sheet with the dot is placed at the right-hand corner of the table, the other at the left corner.

The child is asked to mark a dot on the blank sheet of paper "in the same place that it is on the other."

Stages

1–2a [AR 4–7]: At first, children merely locate the point visually, making no use of the ruler. Gradually they try to "measure," but only to aid visual estimate, which may be fairly accurate but remains intuitive. Right and left may be reversed. Superposing one sheet on the other reveals errors, but the child fails to deduce need for measurement. [Intuitive positions]

2b [AR 6–8]: Children use the ruler but make only one measurement; sometimes this is more or less vertical or horizontal, but usually the child places the ruler obliquely from one corner of the sheet and pays little or no attention to the angle formed. [Qualitative estimates; uncoordinated one-dimensional measurement]

4 [AR 7–10]: Some children learn gradually, after considerable trial and error, to use Cartesian coordinates; often they start with a single oblique measurement from a corner, become progressively aware of the need to determine the angle, then recognize the *two* angles formed with adjacent sides and measure both along coordinate axes parallel to the sides. Other children proceed right away to Cartesian measurement. [Operatory and systematic metrical composition]

LOCATING A POINT IN THREE DIMENSIONS

Task   9 G9

Given: Two identical boxes open at one side and at the top. One box is empty. In other other, a piece of stiff wire is secured in a vertical position, tacked to the base of the box, and a bead is fixed at the top of the wire. At hand: a similar bead, scissors, strips of paper, string, wire, and wooden rods in various lengths, a graduated ruler, and tacks for attaching wire.

The child is asked to replicate the model box using the empty one.

Stages

Note: Development is exactly synchronous with that of measurement in two dimensions (Experiment 8 G8).

1–2a [AR 4–7]: The child uses visual estimates only; makes no use of measuring materials. [Intuitive positioning]

2b [AR 6–8]: Children make one or two measurements only, transferring congruent lengths, without subdivision. [Qualitative estimates; absence of operatory coordination]

3 [AR 7–10]: Some children proceed by trial and error and progressively coordinate and transfer the three dimensions. Other children make 3-dimensional measurements immediately. [Operatory and systematic metrical coordination]

MEASUREMENT OF ANGLES

Task   *10 G10*

Given: Diagrams of the sort shown (Fig. 1), each with a different angle CDB, but without the letters. At hand: pencils, scissors, sheets of paper, a ruler.

The child is shown the diagram, and asked to duplicate it on another sheet of paper.

Stages

1 [AR 4–5]: The child produces very rough drawings, satisfied merely to join one line to another, without any regard to angle formed or the lengths of lines; makes no attempt to measure. [Visual intuitive estimates]

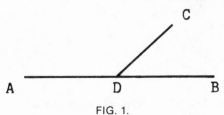

FIG. 1.

2 [AR 4–8]: Children make some attempt to measure lines AB and DC, using their hands or an independent common measure (e.g., a pencil) to transfer lengths. Increasingly, they try also to estimate the angle visually, but although critical of their results, they do not think of any way to measure it. [One-dimensional measure; visual measure of angle separation]

3 [AR 7–10]: The child can measure segment AD or DB to locate the origin of the angle. He may also measure DC and seek to reproduce its slope by trying to hold the independent measure constantly parallel to DC while transferring it from model to copy. Increasingly, seeing the model as a system of angles, children attempt to situate C by measuring and coordinating lengths AC and CB, or they try to measure angles (e.g., by cutting congruent pieces of paper). A few children may attempt perpendicular measure from C to AB. [Difficulty in coordinating subdivision and changes o position; correct or approximate solutions through trial and error]

4 [AR 10–12]: Use of perpendicular measure from C to AB becomes common. Children integrate one-to-many correspondance in the framework of a Cartesian system. They understand that length of angle sides must be related to distance between them. [Correct operatory and formal solution]

MEASUREMENT OF TRIANGLES

Task   *11 G11*

Given: a triangle ABC of the type shown (Fig. 2) by the solid lines in the illustration (it need not be exactly similar). Within reach: pencils, sheets of paper, scissors.

The child is asked to reproduce the triangle on another sheet of paper.

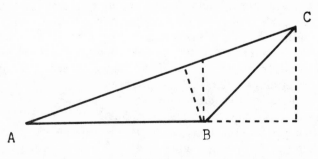

FIG. 2

Stages

1 [AR 4–5]: The child cannot draw a proper triangle and makes no attempt to measure.

2 [AR 4–8]: Some children copy the triangle very roughly, without measurement. Others measure the sides separately but cannot reproduce their slopes; often the sides do not meet at all. [Visual and intuitive estimates; uncoordinated linear measurement]

3 [AR 8–10]: Initially, children try to reproduce the angles (make the sides meet) by transferring the slope of the ruler used to measure the sides, but with increasingly growing precision they adjust the three linear measures to each other by trial and error. Later the child gradually learns to decompose the given triangle, to construct a height perpendicular to one side, and to measure and coordinate all relevant dimensions] Correct solution through trial and error]

4 [AR 10–12]: The child spontaneously uses correct construction methods to reproduce the model. [Correct operatory and formal solution]

SUM OF ANGLES OF A TRIANGLE

Task   *12 G12*

Given: Drawings of several triangles and a set of exactly similar triangle paper cutouts; the triangles are of various sizes and differ greatly in shape, including one that is extremely elongated. The three angles of each triangle are marked with arcs at equal distances from their vertices, so that when the angles are cut off along the arcs, they can be put together to form a semicircle.

The child is shown each triangle in turn (the drawing and the corresponding cutout) and asked what its three angles will look like (what shape they will form) if they are cut off and placed together with their points and arcs touching. (At no time should the questioning be in terms of the sum of the angles being 180°.) The examiner cuts each triangle apart, puts two of the angles together, and then asks the child to predict and then show what will happen when the third is added. The examiner may need to place the third angle and point out the semicircle. The child is also asked what will happen if the angles forming the semicircle are arranged in a different order. With later triangles, parts of this procedure may be repeated, and the child will experiment, arranging and rearranging, *after* he has declared what shape he thinks will be formed. The last triangle is the elongated one. The aim throughout is to assess the child's readiness to reason and generalize from preceding experiences, but without explicitly asking about "all triangles" or "any given triangle" unless the child is already making consistently correct predictions.

Stages

1-2 [AR 4-7]: The child fails to see the relations between the angles as such and the parts of their "half moon" sum. At first, he does not even conserve the sum when observed. Later, he learns that the angles of a *given* triangle will still make a semicircle however rearranged, but his predictions continue to be erratic and are usually wrong. [Gradual conservation of observed sum; no generalization]

3 [AR 6-10]: Children begin to consider the relative sizes of angles and gradually arrive at the generalization ("It's always a semicircle!"): some by discovering the complementary (compensatory) relations between angles as new triangles are compared with preceding ones ("The bigger it is here, the smaller it is there."); some by repeated successful abstraction and composition of angles. [Gradual generalization by inductive discovery]

4 [AR 10-12]: The correct prediction is made right away and consistently, with awareness of reasons of why it must always be true. [Formal generalization governed by logical necessity]

GEOMETRICAL LOCI: LINE AND CIRCLE

Task   *13 G13*

Given: A table with two chairs opposite each other; a set of 10 or more small marker objects (such as pennies or dried peas); other objects to serve as two "trees," a "target," and so on; paper and pencils (for older children).

Two loci are studied:

1. *The locus of points equidistant from two points A and B,* that is, the line bisecting and perpendicular to AB. The experimenter indicates two "trees" (A and B) and asks the child to show where he could stand so as to be "just as far" from one as from the other. (With very young children, the experimenter sits opposite the child at the table and asks him to place a "target" where it will be the same distance from each of them.) If the child indicates one correct position, he is asked whether there are "other places just as far...." If he indicates other points correctly, he is questioned about filling in the gaps between them (continuity) and about how far they could go (infinity) and in what directions (symmetry). His understanding is checked by asking whether any points *not* on the line would satisfy the condition.

2. *The locus of points equidistant from a point P,* that is, a circle with P as its center. The experimenter indicates a "target" (P), gives the child 10 or more markers ("children"), and asks him to show where the children could stand so they all can shoot at the target from the same distance. When appropriate, he is questioned further about the nature of the locus.

Stages

1 [AR 4–6]: The child indicates points seemingly at random, with no regard for distance: (I) one point, probably more-or-less "between" A and B; (II) points loosely but erratically related to P. [Distance is conceived only as an empty space; equidistance has even less meaning]

2 [AR 4–7]: (I) Children locate an equidistant point, usually the midpoint between A and B, fairly accurately but without measuring; later they add other points to the locus, but usually only on one side of the first point. (II) Children begin by arranging points in rows or in an irregular ring or in pairs around P, and gradually approximate the locus by trial and error. [Qualitative estimates based on perception; beginnings of generalization through repetition]

3 [AR 7–10]: Children construct the loci with ease, after locating only a few points by correct reference to the given equidistance condition, and conclude immediately that all points on the line or circle must have the same property. Conditions of infinity, symmetry, and continuity are then generalized. [Operational solution through reasoning by recurrence]

4 [AR 10–12]: The loci are identified by definition; their composition is understood in terms of a refined notion of geometric points.

CURVES OF MOTION

Tasks   *14 G14*

Given: Paper and pencils; cardboard or thin wooden cut-outs; a disk, a triangle, and a square.

1. The disk is pinned to a sheet of paper so that it will rotate around its center. The child is asked to predict and draw the kind of line that will be drawn by a pencil attached to the edge of the rotating disk. The experimenter then demonstrates, with the pencil attached, and questions the child further, specifying different positions for the pencil. These procedures are repeated with the triangle and the square.

2. The disk is to be rolled along a straight base, with a sheet of paper behind it, so that if a pencil is attached it will draw some cycloid form (if the pencil is at the center, the form will be a straight line). The child is questioned, one case at a time, about what shapes will result with the pencil in three different places on the rolling disk: on the edge; at a point between center and edge; at the center. The experimenter demonstrates each case, first without and then if necessary with the pencil, before going on to the next.

Stages

1 [AR 4–6]: The child is unable to imagine a motion before it occurs and simply draws the object at rest. Movement itself cannot be represented. [Static configurations]

2 [AR 5–7]: The child begins to imagine curves of motion, but is often unable to draw such a curve as distinguished from the outline of the object (e.g., in task I, asked what shape the rotated triangle will make, he draws a triangle or rectangle; in task II he draws a circle or series of circles). [Intermediary solutions; beginning dissociation of object and motion]

3 [AR 7–10]: The child reaches correct solutions after trial and error and some hestitation. He does not necessarily deduce or generalize, but offers a concrete solution for each task.

4 [AR 10–12]: The child does not hesitate or proceed by overt trial and error. [Correct induction and correct anticipation of the curves]

CONSERVATION OF AREA: "COWS IN THE FIELDS"

Task   *15 G15*

Given: Two identical pieces of green cardboard (A and B), each about 20 × 30 cm. Two small toy cows and 30 little "houses" (toys or blocks or pieces of paper, each about 1 × 2cm).

The child is shown the two cardboards placed side by side; they are described as fields with grass for cows to eat. There is one cow in each field. The child is first asked whether both cows have the same amount of grass to eat. A farmhouse is then placed on each field and the question is repeated. Other houses are then added, at least 4 or 5 times, one more at a time (always the same number on A and B) until 30 houses have been placed. On A, the houses are arranged in one or more tight rows, touching; on B they are widely scattered at random. Each time, after houses have been added to both fields, the child is asked whether both cows still have the same amount to eat.

Stages

1 [AR 4–6]: When confronted with different configurations, the child negates equality. Judgment is based entirely on perception. [Absence of conservation; sometimes, failure to understand the question]

2 [AR 5–8]: Up to a certain number of houses, the child recognizes that the remaining grass areas on A and B are equal; beyond that number, the perceptual configurations are too different; the number varies from one child to another. Thus conservation is conceived as a possibility but not as a necessity. [Perceptual intuition and intermediate responses; no operational composition]

3 [AR 7–9]: The child recognizes that the areas are always equal no matter how A and B are perceived. [Conservation is a necessity]

CONSERVATION OF AREAS: COMPLEMENTARY SHAPES

Task   *16 G16*

Given: Two identical rectangles, one of which is cut along its diagonal into 2 small triangles, which are then arranged into a large triangle. The child is asked whether the areas of the rectangle and the large triangle are equal. (Is there just as much "room," the same "amount of space,"...?)

Stages

1 [AR 4–6]: The child confines himself to perceptual judgments and negates equality when the parts are rearranged and the shape altered. There is no attempt to measure. [Absence of conservation]

2 [AR 5–8]: The child makes some correct judgments, but they are the consequence of intuitive adjustments and are lacking in generality. There is some degree of transitivity, but it is limited. [Absence of necessary conservation; intermediate responses]

3 [AR 6–9]: The child understands conservation of total area. A middle term (the diagonal of the rectangle)is now used as a common referent. [Conservation is generalized to cover complementary areas. True measurement, involving unit iteration, is displayed]

SUBDIVIDING AREAS

Task   *17 G17*

Given: Circular, rectangular, and square "cakes" (several of each shape and size, more to be made as needed): The first few might be clay patties, to be cut with a wooden knife; but most may be paper, to be marked with a pencil and cut with scissors, or marked off with matchsticks.

The child is first given a circular "cake" and asked to divide it up for 2 people (so "they will eat up all the cake, and one will have just as much to eat as the other"); then he tries it with a rectangle and a square. If he seems able or nearly able to cope with the problem of bisection, he is given other "cakes" (again first a circle) and asked to divide each one for 3 people. These procedures are repeated as the child is asked successively to divide cakes into 4, 5, and 6 equal parts. Each time, he is asked whether the separated parts, if recombined, will make up the whole cake.

Note: Ways in which problems of subdivision relate to the concept of fractions are defined implicitly here.

Stages

1 [AR 3-5]: When children are asked to divide the cake into 2 (or 3) parts, they generally cut off 2 (or 3) small pieces, leaving a large remnant that is ignored; some do not even stop with 2 (or 3) cuts but continue indefinitely. Soem children succeed in dividing a cake into 2 parts (with no remainder), but the "halves are far from equal. [Failure to relate parts to whole and/or to compare parts with each other]

2 [AR 4-7]: Especially if a cake is fairly small, the child can readily divide it into 2 approximately equal parts, and sometimes into 4. Division into 3, 5, or 6 parts is still difficult, especially with a circle; but division into 3 is accomplished sometimes fairly readily with a rectangle or square, and after trial and error with a circle. In trisecting, the child usually begins by producing 3 small portions plus a large remainder (as in stage 1), or by two disections resulting in 4 quarters; but in both cases he proceeds to subdivide and distribute the extra piece. [Partial solutions; intuitive, nonoperational conservation of the whole]

3 [AR 6-10]: The child succeeds with division into 3 parts without difficulty; and division into 5 or 6 is accomplished after trial and error or by using schemas already learned (bisection and trisection). [Understanding of part-part and part-whole relations, including associativity (parts are also wholes: will be subdivided)]

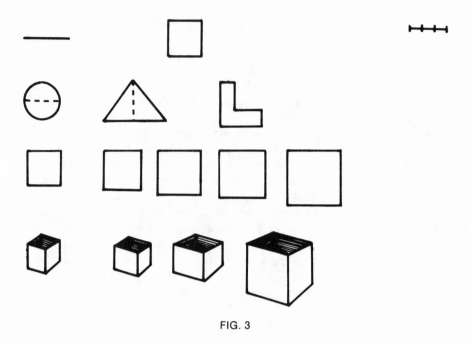

FIG. 3

DOUBLING AREAS AND VOLUMES

Task   *18 G18*

Given: Pencil and paper; rulers; scissors; sand. Drawings as shown in Fig. 3; and cubical boxes (E) that can be filled with sand. (Dimensions need not be those suggested.)

The child is presented successively with the following problems: (A) Draw a line twice as long as the one shown; (B) Draw a square twice as big as the one shown (having "twice as much room on it"); (C) Double other figures (circle, triangle, L-shaped "field"); (D) Select the square that is twice as big as the model; (E) Select the box that is twice as big ("will hold twice as much") as the model box. When the child has made a choice, he is questioned about how many small boxes full will go into the bigger box chosen; and the model box is filled with sand which is then emptied into the chosen box.

Stages

1 [AR 4–5]: No understanding of the problem itself.

2 [AR 4–7]: In attempts at doubling, the child simply produces a small but arbitrary increase in size: draws a straight line (and tries unsuccessfully to draw a square) that projects a little beyond the model in some way, without

imposing any metrical relationship. When asked to select the square or cube twice the size of the model, the child may choose the right one at random but has no rationale. [Additive composition]

3 [AR 6-11]: The child produces a figure consisting of 2 juxtaposed model areas (e.g., 2 squares), forgetting the requirement of shape, or simply doubles all dimensions. His success in reproducing and doubling linear dimensions (with or without true measurement) does not transfer to area or volume; the child overcomes with difficulty his belief in direct proportionality between the lenghts of boundary lines and the areas or volumes they enclose. [Partial and empirical solutions]

4 [AR 10-13]: The child at least begins to understand that determination of area or volume involves mathematical multiplication. Some children already grasp the metric relationships between line length, area, and volume. [Formal multiplicative composition]

CONSERVATION AND MEASUREMENT
OF VOLUME

Task   *19 G19*

Given: A "lake" (large square of corrugated cardboard about 30cm² in area). Several "islands" (small pieces of stiff cardboard pasted to the "lake"; one measures 3 × 3cm; suggested dimensions for others: 2 × 3cm, 2 × 2cm, 1 × 3cm). A "house" (wooden block), 4cm high and just covering the 3 × 3cm island base (volume: 36cm³). At the side: at least 36 1-cm cubes ("bricks" or "rooms") (see Fig. 4).

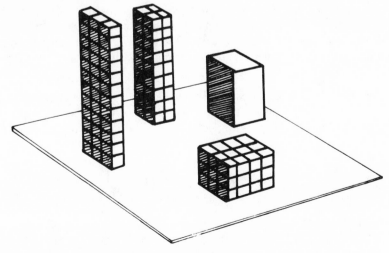

FIG. 4

The child is asked to build a new house with "just as much room in it" as the model house but on a different island (2 × 3cm or 2 × 2cm); the new house is to be built with the unit cubes. Repeat with other base(s) if further exploration seems indicated.

Finally, the child is asked to replicate the model (3 × 3 × 4cm), using the unit cubes. When this is actually made (with adult help if necessary), it is then dismantled as the child watches the adult use the same 36 cubes to build something of a quite different shape; then another; each time the child is questioned: (*a*) Is there the same amount of room in this new house as in the old one (the model)? (*b*) Could we use these same bricks to make a house just like the old one, with the same amount of room?

Stages

1 [AR 3–7]: Experiment techniques not useful at this age.

2 [AR 5–7]: The child fails to coordinate dimensions, attending mainly to one at a time although gradually becoming aware of 3 to deal with. Some children judge equality only by the largest dimension and refuse to build a new house taller than the model. More advanced children may try to compensate for loss in width or depth by increasing height slightly but not sufficiently. [Topological and ordinal judgments; qualitative compensations]

3 [AR 6–12]: Some children can relate and correctly adjust 2 or even 3 dimensions (e.g., by counting and rearranging unit cubes) but do not measure. Other children make correct unit measurements and use these to justify successive constructions (e.g., "twice as high") but not to calculate volume. The most advanced subjects know that volume is determined by mathematical multiplication, but are not sure how (e.g., they may multiply 2 lengths and a surface area). [Quantitative compensation: logical multiplication with metrical relations; conservation of "internal" volume only]

4 [AR 10–13]: The child establishes the correct mathematical relations between contained space and the dimensions of the areas that bound it. [Spontaneous decomposition; logical and mathematical multiplication; conservation both of "internal" and "occupied" volume]

Space

INTRODUCTION

Space has numerous perceived properties and various connotations at many levels of our experience. At the most basic intuitive level, it is a universal; we live in it, it is there, outside, everywhere; we think of it as "having air." But "space" itself is not a school subject, or even a topic studied as such, although space is an inherent aspect of almost any given aspect of study.

The concept of space has of course been treated by philosophers. For Aristotle, space is the container of all objects; for the Cambridge Platonists, the sensorium of God; for Kant, the a priori form of intuition of external phenomena. In modern mathematics, "space" is the name for certain invariant systems of abstract entities and operations (e.g., a vector space).

Space perception theories are equally varied. Consider the two extreme views. The nativistic point of view endows the mind with a primitive intuition of space which becomes qualitatively differentiated through sense experience, whereas the empirical point of view assumes that perceptual space emerges from the coordination of the spatial features of the different senses.

Piaget's findings suggest that space is neither a primitive intuition nor the result of perceptual experiences alone. Space is constructed; space, like all other concepts, results from an interplay between assimilation and accommodation. Thus, although space involves perception, it is not the result of perception alone. One of the main obstacles to a developmental study of space derives from the fact that the evolution of spatial relationships proceeds at two different levels. It is a process that takes place at the perceptual level and simultaneously at the level of thought and imagination.

Generally, the cognitive approach to the problem assumes that the concept of space develops under the influence of motor and perceptual mechanisms. As far as the generality of such an assumption goes, it is quite correct. But it often leads to the further assumption that representational images are no more than copies of existing sensorimotor constructs. This oversimplifies and in a fundamental sense constitutes a misinterpretation of the findings of the Geneva school. According to Piaget, knowledge is not a copy of the real but a construction of it, involving assimilation and active coordination by the subject. The beginning of life is marked by an absence of coordination between the various sensory spaces and in particular by a lack of coordination between vision and grasping: visual and tactilo-kinesthetic space are not yet related to one another in any unified structure. Thus, it is not surprising that in the early months of life there exists no permanence of solid objects or persons. This concept will come into existence during the sensorimotor period of development.

The fact that sensorimotor structures involving the permanency of objects and persons anticipate future achievements of spatial representation and therefore constitute necessary prerequisites is not enough to indicate the exact relationship between perceptual and representational space. The child can perceive things projectively, can grasp certain metric relationships by perception alone, long before he can deal with perspective in thought or measure objects through operations. Furthermore, his ability to perceive forms (e.g., as lines or curves, squares or circles) is far in advance of his capacity to think about them—to reconstruct them at the level of mental imagery or symbolic representation.

Thinking has the task of reproducing at its own level everything that perception has achieved in the limited field of direct contact or immediate proximity with objects. There is a gap of several years between these two constructions. It is not until 7 or 8 years of age that measurement, the conceptual coordination of perspectives, results in the construction of a conceptual space, marking a real advance beyond perceptual space. It is essential to note that despite their differences and the time lag that separates them, perceptual and representational constructions are to some extent repetitive and possess a crucial factor in common. This common factor is motor activity.

Motor activity (eye movement, grasping, reaching, walking, and so on) is first a governing factor in the infant's most elementary perceptions of spatial properties and relations (shape, size, distance, location) and then in the formation of mental images of these; and motor activity (drawing, measuring) also becomes the basis for operational coordination of such properties and relations in representational space. This continuous functioning of motor activity, through all stages in the developmental construction of space, implies, among other things, that this development involves factors of internal assimilation, not merely external encoding of perceptual data. It is of great importance for the understanding of spatial thinking.

Indeed, an essential aim of Piaget's studies in *Geometry* as well as in *Space*, is to show how, when, and with what effects motor activity intervenes in the child's construction of space. And his developmental findings about that intervention strongly indicate that the truth about space perception lies midway between the two extreme theoretical views (nativistic and empirical): that the child is actively involved, through his motor factor, in the construction of space. Observe that here again Piaget uses a philosophical framework as a point of departure and proceeds to study the problem from a developmental point of view, with results that in turn come to clarify the philosophical issue itself.

RECOGNITION OF SHAPES BY TACTILE EXPLORATION

Task   *20 S1*

Given: Paper or cardboard stand to screen objects from child's view. A collection of two kinds of objects: (1) Familiar three-dimensional things (pencil, key, comb, spoon...) to be used with young children only. (2) Stiff cardboard cut-outs of various abstract shapes to be presented in the following order: (A) geometric figures: circle, rectangles, rhombus,...; (B) more complex but symmetrical figures: four-pointed star, crosses, swastika, semicircle,...; (C) asymmetrical figures with straight sides: trapeziums, trapezoids,...; (D) topological forms: irregular areas with one or two holes, closed and open rings, intertwined rings, superimposed rings.

The child is handed one object at a time, behind the screen, and is asked to explore and identify it by touch. First he is asked to name it if he can, then to recognize it among a collection of objects or drawings and/or to draw it on a sheet of paper.

Stages

1 [AR 2–4]: Some children recognize familiar objects but no flat shapes; others can distinguish some shapes in topological terms (open, closed, with or without holes, etc.), but not Euclidean ones (square, triangle, circle). Drawing progresses from mere scribbles to shapes with rough topological correspondence with models (e.g., drawings of circle and square are similar closed figures). Exploration is passive or incomplete. [Recognition of common objects and topological features]

2 [AR 4–7]: Exploration is more active, sometimes even persistent, but unsystematic and without points of reference. There is progressive differentiation between geometric features, first between straight and curved lines and later in terms of angles, but limited success in recognizing or drawing the more complex shapes. [Perception both of topological and Euclidean features; empirical analysis only: lack of coordination between reasoning and perceptual data]

3 [AR 7–9]: Exploration and drawing are now systematic: the child establishes a fixed point of reference to which he can always return, and assimilates perceived elements to a plan of action required to construct shape. He can represent complex shapes, accounting correctly for order and distance relations among elements. [Operational method]

DRAWING GEOMETRIC FIGURES

Task   21 S2

Given: The 21 illustrated model figures (Fig. 5), some of which emphasize simple topological relations (1, 2, 3, where the small circle is *outside, inside,* or *on* the larger figure), some Euclidean shapes (4–8, 18), and some a combination of both (9–17, 19–21). Note that models 4–8 also represent a simple topological property (*closed,* as distinguished from models 20 and 21, which are *open*).

The child is first asked to draw a man or something else of his choice; this helps to put him at ease and provides an indication of his natural drawing ability. Then he is asked to copy a model figure; then another; and so on.

Stages

1 [AR 3–4]: The child produces scribbles or rough drawings that somehow distinguish between open and closed figures (e.g., cross and circle) but not between straight-sided and curvilinear closed figures (e.g., drawings of circle, square, and triangle are roughly similar closed curves). Drawings accurately represent the topological relations in models 1–3 (outside, inside, on). [Correct representation of topological relations; disregard of Euclidean ones]

2 [AR 3–7]: Straight-sided figures are now clearly distinguished from curves, and the child gradually learns to coordinate angles and dimensions, producing essentially correct drawings, often after considerable trial and error, of all models (except, in most cases, 16—and after great difficulty with model 18). [Progressive differentiation of Euclidean relations]

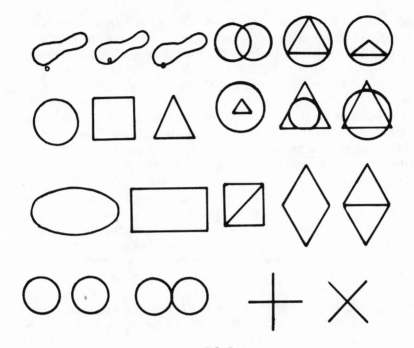

FIG. 5

3 [AR 6–8]: Problems of model 16 are solved now if not before; all other models are correctly drawn without difficulty. [Operational representation of shapes]

ORDER: LINEAR AND CIRCULAR, DIRECT AND REVERSED

Task   22 S3

Given: (a) A set of 7 or 9 rather large beads, with at least 5 or 6 different colors represented, arranged as a model. Also, a collection of loose beads, greater in number than the model set but containing an identical set. Also, stiff wire rods of equal length and lengths of cord or flexible wire. (b) two "clotheslines," one—the model—rigged a little higher than the other and hung with 7 small paper "clothes": blue shirt, red dress, . . . ; also, a larger collection of similar "clothes."

1. *Reproducing linear order.* (a) The beads of the model are strung on a rod. The child is asked to reproduce the model by selecting and stringing loose

beads on another rod. The rod is also placed near and directly opposite the model; it also may be presented somewhat displaced to one side. (b) The child arranges clothes on a line to correspond with those on the model clothesline.

2. *Circular into linear order.* The beads of the model are strung on a circular loop. The child is to string beads on a straight rod in corresponding order.

3. *Reverse order.* (a) Given the linear bead model, the child is to string beads in reverse order on another rod. Given a circular string of beads, the child is to string beads on another loop in reverse order. (b) The child arranges clothes on a line, reversing the order of the model.

4. *Stacking: direct and reverse order.* Given the model clothesline hung with clothes, the second line is correspondingly arrayed (by the experimenter if necessary). The child is told he is to take the clothes off of "his" line one at a time, going from one end to the other, and stack them in a basket. But before and in the course of stacking, he is to predict where pieces will be in the stack (what will be under the blue shirt? . . . in the middle? . . . on top?). Then he is to transfer the clothes to another basket (reverse order: top to bottom), again making predictions in answer to questioning.

5. *Figure eight.* The 9 beads of the model are strung, with spaces between them, on a cord or flexible wire arranged in a figure eight. The child is to reproduce this, using cord or wire of equal length and then to string the beads in the same order but on a straight rod perhaps half as long.

Stages

1 [AR 3–4]: The child can select elements corresponding to those of the model; but either pays no attention at all to how they are arranged or succeeds only in pairing some elements in terms of contiguity, not necessarily ordering them correctly and not coordinating pairs with each other. [Intuitive correspondences without order]

2 [AR 4–7]: Some children can reproduce order only when a linear model is to be exactly copied and when the copy is squarely opposite or under the model. More advanced children can always copy direct order (even without perceptually adjacent correspondences) and are mainly successful transposing circular order to linear; but reverse order is accomplished only partially or after much trial and error, and the figure eight is even more difficult. [Intuitive representation and trial-and-error construction of order]

3 [AR 6–10]: The child sees elements as parts of a coordinated whole. Reverse order is readily reproduced; conceptual reversibility guides motor activity. Difficulties of the figure eight are solved now if not before; child understands it is a circle transformed. [Operational correspondence]

RIGHT AND LEFT

Task   *23 S4*

Given: Objects on a table (pencil, key, coin, card); a bracelet or wrist watch to be worn by the experimenter.

The experimenter asks 5 series of questions:

1. (Experimenter sitting opposite child) Show me your right hand. Now show me your left hand. Show me *my* right hand. Now my left.
2. (Arranged left to right: coin pencil.) Is the pencil to the right or left of the penny? Is the penny to the right or left of the pencil?
3. (Experimenter, sitting opposite child, has a coin in his right hand and a bracelet on his left arm.) Is the penny in my right or left hand? Is the bracelet on my right or left arm?
4. (Arranged left to right: coin, key, pencil.) Is the pencil to the left or right of the key?... of the penny? Is the key to the left or right of the penny?... of the pencil? Is the penny to the left or right of the pencil?... of the key?
5. (Arranged left to right: key, card, pencil. Objects are shown to the child for about 30 seconds and then covered.) Now tell me by heart how the things are arranged. (This is followed by questions like those of series 4.)

Stages

1 [AR 5–8]: The child considers left and right only from his own point of view. [Egocentric reference]

2 [AR 8–11]: Increasingly, the child can consider left and right from the point of view of another person and in terms of objects themselves. He is gradually constructing a system of reference. [Progressive decentration]

3 [AR 11–12]: All aspects of left and right can be dealt with; the child has established a coordinated system of reference. [Operational method]

KNOTS AND THE RELATION OF "SURROUNDING"

Task   *24 S5*

Given: Lengths of cord for making knots.

1. The child is shown (Fig. 6) a simple knot (a) and asked to make one like it.

FIG. 6

2. The child is shown a looser simple knot (b) and asked if it is the same as the first. Then he is asked to make one like it and to tell what will happen if the ends are pulled.

3. Knot b is loosened still more and shaped like a bow (c); the child is questioned as before. Does the child by now understand the perceptual continuity between knots a, b, c?

4. Knot c (a right overhand knot) is shown with a left overhand knot (d). The child is asked if they are identical; he may judge by eye and/or by running his finger along the knots.

5. The same procedure is followed as the child is asked to compare true and false overhand knots (d and e).

6. Similarly, the child compares a figure eight (f) with a "false figure eight" (g, an overhand knot with its long ends joined and arranged to form two loops).

7. The child is shown (h), two overlapping loops and two linked loops and is asked what will happen in each case if the two loops are pulled in opposite directions.

Stages

1 [AR 3–5]: Some children cannot tie a knot even after watching it done and hearing the process explained; having formed a loop, a two-dimensional "surrounding" (enclosure), they do not understand how to

make it three-dimensional by intertwining (passing one end over-and-under through the loop). More advanced children do learn to do this but do not generalize the learning; they may distinguish at sight between overlapped and intertwined loops, but not between true and false knots (d and e). [Correct direct order, intuitive recognition]

2 [AR 4–7]: Children can copy a simple knot without help. Some do and some do not recognize the correspondence between knots a and b; some of those who relate a to b do not see their correspondence with knot c, or the difference between true and false knots (c and e), except after trial and error. Motor anticipation and thought are tied to image and confined to limited transformations. [Perceptual exploration without operational flexibility; partial intuitive correspondences]

3 [AR 6–8]: The child recognizes the reversibility correspondence between knots a, b, c, and therefore can distinguish these from the false knot (e) and sees the difference between the left and right overhand knots (d and c) and between the true and false figure eights (f and g). Figures are perceived in a framework constituted by their potential transformations in terms of motor activity and mental representation. [Perceptual activity is directed by a systematic operational method]

SUBDIVISIONS, POINTS, AND CONTINUITY

Task   *25 S6*

1. Given: A straight line (later, one or more other figures: square, triangle, . . .). The child is questioned about what will happen if the figure is repeatedly subdivided until it can't be divided any more. The child may use any mode of subdivision (to get something half as big, then half of that, etc., *or* to divide into smaller pieces, then still smaller pieces, etc.) and demonstrate either by drawing figures or cutting them up. Eventually he must continue the process (as long as he can) only in his imagination. What will there finally be at the end? What shape is it (even if the child specifies a "point")?

2. Given: A collinear series of points drawn with space between them (perhaps 3–5cm). The child is asked to put more points, and still more, in the spaces, and is questioned about how many there can be, whether they are touching, whether they could eventually form a line (is a line made up of points?).

Stages

1–2 [AR 4–8]: Children either cannot imagine and draw the smallest (2-3mm) and largest squares or do so only by successive trials, often beginning with squares not much smaller or larger than the given one. The child makes very few subdivisions of figures and imagines the end product as having shape determined by the figure. Points perceived as separated are not a line; contiguous points forming a perceived line are no longer points. [Absence of operational mobility and reversibility]

3 [AR 7-11]: The child envisages a large but not infinite number of subdivisions, and ultimate elements are still somehow tied to perceptual forms. Assembling a line from points is seen intuitively as the reverse of subdivision, but discontinuity of points is still not reconciled with the continuity of a line. [Concrete operations involving order, proximity, enclosure, and separation; partial and intuitive notion of continuity]

4 [AR 11-13]: The child can now perform abstract operations extending analysis (subdivision) and synthesis beyond physical limits. Ultimate elements are hypothetical points, shapeless, neither tangible or visible, which he can mentally separate and combine to the limits of infinity. The continuous line is composed of infinitely many such points. [Hypothetico-deductive thought: operations freed from material content and functioning only in terms of logical structure]

SMALLEST AND LARGEST SQUARES:
SQUARES WITHIN SQUARES:
ORDER AND ENCLOSURE

Task   *26 S7*

Given: A square drawn on a sheet of paper. The sides of the square should be about a third as long as the short dimension of the paper.

The child is asked first to draw the smallest square that can be drawn, so small that nobody could make a smaller one (for purposes of the experiment, this is about 2–3mm). Then he is asked to draw the largest square that will fit on the paper. He may do this drawing wherever he chooses: on the sheet with the given drawing or on a separate sheet.

Note: If a child draws the smallest and/or the largest square, it implies that he sees in his mind an ordered series of squares intermediate in size, with smallest and largest constituting an enclosure. These operations of ordering and enclosing are parallels of operations involved in mentally subdividing a line into a continuous series of points, the problem dealt with in Experiment 25 S6. Perception of continuities is modified in terms of increasing fineness and thus by evolution and synthesis of relationships of proximity and separation as well as those of order and enclosure.

Stages

1-2 [AR 4-8]: Children either cannot imagine and draw the smallest (2-3mm) and largest squares or do so only by a series of successive approximations, often beginning with squares not much smaller or larger than the given one (some younger children soon forget whether the next attempt in such a series should be smaller or larger). [Lack of operational mobility and anticipatory schema of seriation]

3 [AR 7-11]: The child draws the smallest and largest squares with little or no difficulty, sometimes at the first attempt. He anticipates the end result through internalized reversible actions using correct mental images. If questioned about what would happen if the smallest square were made smaller still (and sometimes even if not questioned thus), he may say the result would be a "point," but this is conceived in perceptual terms as having size and/or shape. [Concrete operational transformations]

4 [AR 11-13]: The child spontaneously draws or describes the smallest possible square as a point, and can envisage an infinitely diminishing series of such points. [Abstract operations]

CONSTRUCTION OF STRAIGHT LINES

Task   *27 S8*

Given: A rectangular table and a round table (or a circular piece of cardboard about 25cm in diameter). Also 10 matchsticks ("telephone poles" or "trees") standing in small plasticene bases.

The experimenter places 2 poles (A, Z) on the table as end points of a straight line parallel to the table edge and about 2 or 3cm from it. The child is asked to place other poles between these to make a straight line running along a straight road. (He may also be asked to place poles in a line right *at* the table edge.)

This procedure is repeated with end points forming a line diagonal to the table edge.

At some point, the child is shown a curved or zigzag line of poles on the round table and is asked to straighten it out. If he does not spontaneously use the method of placing himself at one end and sighting along the line ("projecting" it), he is encouraged to stand at various positions around the table and questioned about their helpfulness as vantage points.

Stages

1 [AR 3–4]: Children of this age know the difference between straight and curved lines, but they are able to construct a straight line of poles only right on the edge of the table—not when the poles are to form a parallel line 2 or more centimeters from the edge. They succeed in making a topological line when placing elements very close together. [Intuitive representations]

2 [AR 4–7]: The child can make a line parallel with a straight edge, perceiving the edge as a line and imitating it. When the end points require a line in conflict with surrounding straight or curved lines, younger children are strongly influenced by their perceptions of these (e.g., making their "line" turn the corner or follow the arc of the table edge); more advanced children gradually avoid this and may approximate a straight line fairly closely, also becoming increasingly aware that point of view might make a difference. [Intermediate reactions]

3 [AR 6–8]: The child spontaneously lines himself up with the two end poles and constructs a straight line (regardless of the surroundings) by "aiming" from one to the other. [Systematic operational coordinations]

PERSPECTIVE

Task   *28 S9*

Given: A thin cardboard or metal disk and a pencil or stick; drawing materials; prepared drawings; a doll.

The purpose is to find out how the child will represent objects seen in different perspectives. (The experimenter must emphasize that questions are about *apparent* shape, not actual shape. Various views of pencil and disk are shown in Fig. 7.) This is done in two ways (with and without a second "observer" whose perspective is different from the child's).

1. A doll ("man," "person,"...: the other observer) is placed slightly in front of the child and at one side, with its line of vision at right angles to his. An object is placed before the child (e.g., pencil: vertical) and he is asked *how it looks to the other person;* then it is placed in one or more other positions in turn (e.g., pencil extended horizontal to the doll, end-on to the child), and with each change the same question is asked. Repeat with other object. To question the child responds in to ways: (*a*) by drawing; then (*b*) by selecting from prepared drawings, some correct and some incorrect, the one he thinks represents the apparent shape of the object in the given perspective.

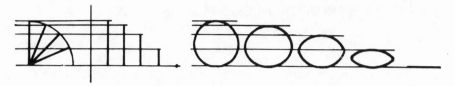

FIG. 7

2. (The doll is removed.) The child watches as an object's position is altered and is asked to *imagine or predict* the apparent shapes it would assume ("the shapes he would see") with other changes in its position (e.g., the object is turned through 90° and the child then asked what it would look like in intermediate positions; or it is very slowly turned and the child asked what its shape will be after the motion has continued to a later stage.) The child responds in the same two ways as before.

Stages

1 [AR 4–5]: Inability to represent shape by drawing or to understand perspective.

2 [AR 5–8]: The child is unaware of or generally confused by the different viewpoints of the doll and himself. Younger children cannot ignore actual shape, and represent the object as having the same shape and size regardless of its relative position. More advanced children begin to distinguish between different views, but usually when selecting from comparison drawings rather than in their own; they are realizing that perspective makes a difference but are unable to represent it adequately in their drawings (e.g., views a, c, and e of the disk may be drawn as 3 circles of diminishing size). [Egocentric reactions with attempts at decentration; total or partial failure to distinguish between different viewpoints; representation lacking perspective]

3 [AR 7–12]: The child now distinguishes clearly between different views, even in his own drawings: at first partially and only with respect to general shape (e.g., circle becomes ellipse), later in terms of quantification as well (relative proportions of different ellipses and straight lines). Children are increasingly imagining perspective in terms of continuous transformations, seeking and articulating laws governing these; eventually they apply perspective systematically in drawing. [Operational coordination of points of view; visual realism]

PROJECTION OF SHADOWS: CONES

Task   *29 S10*

Given: Objects consisting of simple, combined, or modified cones, to be mounted in turn on a support between a lamp and a vertical white screen. Also: paper and pencil; prepared drawings.

The child is shown each mounted object in place and asked to predict what its shadow will look like on the screen when the lamp is turned on. He responds by drawing and/or by choosing from prepared drawings (some correct, some incorrect). Following each response the experimenter turns on the lamp to show the child the shape produced, then turns it off before presenting the next object (or the same object in a different position).

Objects are presented in this order: (1) Simple cone, upright or inverted. (2) Bobbin—two cones attached point-to-point or base-to-base—vertical. (3) Simple cone, horizontal, sometimes with point and sometimes with base opposite the light source, to project a circular shadow. (4) In the same positions, a cone with a hole through the vertical axis, to make a ring shadow. (5) Bobbin placed to project a circular shadow.

Note: Piaget's experiments also used these procedures with the disk and pencil of Experiment 28 S9 placed to makes various shadows. (See Experiments 30 S11 and 31 S12.) They found the same stage behaviors as before. But equivalent behaviors were achieved later with the conical objects because each of these had to be imagined as a series of varying cross-sections. Correct solutions were achieved at Stage 3 with the sample shapes but not till Stage 4 with the cones.

Stages

1 [AR 4–5]: Inability to represent shape by drawing or to understand shadow projection.

2 [AR 5–7]: The child cannot predict shadow shapes except when they are in fact copies of the objects as perceived by him (as in cases 1 and 2). For example, even after he has seen the circular shadow of the horizontal cone with base toward the light, he does not predict a circle when the cone's point is turned to the light. [Egocentric reference and direct copy of object]

3 [AR 6–10]: The child begins by making mistakes with case 3, that is, thinking the point will show if it is toward the light, but learns from experimenting to predict correctly in all cases; he is beginning to understand that the larger cross-sections block the light enclosing the smaller ones, as it were), thus determining shadow shape. [Progressive decentration; correct solutions through trial and error]

4 [AR 10–12]: The child knows how shadows are proejcted, and draws the correct shapes without difficulty. [Operational coordination]

PROJECTION OF SHADOWS: DISK

Task   30 *S11*

Given: A cardboard mounted on a support and placed between a lamp and a vertical white screen. Also: paper and pencil; prepared drawings.

The disk is placed successively in several different positions including upright and parallel with the screen to produce a circular shadow, perpendicular to the screen to cast a line shadow, and tilted for elliptical shadows. In each case, before the lamp is turned on, the child is asked what the shadow will look like. He responds by drawing and/or by choosing from prepared drawings (some correct, some incorrect). Following each response the lamp is turned on to produce the shadow, then turned off while the placement of the disk is changed.

Note: The stage behaviors found correspond with children's representations of the disk seen in different perspectives in Experiment 28 S9.

Stages

1 [AR 4–5]: Inability to draw shapes or understand shadow projection.

2 [AR 5–8]: Younger children predict and draw (or choose) a circle regardless of how the disk is placed. Others know the shadow will be different but cannot correctly represent what they will be when the disk is perpendicular or tilted. For example, they draw an arc instead of a straight line or a broken or smaller circle instead of an ellipse. [Egocentric reference; total or partial failure to represent shadow shapes]

3 [AR 6–9]: The child represents vertical and perpendicular positions correctly, and clearly distinguishes the tilted position from both; his drawings for the ellipses are at first rather rough and more or less alike, but later he correctly draws their different proportions. [Operational coordination]

PROJECTION OF SHADOWS: STRAIGHT LINE

Task   31 *S12*

Given: A pencil mounted on a support and placed between a lamp and a vertical white screen. Also: drawing materials and prepared drawings.

The pencil is placed successively in different positions: (1) vertical; (2) flat, point toward screen, to make a small circular shadow; (3) tilted toward the screen, to make vertical shadows of different lengths. In each case, before the lamp is turned on, the child is asked what the shadow will look like. He responds by drawing and/or by choosing from prepared drawings (some correct, some incorrect). Following each response, the lamp is turned on to produce the shadow, then turned off while the placement of the pencil is changed.

Stages

1 [AR 4-5]: Inability to draw shapes or understand shadow projection.

2 [AR 5-8]: Younger children still have no understanding of shadow projection, and they predict shadows representing only how they see the pencil itself: vertical; horizontal left to right; tilted left to right. Others begin to expect some different shapes (e.g., small circle, or small acute angle representing pencil point, for flat position; tilted lines, sometimes longer instead of shorter, for oblique positions). [Egocentric reference; total or partial failure to represent shadow except as copy of object as perceived]

3 [AR 7-9]: The child now predicts correctly for vertical and flat positions. Some children still draw tilted lines for oblique positions but may make them somewhat shorter than the pencil; still others draw correctly and explain a series of increasingly foreshortened vertical line shadows. [Progressive decentration; operational coordination]

PROJECTION OF SHADOWS: RECTANGLE

Task   *32 S13*

Given: A cardboard rectangle is supported directly below a lamp so that its shadow will be case downward onto a horizontal screen. Also: paper and pencil; prepared drawings.

The rectangle is placed successively in different positions: (1) horizontal, to make a shadow copy of itself; (2) vertical, to make a line shadow; (3) tilted, to make rectangular shadows of decreasing width. In each case, before the lamp is turned on, the child is asked what the shadow will look like. He responds by drawing and/or by choosing from prepared drawings (some correct, some incorrect). Following each response, the lamp is turned on to produce the shadow, then turned off while the placement of the rectangle is changed.

Note: This method differs from that of Experiments 30 S11 and 31 S12, more completely dissociating the plane of projection from the child's viewpoint and serving as a cross-check. Nevertheless the same stages were found as in those experiments and in Experiment 28 S9.

Stages

1 [AR 4–5]: Inability to draw shapes or understand shadow projection.

2 [AR 5–8]: Some children always draw a copy of the rectangle itself; others try to discriminate but make various mistakes with oblique and vertical positions, not predicting a line shadow for the latter. [Egocentric reference; total or partial failure to represent shadow shapes]

3 [AR 7–9]: The child predicts the line shadow correctly but may have trouble with oblique positions at first. Later, these are drawn correctly and explained without difficulty. [Progressive decentration; operational coordination]

COORDINATION OF PERSPECTIVES

Task   *33 S14*

Given: A 3-dimensional model (Fig. 8), about 1 meter square, of 3 mountains (roughly pyramidal) ranging from 12-30cm high: the smallest (at right front as seen from position (*a*) is green and has a little house at the summit; the one at left is brown and topped with a red cross; the largest is gray, with a snowy peak. Also: 3 roughly triangular pieces of cardboard of sizes and colors corresponding to those of the model mountains. Also: 10 pictures showing the mountains from various perspectives (some possible, some not). Also: a doll (another "observer").

FIG. 8

Three methods of questioning may be used:

1. After the child represents the scene as it looks to him from position *a*, using the pieces of cardboard, the doll is placed successively at *c, b,* and *d,* and the child is asked each time to show how the mountains look to the other person from the given position. (After each response, he may check by moving to the given position.)

2. The child looks at some or all of the pictures and is asked to choose the one that could have been "taken" or "painted" by the doll from a given position; then from another 2 or 3 positions in turn.

3. The child is shown a particular picture and asked to place the doll where it could "take" that picture. Repeat several times.

Note: Piaget's presentation gives examples of all stages for each method of questioning.

Stages

1 [AR 4–6]: The child does not understand what is wanted.

2 [AR 6–9]: The child fails to realize that observers see different things from different points of vantage; he may make some attempts to represent views different from his own, but only in terms of one dominant feature in relation to an observer, and usually he soon relapses to reproduce his own point of view. [Egocentric reference; transitional reactions]

3 [AR 7–12]: The child knows that certain relations (left and right, in front and behind) vary with point of view, and tries to represent this: with limited success at first (dealing correctly with some relations among mountains but ignoring others); later all points of reference are systematically coordinated. [Progressive relativity; operational coordination]

GEOMETRIC SECTIONS: CYLINDER, PRISM, BLOCK, BALL

Task   *34 S15*

Given: Objects made of plasticene or styrofoam: cylinder; prism; a rectangular block; hollow ball. Also: a knife with a wide, flat blade; drawing materials; and prepared comparison drawings.

Each object in turn is placed before the child. The experimenter holds the knife over the object, clearly indicating the direction either of a transverse cut or a longitudinal cut. The child is asked to predict what the surface of the cut section will be if the cut is made. He responds by drawing and by choosing from prepared drawings; if necessary, the cut is then actually made, to show him the result. The following order of presentation is suggested: (1) *cylinder*, transverse cut, to make a circular section; (2) *prism*, transverse cut, to make a triangle; (3) *block*, transverse cut, to make a square; (4) *ball* clearly described as hollow, any cut; (5) *cylinder*, longitudinal cut, using a part remaining after the transverse cut, to make a rectangle, and so on.

Stages

1 [AR 4–5]: The child does not understand the problem, partly because he can at most distinguish topological features of shapes (e.g., closed or open) but not those determined by point of view relative to a plane (projective) or by real or imagined movement, as in measuring, in or on a surface (Euclidean).

2 [AR 4–8]: The child may draw something that somehow represents both the whole object and the section (e.g., for the transverse section of the cylinder, a rough rectangle with a circle inside each end, or a long oval with a straight line across it), failing also to select the correct sample drawing; or he may succeed partially in representing a section separately, through imagining first the plane of the cutting action and later the periphery produced. [Total or partial failure to distinguish internal and external points of view; progressive development and interaction of projective and Euclidean operations]

3 [AR 5–9]: The child represents the sectional surfaces directly and without difficulty. [Operational coordination]

CONIC SECTIONS

Task   *35 S16*

Given: Several solid styrofoam cones; a knife with a wide, flat blade; drawing materials; prepared drawings.

The experiment is designed to find out how the child will represent in advance surfaces produced by various sectionings of the cone: (1) parallel with the base, making a circle; (2) vertical bisection, making a triangle; (3) oblique, making an ellipse; (4) oblique through side and base, making a parabola. Procedures are the same as for Experiment 34 S15.

Stages

1 [AR 4–5]: The child does not understand the problem.

2 [AR 4–8]: Characteristics of individual behaviors correspond exactly with those found in the preceding experiment. [Total or partial failure to distinguish internal and external points of view; progressive development and interaction of projective and Euclidean operations]

3 [AR 6–9]: The child represents the sections directly and without difficulty. [Operational coordination]

SECTIONS OF COMPLEX OBJECTS

Task   *36 S17*

Given: Knife, drawing materials, prepared drawings, and objects made of plasticene or plastic foam as described below.

The experiment is designed to find out how the child will represent in advance the surfaces produced by transverse or longitudinal sections, and procedures are the same as for experiment 34 S15. Objects are presented in this order: (a) A thick ring with circular cross-section. (b) A ring with square cross-section. (c) Two disks connected by a parallelepiped; transverse section is a square or short rectangle, longitudinal section a longer rectangle. (d) Four-pointed star with thick straight edges; section from point to point is a long rectangle, across the root a square or short rectangle. (e) A cornet made by rolling up together two sheets of differently colored plasticene as the child watches. (f) A twist made by intertwining two strands of differently colored plasticene. (g) A helix made by winding a strand of plasticene into the shape of a pointed snail shell.

Stages

1 [AR 4–5]: The child does not understand the problem.

2 [AR 5–7]: As in Experiment 34 S15, the child cannot usually distinguish whole objects from projected surfaces that would be produced by sectioning. [Total or partial failure to distinguish internal and external points of view: intuitive representations]

3 [AR 7–11]: Sections of the simpler shapes are represented fairly well (better for A and B than for C and D); those involving spirals (E, F, G) are not mastered even with persistent effort. [Systematic concrete coordinations]

4 [AR 11–12]: The child readily represents all sections except that of F, which still gives some trouble. [Formal coordinations]

ROTATION AND DEVELOPMENT OF SURFACES: CYLINDER AND CONE

Task   *37 S18*

Given: A paper rectangle folded once to make a "ridge roof"; a paper cone with a base, and a paper cylinder. Also: pencil, scissors, and extra paper.

The child is first asked to draw the shape the "roof" will be in if it is opened out flat. After he responds, the paper is unfolded to show him the result. He is then shown the cylinder and the cone, one at a time, and in each case he is asked first to draw the object itself and then to draw the flat shape that would result from "unrolling" the paper. Responses may be checked by unfolding the object and/or by cutting out the child's drawing to see whether indeed it can be folded to make the object.

The child may also be asked to draw a man with a cart (seen from above), to show whether he spontaneously "rotates" wheels or surfaces into a different plane.

Note: Piaget's presentation includes typical drawings for stages 2a, 2b, and 3a; and he points out that children who have had school experience with paper folding are more advanced than others by 2 or 3 years.

Stages

1 [AR 4–5]: The child does not understand the problem.

2 [AR 5–8]: The child's drawings of an object intact and unfolded are either alike (cylinder, rough rectangle with rounded ends; cone, rough circle or triangle) or are different in some way but with development (unrolling) indicated quite inadequately, as by a line showing direction of intended unfolding action or by reorienting the first drawing or representing some different aspect or ill-defined additional surface. [Total or partial failure to distinguish different points of view; intuitive representation]

3 [AR 6–10]: The child arrives at correct solutions after some trial and error, eventually coordinating two kinds of responses: different surfaces represented in a discontinuous way; parts shown suitably integrated in one figure but with rotation incompletely indicated. [Discovery of true rotation; operational coordination]

ROTATION AND DEVELOPMENT OF SURFACES:
CUBE AND PYRAMID

Task   *38 S19*

Given: A rectangular sheet of paper folded once to make a "ridge roof"; a
paper cube, a paper pyramid or tetrahedon. Also, pencil, scissors, and extra
paper.

The child is first shown the "roof" and asked to draw the shape it would be if
opened up flat. He is then shown the cube and the pyramid, one at a time, and
asked to show how each would look if unfolded.

Note: Piaget's presentation includes drawings representing stages 2a, 2b,
and 3a; and he points out that children who have had school experience with
paper folding are more advanced than others by 2 or 3 years.

Stages

1 [AR 4–5]: The child fails to understand the problem.

2 [AR 5–7]: Children generally draw the developed ("unfolded") figure as
   identical to the intact figure, or as similar but smaller (the loss of one
   dimension from solid to flat being represented as a reduction in size). Some
   children begin to distinguish the intact from the developed figure (e.g., by
   indicating one or more additional surfaces in a vague or disconnected
   way). [Intuitive representation]

3 [AR 7–11]: Some children arrive at partial solution, showing in their
   drawings either all surfaces correctly drawn but wrongly combined, or a
   static representation of an uncompleted stage of development and/or an
   indication of the unfolding action itself in which surfaces are only partly
   opened out (e.g., as if seen in perspective). More advanced children
   produce correct drawings for the cube, but not for the pyramid.
   [Progressive discovery of true rotation; systematic concrete coordinations]

4 [AR 11–13]: The child draws the opened-out pyramid with little or no
   difficulty. [Formal solutions]

CONSERVATION OF PARALLELISM:
TRANSFORMATIONS OF THE RHOMBUS

Task   *39 S20*

Given: "Lazy tongs" and drawing materials.

As an introduction, the child is first shown the tongs in their extreme
contracted position (handles and rods vertical, no open spaces) and asked to

guess what will happen if the scissor handles are moved a little (experimenter gestures to show slight motion that would produce very narrow vertical rhombuses. When the child has responded, the experimenter makes the actual transformation as the child watches.

These procedures are carried out in small increments again and again, until the tongs are fully extended (narrow horizontal rhombuses or straight line). Each time the child is questioned about what the rhombuses will look like if the handles are drawn slightly closer together. The child responds (always before demonstration) by describing and drawing the shapes he thinks will be produced with each movement.

Stages

1 [AR 4–5]: The child cannot draw a rhombus at all, or anticipate any transformation of one.

2 [AR 4–7]: Some children can imagine the transformations, if at all, only as a series of figures getting larger and larger indefinitely, and their drawings are not rhombuses (they may draw a series of crosses, or closed figures such as rectangles or roughly elliptical pointed forms). More advanced children, shown the tongs moved to produce narrow rhombuses, can predict that these will get wider as the tongs are further extended, and even later that they will get smaller; however, although their drawings may approximate rhombuses pretty well, they usually do not conserve length and parallelism of sides or represent a continuous series of changes. [Gradual abstraction of the rhombus; beginnings of anticipatory schema]

3 [AR 6–9]: The child can (possibly after a few mistakes at first) correctly represent the transformations as a continuous series, showing the inverse relation between varying height and width ("The height gets less and the width gets greater"). He also comes to realize that length of sides must be constant and opposite sides parallel. [Operational construction; conservation of parallelism and length]

4 [AR 9–12]: The child understands clearly and can explain the relationships of the transformations, and often even deduces the whole series in advance. [Explicit formulation and anticipatory deduction]

SIMILAR TRIANGLES: PARALLEL SIDES AND EQUALITY OF ANGLES

Task   *40S21*

Given: A series of cardboard triangles of different shapes and grouped in different series. (5 similar isosceles triangles with acute apex angles, 3 similar isosceles triangles with obtuse apex angles, 3 isosceles triangles with different bases, 3 dissimilar isosceles triangles with same base but varying in height, 1 scalene, 1 right triangle and 8 equilateral triangles).

The child is asked to compare these figures and draw them on another sheet of paper.

Note: Two problems are being explored here, the first one should emphasize the idea of parallelism of the sides, the second one should stress the concept of the equality of angles.

Stages

2a. (AR 4-7) Neither the parallelism nor the equality of angles are understood as concepts. (Intuitive Representation).
2b. (AR 6-8) Intuitive idea of parallelism in few selected cases such as obtuse-angled triangles with sides but slightly inclined. Marked progress in judging the slope of the sides of triangles.
3. (AR 7-11)Similarity of triangles is based on equality of angles with a progressive analysis of the angles themselves. (Concrete Coordinations).
4. (AR 11-13) The child understands clearly how to compare different triangles and has no difficulty reproducing them. (Formal solutions).

SIMILAR RECTANGLES

Task   *41S22*

Given: Horizontal rectangle and larger rectangles, one of which is used as standard. The standard and comparison figures are presented in random order. The child is asked whether the large one "looks like" the little one or not and particularly whether it is "the same shape but bigger." Later the child is asked to produce pictorial constructions and compare them.

Stages

1. (AR 4-5) The child fails to understand the problem.
2. (AR 4-8) The child provides global comparison often resulting in overestimation of length. Difficulty in perceptual transposition of dimensional relationships. Often increase in one dimension in forgetting the other.
3. (AR 7-11) Intuitive transposition of dimensional relationships within the framework of perceptual comparisons but not in the drawings.
4. (AR 10-13) Proportions generalized operationally and synthesis between perception and reproductions. (Formal solutions).

Note: Any rectangle can serve as a standard but it is preferable to use an intermediary figure.

HORIZONTAL AND VERTICAL AXIS

Task   *42S23*

Given: 2 bottles, one *A* with straight, parallel sides and the other *B* with rounded sides, each about one-quarter filled with colored water. A cache or semi-opaque screen. Drawings of different orientations of the bottles. The child is shown the 2 bottles, which are then placed behind a cache so that the child can distinguish the general contour of the bottles but not the water level in them. The child is asked to anticipate the position the water will assume when the bottles take different orientations. The child is asked to draw each of his anticipations indicating with a cross where the water will be and with a line where the level will be. Bottles are then shown directly to the child and moved into different orientations which the child has to copy when the bottles are actually visible. The bottles are then placed behind the cache again and the child is asked to assess his previous performances. The same manipulations are repeated with bottle *B*.

The same set-up is used but this time a small cork with a matchstick rising vertically from it and a plumb line with a fish-shaped bob and a sand or plasticine mountain and posts that can be planted in them. To test the discrimination of vertical axes the child is asked to draw the positions of the mast of his "ship" at different inclinations of the bottles and then to correct his drawings after having seen the experiment. The child is later shown a plumb line suspended inside an empty bottle; the plumb bob is shaped to represent a fish. The child is asked to predict the line of the string when the bottles are tilted at various angles. This done, tilting of the bottles is actually performed and the child is asked to assess his changes.

Finally the child is presented with a mountain of sand or plasticine and asked to plant posts "nice and straight" on the summit and the slopes of the mountain.

Stages

1. (AR 3-6) The child is unable to distinguish surfaces or planes for fluids or solids. He cannot represent either the water or the mountain as a plane surface. Consequently the child shows liquid neither as line or surface but as a ball. He shows poles as solids lying on the "mountain." The child thinks of fluids and solids in purely topological terms as something inside or on and not according to Euclidian concepts of straight lines, planes,

arranges items in straight or curved lines or spreads them out with large spaces among them. He usually fails to use the surroundings as a frame of reference. He merely frequently constructs incomplete groups of objects unrelated both from the general collection and its setting. The child often reverses left and right viewpoints and always fails to coordinate various perspectives. The child does not recognize geometric similarity and distances as well as proportions are ignored. (Partial Coordination).

3. (AR 6-11) The child can now reproduce the model well, although not to exact measurement and scale. The child coordinates all positions within a single point of view embracing both surroundings and objects located in them. Gradually the child masters the task of making pictorial layouts in terms of both position/distance and perspective/proportions. The child produces a drawing of the objects but does not use exact measurement to establish their proportions. (Operatory qualitative compositions).

4. (AR 11-13) The child uses comprehensive three dimensional organization of space. Euclidian and projective relationships function now jointly in applying the concept of similar shape or ratio. Accurate measurement of distance and proportional reduction of scale is frequently used and introduced spontaneously. (Operatory quantitative composition).

Number

INTRODUCTION

The rate of monetary inflation is a number, and when it jeopardizes my lifestyle I am likely not only to think some new thoughts but to lose my temper as well. My Social Security is summarized by one nine-digit number! Obviously we all deal with numbers; they are everywhere in our daily lives. They indicate streets and addresses, they order events, objects, and persons. In a highly technological society, especially, there is hardly any part or aspect of life that is not subject to symbolic representation and statistical analysis through use of numeric codes.

Generally, we conceive of numbers as discrete units whose reservoir is infinite. As adults, we find it easy to understand that an object can be represented by a number—and even to believe that for any object or collection of objects (real or imagined), no matter how large or small, there is some number to represent it. We might define "a number" as a symbol that represents or describes something quantitatively; numbers are used to count things, or to rank them in order, or to evaluate the properties of things in terms of "how much" or "how many."

But the important point about numbers is that they are really defined by the internal structure of the *number system* to which they belong. There are of course various number systems (cardinal numbers, integers, rational numbers, real numbers, and so on) and each has some distinguishing properties and features; but all have a basic internal structure with certain invariant properties. For instance, although numbers exist in a continuum, they are nevertheless always discrete units, distinct from each other, unlike the parts into which we divide the continua of space, time, and matter. Moreover, numbers are always *ordered,* by a relationship of "not greater than." (This is easiest to see in the simplest of the familiar number systems, the positive integers, the numbers we use for counting.) And from this invariant ordinal relationship, the basic operations (addition and multiplication) with their basic laws are derived.

It takes 7 to 8 years of existence for the child to complete the construction of the system of the positive integers, and to Piaget we owe the demonstration of this developmental unfolding.

To understand the meaning of this development, let us consider an example. Suppose that I have three cats at home. They all have different names, but I know they are all "cats." One is white, another grey, another striped; one is fluffy, two are sleek; one is cuddly, one aloof, one playful. In short, they are very clearly different in various ways. What am I doing, then, when I group them together by calling them all "cats?" I am ignoring their differences and paying attention only to their similarities—properties shared by all cats (including, of course, some shared *only* by cats). In other words, I am classifying my animals as members of "the set of all cats"; I am making abstractions out of them, abstracting their characteristics to the point where they are the same as those of all other cats. "The set of all cats" is for me an abstraction, an idea based on the establishment of correspondences. It contains all possible cats, all conceivable cats—but cats that have discarded all their properties except those that all cats have in common. Obviously, I cannot have in my head an image of all *real* cats, with all their different features; and those differences are irrelevant, anyway, to the process of distinguishing a cat from a noncat, or deciding whether anything is or is not a member of the set of cats.

But since all the members of this abstract set of cats are identical, how am I to differentiate among them? Suppose I want to think about assigning some of them to owners. How can I proceed, to be sure I'm dealing with a different one every time? The only available way is to introduce an ordinal referent, a system for dealing with them in order. In the abstract, what this comes to is using the ordinal aspect of the number system: I can think of and treat the members of the set of cats as "first cat, second cat, third cat," and so forth, identifying and differentiating among them on the basis of a serial order.

This example illustrates some of the difficulties the child has to overcome in order to operationally understand the concept of number. It is quite evident that very early the child can verbalize the numerical succession. But it is one thing to thus represent the set of integers verbally and quite another to understand its conceptual meaning, its operational properties, and its invariant features.

The child's construction of number consists in understanding the dual aspect of the system of positive integers: Operations of correspondence (classifications) are necessary for the establishment of sets, and operations of order (seriations) are equally essential. Yet the number is neither ordinal entity only nor a cardinal entity only. The system of number has both properties at the same time.

In *The Child's Conception of Number* Piaget demonstrates developmentally that the number is the result of the synthesis between these two aspects of thinking. The number of simultaneously a set and a relation, and it is only when the child can do both classification and seriation that he will come to correctly conceptualize the number.

Yet the number is not only a synthesis. As a synthesis it gives birth to new properties which are neither part of a classification nor part of a seriation. The set of integers has properties that define a number system, not a classification or a seriation. It is in this sense that according to Piaget a new structure has new properties that are not reducible to the entities from which they emerge. Yet one can also return to a classification or a seriation from the set of integers. In short, although this structure is new, it is not irreversible.

Observe that here again Piaget attempts to solve through psychological enquiries an epistemological, philosophical problem: the number is neither known a priori nor the result of experience alone. It involves again an active construction by the child. The number is the result of the child's own actions upon objects in terms of their ordering, their classification, and their synthesis into the concept of number.

CONSERVATION OF SUBSTANCE

Task   *45 N1*

Given: Two identical balls of clay.

The child is asked to observe the equality of the quantities of both balls of clay. If the child disagrees with the idea of the balls being of equal quantity, he is asked to add or take away some clay so that his perception of them is that they consist of the same amount ("to eat"), whether or not that is objectively true. Once equality in the child's mind is established:

The experimenter transforms one of the balls of clay into a sausage shape and asks, "Do we still have the same amount to eat?" The experimenter then returns the clay to its original shape and repeats the question. This may be repeated, employing different shapes, or dividing the ball into several little pieces, and then returning it to the original form.

Stages

1 [AR 4–7]: When the shape of the ball is altered so that it is no longer identical with the second, the child maintains the amounts are no longer equal. Judgment is tied to one dimension; different shapes are different amounts. [Absence of conservation]

2 [AR 6–8]: The child vacillates in his answers and usually fails to conserve. He focused on one dimension at a time and continues to find one object having more or less than the other. He might affirm conservation for one transformation, but this is not generalized and justified for all transformations. [Conservation is a possibility]

3 [AR 7–9]: The child affirms conservation. To justify his responses, he uses one of several available arguments: reversibility (object returned to original shape is again equal in amount); compensation (what object has lost in height has been gained in width); or identity (substance is the same as it was before, since nothing was added or taken away). [Conservation is a logical necessity]

CONSERVATION OF WEIGHT

Task   *46 N2*

Given: Two balls of clay and a balance.

The child is asked what the balance is and how it works. If he does not know, the experimenter explains it to him. Then the experimenter, asks, "If I were to put this ball here and that one there, would they weigh the same? Would they balance?" "Why?" The experimenter does not actually put the balls on the balance unless it is necessary to show the child that they do weigh the same amount.

The experimenter transforms one clay ball into a sausage shape and asks, "If I were to put this sausage shape on the balance and this ball on the balance, would they weigh the same amount or would one weigh more than the other?" "Why?" The experimenter restores the sausage to ball form and asks the questions again.

The procedure is repeated as one ball of clay is transformed to pie (wedge) shape, to ball, into many pieces, and to ball. After every change in shape the same questions are asked.

Stages

1 [AR 4–8]: The child concludes that the two balls are equal in weight when their shapes are the same. When the shape of one is altered, he concludes that the two are not equal in weight. He attends to a single dimension only. [Absence of conservation]

2 [AR 6–10]: The child is unsure of his response to the task; he usually fails to conserve. He can see other dimensions but is easily confused and relies then only on one dimension at a time for his response. He still sees most of

the time one object as heavier than the other when the shapes differ. [Conservation is a possibility]

3 [AR 7–11]: The child is capable of conservation. He uses one of three arguments to justify his response, as he did for conservation of substance (45 N1): (a) reversibility—if the transformed object is returned to its original shape, the two are then equal; (b) compensation—what the object has lost in one dimension has been compensated in another; or (c) identity—substance is the same before and after transformation. [Conservation is a logical necessity]

CONSERVATION OF VOLUME

Task   *47 N3*

Given: two balls of clay; one metal ball equal in size to the clay balls; two identical glasses equally full of water; two rubber bands.

The balls are presented to the child who is asked whether they are equal in size. The balls are adjusted until he agrees that they are equal. The same procedure is followed for the water level in the glasses. The agreed upon level is marked with a rubber band on each glass.

The child is asked the following questions: "If I dip this ball in the glass what will happen?" "Why does the water level rise?" "If I dip a ball in each glass will the water rise the same distance in both or in one more than in the other?" "Why?" If the child is not sure of an answer, the procedure is carried out.

Then a clay ball is transformed into a sausage shape in front of the child and the question asked, "If I dip the ball in one glass and the sausage in the other, will the water rise the same distance in both, or in one more than the other?" "Why?" The sausage is returned to ball form and then flattened into pancake shape. The same questions are asked. Finally, one ball is broken into several parts and the questions asked again.

The child is shown the metal ball and a clay ball of equal size. He is allowed to feel their respective weights. The experimenter says, "here is a metal ball the same size as the clay ball. If I dip the clay ball in one glass of water and the metal ball in the other, will the water rise the same distance in the two glasses or more in this one than in that?"

Stages

1 [AR 4–9]: When one object of a pair is altered in shape, the child maintains that they are no longer equal in volume. S attends to only one dimension. [Absence of conservation]

2 [AR 7–10]: The child usually fails to show conservation. He gradually begins to focus on more than one dimension while continuing to give answers in terms of a single dimension; he sees one object as larger. [Conservation is a possibility]

3 [AR 9–12]: The child uses one of several responses to justify his answers: (a) reversibility—if the second object is returned to its original shape, the two are equal; (b) reciprocity or compensation—what object has lost in one dimension has been compensated in another; or (c) identity—substance is the same as it was before being transformed. [Conservation is a logical necessity]

CONSERVATION OF CONTINUOUS QUANTITIES

Task   48 N4

Given: Two cylindrical containers of equal dimensions (A_1 A_2) containing equal quantities of liquid, and a third container (B), taller and narrower.

First, contents of A_2 are poured into (B). The child is asked if the quantity in B is equal to that in A_1. The child is again shown that A_1 and A_2 are equal. Then the liquid is returned to A_2. The content of A_2 is divided among several smaller containers. The child is asked whether the quantity in these equals that in A_1.

Stages

1 [AR 4–6]: The child says the quantity of liquid increases or decreases according to size and number of containers. He tends to one dimension only. [Absence of conservation]

2 [AR 5–7]: The child accepts the notion of conservation when differences in levels are slight or when there are only two smaller containers, but is doubtful in other cases. He begins to attend to more than one dimension. [Conservation is a possibility]

3 [AR 6–9]: The child states immediately that quantities are conserved, and coordinates height and width, a two-fold aspect. The child justifies his answers using one of the arguments cited in Experiments 45 N1, 46 N2, or

47 N3. [Logical multiplication of relations and mathematical composition of parts and proportions exists and conservation is a necessity]

CONSERVATION OF
DISCONTINUOUS QUANTITIES

Task   *49 N5*

Given: Two glass containers (A_1, A_2) of equal capacity and equal numbers of red and green beads.

The experimenter says, "Every time I put a red bead in my glass you put a green bead in yours." Then, "Will there be the same number of beads in both glasses?" "If you made a necklace with red beads and another with green, would they be the same length?"

The child is shown a third glass container (A_3), taller and narrower than the first two. The experimenter pours the contents of A_2 into A_3 and then asks whether A_1 and A_3 contain the same number of beads.

The experimenter pours the contents of A_3 back into A_2 and compares A_1 and A_2.

The child is shown a fourth container (A_4), shorter and wider than A_1 and A_2. The experimenter pours contents of A_2 into A_4, then asks him whether A_1 and A_4 contain the same number of beads.

Stages

1 [AR 4–6]: The child estimates quantity from uncoordinated perceptual relationships and attends only to height. In spite of the fact that the elements are discrete, he thinks that their number increases or decreases with change in the shape of the container. [Absence of conservation]

2 [AR 5–7]: The child tends to think that there is conservation either because beads were in identical containers (identity) or because they were in one-to-one correspondence, but appearance (difference of levels) conflicts with this tendency. He begins to coordinate relations, but his attempt at multiplication is not developed; and he may forget one dimension. He might affirm conservation for one transformation but it is not generalized to all situations. [Conservation is a possibility]

3 [AR 6–9]: The child bases responses on correspondence of relations and immediately recognizes conservation. [Conservation is a necessity]

ONE-TO-ONE CORRESPONDENCE

Task   *50 N6*

Given: Six bottles in a row on the table and a set of glasses (more than six) on tray.

The child is asked to remove from the tray one glass for each bottle and to place one glass in front of each bottle. Once correspondence is established, six glasses are grouped apart from the bottles and the child is asked if there are as many glasses as bottles.

Stages

1 [AR 4–6]: The experimenter evaluates through a global comparison of lengths of sets and has no notion of lasting equivalence. [No exact correspondence]

2 [AR 4–7]: The child is capable of making one-to-one correspondence between bottles and glasses without hesitation. He is certain that number of bottles and glasses is equal when he sees them paired, but ceases to believe in equivalence when rows are not longer of equal length. Correspondence is visual. Spatial alterations appear to affect qualifications of elements. [One-to-one correspondence but without lasting equivalence for corresponding sets]

3 [AR 5–7]: Once sets become equivalent through one-to-one correspondence, they remain so. The child discovers and states explicitly that grouping or spacing elements in no way affects their numbers. [Equivalence and conservation]

CORRESPONDENCE

Task   *51 N7*

Given: A number of vases and a greater number of flowers.

The child is asked to take one flower for each vase. After he makes this correspondence, he is asked to check his results by putting one flower into each vase. Flowers are then taken out and bunched together. The child is asked, "Are there still the same number of both?"

Given: A number of eggs cups and a larger number of eggs. Procedure is as above. In addition, eggs are first clustered close to egg cups and then some distance away to test whether optical contact affects estimate of equivalence.

Stages

1 [AR 4–5]: The child is not capable of making one-to-one correspondence by himself; he only discovers it when forced to look at relations between container and content. Equivalence is a result of perceptual comparison of lengths of rows. When one set of elements is grouped more closely or spaced more widely then the other, equivalence is not recognized. [Global comparison without one-to-one correspondence or lasting equivalence]

2 [AR 4–6]: The child can by himself produce a one-to-one correspondence, but it is still intuitive. He no longer sees equivalence once configuration of set is changed. Gradually, he begins to free himself from perception. The closer one-to-one correspondence between elements, the more lasting the equivalence will be—therefore, if a flower is put into vase, or an egg into egg-cup, the link between corresponding elements will be closer than when glass and bottle are simply paired. Beginnings of construction of operational correspondence. [Intuitive one-to-one correspondence without lasting equivalence]

3 [AR 5–7]: The operation is no longer affected by intuition. The child grasps both reversibility and equivalence. [Operational correspondence and lasting equivalence]

ONE-FOR-ONE EXCHANGE

Task   *52 N8*

Given: Pennies with which to buy a number of objects, the price of each object being one penny.

The child is asked to estimate how many things he will be able to buy (one-to-one correspondence). The actual exchange then takes place.

The experimenter tries to discover whether or not the child sees equivalence between number of pennies and objects he has bought.

Stages

1 [AR 4–5]: The child can make one-for-one exchanges, but he cannot make correspondence between pennies and objects before the exchange is made. He estimates quantities by space objects occupy. He is also unable to see that the sets are necessarily equivalent after exchange. [Global comparison and lack of equivalence]

2 [AR 4–7]: The child is capable of making correct estimates of number of elements to be exchanged through visual correspondence. However, even after the exchange is made, he does nto believe that the sets are equivalent. He begins to use abstract operations to combat perceptual appearances. [Correct correspondence but no lasting equivalence]

3 [AR 5–7]: Equivalence becomes obvious and logically necessary for the child. [lasting equivalence]

ONE-FOR-ONE EXCHANGE IN CONJUNCTION WITH COUNTING ALOUD

Task   *53 N9*

The experimenter finds out how far the child can count without difficulty. Then experiment of one-for-one exchange of pennies and objects is repeated (52 N8). This time using a number of pairs of objects smaller than highest number to which the child can count. The child is asked to count objects he has been given while pennies he has given in exchange are covered (so he cannot count them).

The child is then asked to guess how many pennies are hidden.

Stages

1 [AR 4–5]: The child makes a global comparison of the sets and does not see equivalence. [Lack of equivalence]

2 [AR 4–6]: The child makes correspondence before actual exchange is made, but is still unable to see equivalence. Gradually, the child recognizes equivalence of sets in questions, but views it as an action of moving an object and an action of moving a penny. He, therefore, accepts correspondence as lasting, but when he tries to abstract cardinal numbers from the operation by which he arrived at it, he does not yet see that equivalence is necessary. [Correct correspondence without lasting equivalence]

3 [AR 5–7]: The child sees sets as equivalent in all situations. [Lasting equivalence]

Note: The verbal factor (counting aloud) has little affect on development of correspondence and equivalence. When correspondence becomes quantified, giving rise to beginnings of equivalence, counting aloud may hasten process, but process is not begun by numerals as such.

SPONTANEOUS CORRESPONDENCE

Task   *54 N10*

Given: A succession of figures made with counters and a box of fifteen or more counters like those used to make the figures. The figures are of five types. 1. Poorly structured (counters randomly distributed, not touching or overlapping); 2. Open figures; 3. Closed figures (no specific number of counters used); 4. Closed figures (the space enclosed depends on the number of counters used); 5. Complex closed figures (unfamiliar to the child).

One figure at a time is placed in front of the child. He is asked to look at the figure and to pick out of the box the number of counters used. The experimenter does not name the geometric figure formed by the counters.

Stages

1 [AR 4–5]: The child does not feel the need of qualitative evaluation since he has no precise notion of cardinal numbers and makes perceptual evaluations. His comparisons are global and qualitative, without coordination of the qualities being compared. [Global comparisons]

2 [AR 4–6]: The child again shows intuitive qualitative correspondence, but as the copying of models becomes more exact the one-to-one correspondence becomes more precise. Correspondence is still perceptual; when configuration is altered the child is no longer convinced of equivalence. [Intuitive correspondence]

3 [AR 5–7]: Correspondence no longer depends on intuitive figure. The child begins to break up figures and arrange them in series as a check. Correspondence becomes either qualitatively or numerically operational. [Operational correspondence]

SPONTANEOUS CORRESPONDENCE

Task   *55 N11*

Given: A row of 6 beans, 1 to 2 cm apart. The child is asked to pick out the same number of beans from a given, larger amount.

Stages

1 [AR 4–6]: Instead of making the one-to-one correspondence, the child bases his evaluation of perceptions on one of the two global qualities of the

row—its length or the density of the objects in it—instead of coordinating them. [Global comparisons]

2 [AR 4-6]: The child immediately makes optical spatial correspondence. What he discovers in making this correspondence is the beginning of seriation and of multiplication of qualitative relations of position, but nothing more. When the density or length of a row is altered he ceases to affirm correspondence. When the correspondence cannot actually be perceived, he negates the equivalence. [Intuitive correspondence without lasting equivalence]

3 [AR 5-7]: Correspondence is freed from perceptual or spatial limitations and persists in spite of any displacement of elements. One-to-one correspondence is quantified (numerical equality is expressed). [Operational correspondence and lasting equivalence]

CONSTRUCTION OF SERIAL CORRESPONDENCE (QUALITATIVE SIMILARITY)

Task   *56 N12*

Given: Ten wooden dolls of clearly different heights (the tallest being at least twice the height of the shortest) and ten sticks also of differing lengths, but with less difference among them.

The child is presented with the dolls and sticks spread randomly on a table. He is asked to arrange them so that "each doll can easily find the stick that belongs to it."

Once dolls and sticks have been arranged in corresponding rows, the dolls are brought closer to each other, the sticks spread more widely so that corresponding elements are no longer so closely paired. Each doll is touched in turn and the child is asked to indicate the corresponding stick.

The order of the series is reversed, each doll is touched, and he asked again to indicate the stick which corresponds.

Next, one series or both are disarranged and he is asked which stick corresponds to a particular doll.

Finally, all elements in both series are mingled, one doll is pointed out, and the child is asked to find sticks corresponding to the remaining dolls.

Stages

1 [AR 4-6]: The child is unable to form isolated series correctly. Neither seriation nor spontaneous correspondence is achieved. [Global comparisons]

2 [AR 5–7]: The child is capable of spontaneous construction of correct series after some trial and error. He solves the serial correspondence task by establishing two distinct series which are then made to correspond. However, seriation and serial correspondence are still intuitive and perceptual. [Intermediary reactions]

3 [AR 6–8]: Seriation and serial correspondence become operational. They are manipulated apart from perception. Correspondence is constructed without trial and error. [Correspondence with truly ordinal and numerical operations]

FROM SERIAL CORRESPONDENCE TO ORDINAL CORRESPONDENCE

Task   *57 N13*

Given: Ten wooden dolls and ten sticks, as in task 56 N12.

Immediately after the child has succeeded in forming the two series, one series is displaced with respect to the other (e.g., the sticks are moved closer together while the dolls are left untouched). One doll is chosen and the child is asked to indicate the corresponding stick.

The order of the series is reversed. Again, one doll is chosen and the child is asked to indicate the corresponding stick. Finally, a stick is chosen and he is asked to indicate the corresponding doll.

Stages

1 [AR 4–6]: The child does not understand seriation. He loses the idea of correspondence when one series is displaced and he merely chooses elements that are opposite one another. [Global Comparison]

2 [AR 5–7]: The child tries to determine the correct correspondence either empirically or by counting, but is confused when he cannot coordinate cardinal and ordinal operations. He understands that in order to find the position of one element he must count the preceding elements as equivalent units; at the same time he does not conceive an element as a unit comparable to others. He does not understand that each position is a number and that this number is inseparable from the aggregate of which it is a part. [Intermediary reactions]

3 [AR 6–8]: The child solves the problem by coordinating his estimate of required position with that of cardinal value in sets in question. Operations of cardination and ordination are now correlated, the former having

become independent of parts and being applied to all terms as equivalent units, and the latter being no longer dependent on quality. The element represents for the child both the nth position and the cardinal value n. [Operational construction of both serial and ordinal correspondence]

RECONSTRUCTION OF
CARDINAL CORRESPONDENCE

Task   58 N14

Given: Ten wooden dolls and ten sticks, as in task 56 N12.

The experimenter sets up the following situations to discover how much correspondence the child retains and how he reconstructs it: One or both series are disarranged and the child is asked which stick corresponds to a particular doll; and all elements of both series are mingled, one doll is chosen, the child is told that all the dolls bigger than this one are going for a walk, and is asked which sticks will stay home in the cupboard.

Stages

1 [AR 4-6]: The child sees no correspondence, nor does he reconstruct the series but chooses elements randomly. He cannot make cardinal correspondence spontaneously. He allots 5 sticks to 6 dolls staying home and leaves 5 sticks for the 4 dolls going for a walk. [Lack of reconstruction of cardinal correspondence]

2 [AR 5-7]: The child makes an effort to complete the task but without systematic reseriation or cardination. He begins to coordinate ordination and cardination, mastering qualitative serial correspondence intuitively, but not yet successful with numerical operations. The attempts to relate the cardinal and ordinal aspects of correspondence can take 4 different forms: (1) The child guesses at the correspondence, or orders one of the series, and then guesses at its correspondence with the other. (2) The child uses cardination but ignores ordination. (3) He uses seriation, but ignores cardination. (4) He uses cardination and ordination simultaneously, but still does not coordinate the position of the element looked for with the cardinal number of the set of elements. [Attempts at reconciling ordination with cardinal value without keeping both in mind simultaneously]

3 [AR 6-8]: Coordination of ordinal and cardinal numbers is complete. The child understands that whatever the order there are always 7 elements before the eighth. [Operational coordination]

SERIATION

Task

Given: Two sets of sticks of graduated lengths. The first set (A–J) ranges in length from 9 to 16.2 cm. The difference between each stick and that of the next size, about .08 cm, is not directly perceivable. The second set (a–i) ranges from 9.4 cm to 15.8 cm and is graduated so that the interval between each stick and that of the next size is also .08 cm. (Accordingly, the interval between A and a is .04 cm, between a and B .04 cm, etc.)

The child is asked to form a series arranging the sticks vertically from the shortest to the longest. When this has been done, she is given, one at a time in random order, the 9 additional sticks of the second set (a–i), and told that these have been inadvertently omitted and are now to be inserted in their proper places in the series. When he has formed the series correctly, he is asked to count all the elements limit.

A number of sticks are removed from the series so that the number of sticks remaining in front of the child should be low enough for him to count comfortably. The experimenter points to one stick and asks how many "stairs" a doll will have climbed when it reaches that point. The child is also asked how many stairs are behind the doll and how many it will need to climb up to reach top.

The series is then disarranged and some general questions are asked. The child is obliged to reconstruct the series before replying.

Stages

1 [AR 4–6]: The child is unable to seriate the sticks. When trying to determine the position of one stick, he does not compare it with the whole set but seems only to look for one that is "big" or "small" in relation to it. He succeeds in making several short series, which he puts side by side without regard to the order of the whole series, or else succeeds in building a staircase that only takes into account the top of each stick. He disregards the base and thus the total length of each element, so that his staircase is regular only at the top, and as the sticks are not placed in a horizontal line they are not in the correct order of size. [Purely intuitive configuration]

2 [AR 4–6]: The child succeeds by trial and error in making a correct staircase, but he has not acquired a system of relationships. He gradually understands the need to reconstruct the disarranged sticks according to an order but has difficulty in dissociating a section of the series from the whole. [Success by trial and error]

3 [AR 6–7]: The child correctly seriates all elements without hesitation. Each element is placed in a position in which it is at the same time bigger than the preceding elements and smaller than those which follow. He understands the relation between cardinal and ordinal numbers once the stairs already climbed have been reseriated and counted. He feels no need to reseriate the remainder to discover how many stairs remain to be climbed. [Systematic operational method]

SERIATION OF CARDS

Task   *60 N16*

Given: Eleven cards, A through K, in which A = 1 unit square (1 × 1), B = rectangle (1 × 2), C = rectangle (1 × 3), through K = rectangle (1 × 10). The cards are placed side by side to form a staircase.

The child is asked to seriate the cards and then to count them as far as he can without hesitating.

He is asked how many cards like A would it take to make B or C, etc. Once the child grasps "unit measuring," the experimenter picks a card at random and the child is asked how many units this card represents.

Stages

1 [AR 4–5]: The child possesses the empirical elements necessary for understanding the law, but he does not understand it. He can count the units of a series without hesitation; he understands that the difference between successive units is one, but he cannot grasp the correspondence between position and cardinal values. The relation between order and cardination is not understood beyond 3 or 4. [Global seriation]

2 [AR 5–6]: The child appears to discover the law when a progressive order is followed, but he is baffled when the order is reversed, when cards are picked at random, and when visual seriation is destroyed. The child's seriation merely produces a rigid series: The positions of the elements depend on the whole set and cannot serve for detailed operations once they are separated from the whole. [Success by trial and error]

3 [AR 6–7]: The child understands the problem completely through operational ordination and cardination. The series ceases to be rigid and becomes operational; each unit can be considered both by itself and in its relation to others, regardless of the order in which the units are presented. [Systematic operational method]

LAG BETWEEN CARDINAL AND ORDINAL NUMBERS

Task 61 N17

Given: A doll, 7 little hurdles of varying heights, and 8 little mats. The mats and hurdles are placed in a row in alternating order beginning with a mat. A doll is made to jump from the first mat (1) over the first hurdle (1) to the next mat (2) so that when it has reached mat 3, it will have jumped 2 hurdles, and so on.

Six questions are asked.

1. "How many mats are needed for each hurdle?"
The doll is made to jump and brought to a stop after one hurdle.
2. The experimenter asks: "How many hurdles have been jumped and how many mats have been touched?" This question is repeated with the doll in various positions.
3. Eight mats and some hurdles are removed. The experimenter asks: "How many mats are needed for the remaining hurdles?"
4. The order of the hurdles is mixed and one is selected. The experimenter asks: "How many hurdles were jumped before this one?"
5. The order of the hurdles is mixed and some of the mats are placed in a row. The experimenter asks: "How many hurdles have been jumped and which are they?"
6. Some of the mats are again put down. The experimenter asks: "Which was the last hurdle jumped?"

Stages

1 [AR 4–5]: The child cannot seriate the mats and hurdles correctly, and he does not understand the relationship in this task between ordinals and cardinals. In spite of the fact that he has the whole series arranged before him, he continues to make a one-to-one correspondence between hurdles and mats. [Global seriation]

2 [AR 5–6]: The child intuitively seriates and empirically discovers the relationship between the number of mats and the hurdles, but he does so without understanding that relationship. When he is concerned with cardinal numbers of hurdles, he either forgets the ordinal aspect or seriates in relation to the last mat only; and when he is concerned with seriating in relation to the last hurdle, he forgets the number of mats. [Intuitive seriation, the success of which depends on actual perception of the series]

3 [AR 6–7]: The child can make the series without hesitation. In the case of isolated elements, he discovers and seriates the preceding elements without forming the whole series. He understands the relationship between the number of hurdles and the mats. [Systematic seriation]

ADDITIVE COMPOSITION OF CLASSES

Task   *62 N18*

Given: B is a set of objects forming a logical class; A is a part of B forming a subclass: a box containing only wooden beads (B), most of them brown (A), but 2 of them white (A'). Thus, A + A' = B.

The child is asked to determine whether there are more elements in B than in A. He is presented with the box of beads and asked whether the box contains more wooden beads or more brown beads.

Note: For the younger child, simplified versions of this experiment should be tried first to ensure that he grasps the difference between A and B.

Stages

1 [AR 4–8]: The child possesses the notion of a total class, but he cannot think simultaneously of both whole and part. He cannot establish a permanent inclusion of parts into a whole. Qualitatively, the child understands that a bead can at same time be both brown and wooden; but quantitatively, he cannot place the same beads in 2 sets simultaneously. As soon as he considers one part separately, the whole as such is destroyed. [Absence of additive composition]

2 [AR 6–8]: The child intuitively and by trial and error discovers the correct answer but not immediate composition. When he is able to think simultaneously of a total class characterized by the attribute "wooden" and of partial classes defined by color, then he gradually discovers correct additive composition and inclusion. [Progressive reversibility of operations]

3 [AR 6–9]: The child discovers spontaneously and immediately, that B has more elements than A. He can see that the part and the whole are defined by some attribute, but that whole also includes the remaining part. Reversible operations allow additive synthesis of parts into a whole. [Logical composition of inverse and direct operations]

RELATIONS BETWEEN PARTS AND WHOLE, AND CHANGES IN COMPOSITION OF PARTS

Task   *63 N19*

Given: Eight beans representing sweets. The child is told that on one day, he will be given 4 sweets in the morning and 4 in the afternoon. The next day, he is to have the same number, but he will be less hungry in the morning, so he will eat only one in the morning and all the others in the afternoon. Beans are put before him to illustrate each statement. Thus 3 beans are removed from one set of 4 and added to the other set to represent the position on the second day.

The child is then asked to compare the 2 sets (4 + 4) and (1 + 7) and to say whether he will eat the same number of sweets on both days.

Stages

1 [AR 5–7]: The child does not regard the 2 sets as equivalent, nor does he grasp the permanence of the second whole in spite of the changes in the distribution of the elements. He is guided by perceptual relationships; he does not attempt to use operations. He does not compare the sum 7 + 1 = 8 with sum of 4 + 4 = 8 [Absence of additive composition]

2 [AR 6–7]: The child gradually comes to see (or can be made to see) that although 7 > 4 and 1 < 4, these inequalities may compensate for each other. Intensive quantification is not yet numerical since the transformations do not require that the elements be counted. The child is involved in addition of classes and not yet in addition of numbers. [Progressive reversibility of operations]

3 [AR 7–8]: Addition of numbers occurs. Subsets are no longer regarded as groups of elements that have some qualitative individuality but as equivalent and distinct units involved in operations. [Logical composition of operations]

EQUATING OF QUANTITIES

Task   *64 N20*

Given: Two sets of counters, one set containing 8, the other 14. The child is asked to make the sets equal. When he believes that they are equal, he is asked if there is now the same number of counters in both sets. If the child continues to have difficulty in equating the sets, the total number of counters should be reduced to simplify task.

Stages

1 [AR 4–6]: The child seems unaware that the total number of counters is constant and, therefore, does not understand that additions and subtractions necessarily compensate for each other. He perceives that one set is larger than the other, and so he adds counters to the smaller set, but he does not expect the set from which they were taken to decrease by same amount. The child takes only a few counters from the larger set, adds them to the other, and makes only a global comparison of the results obtained by this empirical transfer. [Global comparison]

2 [AR 5–7]: The child intuits the beginnings of additive composition. He arranges the counters in comparable figures in order to equate them. Doing this, he is compelled to compare the 2 sets and to notice that each transfer is at same time an addition to one set and a subtraction from the other. However, as soon as the figure is altered, equivalence vanishes. [No lasting operational conservation]

3 [AR 6–8]: The child establishes equivalence by a priori decomposition of sets. Equality is lasting because conservation results from composition, which is now mobile and reversible. [Operational additive composition]

DIVISION INTO HALVES

Task   *65 N21*

Given: A number of counters in a pile.

The child is asked to divide the counters into two groups, "one for you and one for me, so that we each have the same amount."

Stages

1 [AR 4–6]: The child cannot grasp the fact that the sum of the parts is equal to the whole, nor does he recognize the lasting equivalence of halves, even when he has obtained them by distributing elements unit by unit into corresponding sets. [Global comparison]

2 [AR 5–7]: The child compares the two sets but does not acknowledge lasting equivalence or conservation of the whole. [No lasting operational conservation]

3 [AR 6–8]: Additive composition is completed. The child understands that two parts, considered as units, are equal and that the sum of the parts is equal to the initial whole. [Operational composition]

RELATIONS OF EQUVALENCE

Task   66 N22

Given: Ten flowers and ten vases.

The child is asked to place each flower in a vase. The experimenter then removes them from vases and places them in a bowl. The child is given ten more flowers and asked to place these in the vases. They are also removed and placed in a bowl somewhat larger than the first bowl so that the flowers are less closely bunched. The child is asked whether there are as many flowers in one bowl as the other. The bunches are then interchanged, and he is asked the same question.

Stages

1 [AR 4–5]: The child does not understand construction of correspondence or composition of equivalence. He cannot coordinate the equivalences and does not regard each of them separately as lasting. [Global comparison]

2 [AR 4–6]: Composition is intuitive, based on perceptual contact, and not yet operational. The child can make the one-to-one correspondence but does not believe in the lasting equivalences of corresponding sets. The child gradually succeeds, with the aid of suggestions, in discovering lasting equivalence. [No lasting operational conservation]

3 [AR 5–7]: The child now thinks operationally. Composition is an effort at reversibility that runs counter to actual perception. The child succeeds at equivalence and composition. [Operational composition]

MULTIPLE CORRESPONDENCE AND NUMERICAL MULTIPLICATION

Task   67 N23

Given: A set of ten pink flowers, a set of ten blue flowers, and ten vases.

The child put a set of pink flowers into the vases, then the set of blue flowers into the same vases. The child is asked how many flowers would be in each vase if he puts all flowers into the ten vases simultaneously.

Stages

1 [AR 4–6]: The child is incapable of making the 1-to-1 correspondence between the two sets except when units of one are placed inside the units of the second. Although he understands that n blue flowers correspond to n vases and that n pink flowers correspond to n vases, but does not understand that n vases correspond to n pairs. He cannot deduce that X = Y and Y = Z, then X = Z. [Lack of multiplicative composition]

2 [AR 4–6]: The child understands that if each of two equal sets correspond 1-to-1 to a third set, then the first two sets combined will correspond to the third in a 2-to-1 relationship. He does not see this as true multiplication because he has not mastered composition of relations of equivalence or multiple correspondence, nor does he generalize multiple correspondence. [No lasting operational composition]

3 [AR 5–7]: The child is capable of composing equivalences and understands relationships of multiple correspondence. As soon as the 2-to-1 relationship is grasped, it is generalizable to 3-, 4-, and 5-to-1, etc. [Operational composition]

MEASURE

Task   *68 N24*

Given: Two or three containers of different shapes containing equal amounts of liquid, and a set of equal size empty glasses.

The child is asked to determine by perception whether the amounts of liquid in the container are equal. The experimenter then asks him how the determination can be proved. If the child fails to use the glasses spontaneously as a means of measuring, the experimenter suggests that they may be useful for this purpose. If the child still does not react, the experimenter proceeds to pour liquid from the containers into equal size empty glasses.

Stages

1 [AR 5–6]: The child shows no understanding of the conservation so measurement is impossible; quantities that are not conserved cannot be composed. [Absence of conservation]

2 [AR 6–8]: Conservation is demonstrated when changes are only slight and not easy to perceive. The child gradually comes to believe in constancy, even with more obvious changes, as a result of successive verifications. Measurement begins to be possible, but it is not yet systematic. [Intermediary reactions]

3 [AR 6–8]: The child is capable of operational constructions. He discovers common measure and "the unit." He immediately assumes conservation and can measure systematically of his own accord. [Operational conservation]

COMPOSITION

Task 69 N25

1. The child is given a quantity of liquid in a low, wide container and is asked to put the same amount of liquid in a tall, narrow container.

2. The child is asked: If L = A and A = G, does L = G? From this, can L + G = 2A be deduced? If A is filled with 2L, does G = ½A?

Stages

1 [AR 5–6]: The child is incapable of either logical or numerical composition and has no notion of conservation, and therefore no possibility of additive composition. He does not have an intuitive understanding of composition of equivalences. [Absence of composition]

2 [AR 6–8]: The child displays the beginnings of coordination, but his actions are intuitive and without operational composition. He has not yet reached the point at which rational composition dominates perception. [No lasting composition]

3 [AR 6–8]: The child can combine one with another, the units of measure obtained by rigorous equalization of differences. [Operational composition]

Time

INTRODUCTION

"Time is money" says the proverb. This affirmation that represents in essence a socialized common sense use of this concept encompasses a logical substitution. Money is not time as everyone would readily agree, and time can only be money under certain conditions. In short, this logical equation is inaccurate but symbolically correct. In our school history, time was generally considered in the study of physics and was not usually a topic in itself. Conceptually, time represents something that passes, something that one cannot grasp, hold or touch, but that one can measure. One seldom thinks of the contradiction that this term represents: It is another of the abstract concepts that are very much a part of our daily lives. I am too early or too late for an appointment; I have spent too much or too little time with someone; I have devoted enough or not enough time to this or that. Time is an inherent part of our lives, as well as a concept that encompasses one's total life. In reflecting about the concept of time, one may be angry or happy over time; one might use the concept metaphorically, and it might even symbolize life itself. One accepts, uses, or distorts it; one attempts to get rid of it; one talks of good timing or the lack of it. In short, one talks of time as though it were the most banal and practical concept. Yet its essence is of the most abstract character.

Time has been the subject of philosophical debates. The first famous but unresolved controversy arose in ancient Greece between Parmenides who maintained that change was irrational illusion and Heraclitus who believed that there was no permanence and that change characterized everything without exception. Another controversy arose centuries later between disciples of Newton and Leibniz. According to Newton time was independent of and prior to events; in his own words: "absolute time and mathematical time of itself and from its own nature, flows equally without regard to anything external." According to Leibniz, on the other hand, there can be no time independent of events, for time is formed by events and relations among them, and constitute the universal order of succession. It was this later doctrine that gave rise to the doctrine of space-time, in which both space and time are regarded as two systems of relations, perceptually distinct but inseparably bound together in reality.

These controversies have led some people to believe that the concept of time cannot be accounted for unless one distinguishes between perceptual, subjective and objective time. From a psychological point of view, the problem is to determine whether or not our intuition of time is primitive. If time is an intuition, no matter how primitive, it will have epistemological consequences, as well as if time is a construction that uses as prerequisites velocity and space. In short, the determination of time as an intuition or not is both psychologically and epistemologically important.

Let me remind the reader of the apparent paradox that one encounters in defining time. In order to define time, one needs a clock. What is a clock? It is a tool that generates spatial displacement at a constant speed. What is speed? It consists of an interval as measured through a unit of time. The attempt to define time leads to circular reasoning: To define time one needs speed, and in order to define speed one needs a time referent.

To solve this apparent paradox, developmental findings might be of help. It is important to determine which parameter is first achieved by the child, since his hierarchy of construction of the concept of time might finally help isolate primitive factors. If the order of succession is primitive and the organization of events implies an ordinal referent, and if time as a concept appears only after the understanding of the order of succession, then one is in a position to clarify the previous circular pattern of theoretical reasoning.

In effect the concept of time involves three types of operations: The first type concerns the order of succession. If three events A, B, and C occur in succession, it is implied that, as long as one maintains the same referent, C happened after B, and B after A. This order of succession, based upon an extraction of an order in events, although not innate is early achieved, around 4 years of age. During its construction the child tends to confuse the limits of the time interval with the order of succession itself. At the beginning the child takes into account only the last event perceived without relating this last event to the totality of the event itself. In practice this means that the child does not pay attention to the order of succession as representing a beginning and an end, between which an interval of time takes place. For him, what counts is the perception of what came last.

The second type of operation the child needs to master refers to an operation of enclosure. What is meant by this term is the recognition that two events can be compared in terms of their time of departure and time of arrival. If an event A began before and ended before another event B, then there is no question that A lasted for a shorter time than B. In this case the simple comparison of time of departure and arrival of both events is sufficient to provide a correct evaluation of a time interval between two events. Observe that in this case one does not need a comparison dealing with speed or distance covered during this time. The simple comparison between the order of succession of event A and event B is sufficient. In short, the order of succession is but one aspect of the concept of time and it is essential that the child conceives that this order of succession encloses events, that an order of succession involves an interval of time or a duration. The recognition of a duration as a time-interval is the second type of operation that the child achieves when constructing his concept of time.

Thirdly, the child needs to possess a time-metric. In the previous case, let us assume that both events to be compared began at the same time and ended at the same time, but that A (for instance, a car covering a certain distance) and B (another car covering a greater distance in the same span of time) were different in terms of distance covered as well as in terms of their speed. The total durations of both events were equal, not the way they were perceived. Observe that in this case, since car B went faster than A, it necessarily follows that B covered a greater distance if the duration of the two events are equal. There are necessary relationships that are part of the equation: $t = space/speed$. Time metric implies a further understanding of a unit, of a referent (such as the second or the minute) that can be repeated and is unaffected by usual external circumstances.

A young child will believe that if he goes faster, the clock he is looking at to measure time will also go faster. For him, time as a duration and as a measure of events among themselves is dependent upon factors of speed and space. In short, time is developmentally not an intuition. It is a construction that uses spatial referents such as order of succession first, then speed and velocity. Only around 9 years of age will the child come to dissociate time from space and speed.

This observation has again epistemological consequences and demonstrates Piaget's philosophical concern about a category of knowledge whose unfolding is studied in the child's development. Its results, in turn, clarify the philosophical problem itself.

SEQUENCE OF EVENTS

Task   *70 T1*

Given: Two flasks of equal capacity and different shapes (I and II). Flask I is filled with colored water. At regular intervals, a fixed amount of liquid is allowed to flow from I into II until II is full and I is empty. The child is given a sheet of paper on which the series of flasks I and flasks II are reproduced.

1. The child is asked to indicate respective liquid levels by pencilling horizontal lines on drawings of flasks. He is asked about global order of changes.
2. The sheet of paper is cut horizontally and vertically so that each flask is a separated drawing: The drawings are shuffled and the child is asked to put them back in order.
3. The drawings are shuffled again and the child is asked: "Was water here (I_2) before or after it was here (I_3)?" Next: "When the water was here (I_5), where was the water in other flask?"
4. "Does the water take the same length of time to drop from here (I_1) to here (I_2) as to rise from there (II_1) to there (II_2)?"
5. "Which takes longer: for water to drop from here (I_1) to here (I_3) or from here (I_1) to here (I_2)?" "From I_1 to I_3 or from II_1 to II_2?"
6. "Does water take the same length of time to rise from II_1 to II_2 as to rise from II_2 to II_3?"
7. "Is there an equal increase in water level from II_1 to II_2 and II_3, etc?"

Stages

1 [AR 5–7]: Though the child recalls overall motion intuitively and arranges successive levels by their configuration alone, he does not put drawings in order. Once observed events have taken place, he fails to reconstruct order of succession; the child sees a series of static spatial relationships and not the displacement of liquid from top flask to bottom flask. He improves reconstruction through trial and error but cannot yet grasp overall order of events. [Intuitive solution]

2 [AR 6–10]: The child still cannot seriate shuffled drawings; fails to grasp spontaneously the inverse relationship of changes in I and II; does not remember throughout construction of series that as levels rise in II they drop in I. He lacks reversibility of thought. Increasingly he is able to produce both series by trial and error; begins to grasp connection of simultaneity and order of events in time. The child arranges series by height alone, not by height and coordination of two motions. Correct arrangement of unseparated drawings but failure to seriate separated drawings. [Transitional behaviors]

3 [AR 8–10]: The child produces double series in accordance with principle. [Operational co-seriation of the separated drawings and the grasp of succession and simultaneity]

Note: Several levels of reasoning are involved in this experiment:

a. Inverse proportion: decrease in I corresponds with increase in II;

b. Seriation: level of II increases in an ordered way, of I decreases in an orderly way;

c. Time: simultaneity of successive changes in I and II.

SIMULTANEITY

Task   71 T2

Given: Two figures (I and II), moved in the same direction along parallel lines. The figures stop and start simultaneously. However, I is moved faster than II; when the figures stop, I is 3 to 4 cm. ahead of II.
The child is asked a series of questions: "Did they start at the same time?" "Did they stop at the same time?" "Which one stopped first?" "Did they travel the same length of time?" "Why?"

Stages

1 [AR 4-7]: The child generally denies simultaneous arrivals; two motions at unequal velocities lack a common time. The child fails to grasp simultaneity of endings. Often even the simultaneity of starting points is negated. I takes longer than II because it goes further or more quickly; II stops "first" because it covers a smaller distance. [No simultaneity; duration judged proportional to distance]

2 [AR 5-7]: Time articulations remain uncoordinated and unstable. The child establishes a direct time-speed relationship ("the faster, the more time") or an inverse relationship ("the faster, the less time"). He gradually begins to coordinate the direct and inverse time-space relationships. Generally the child denies the simultaneity and equality of the synchronous duration. II goes on for a longer time because it moves less quickly. [Differentiation of intuitive conceptions]

3 [AR 7-9]: The child immediately coordinates simultaneity and synchronism; he no longer uses trial and error. [Operational coordination]

EQUALIZATION OF SYNCHRONOUS DURATIONS

Task   72 T3

Given: A reservoir containing water that flows through a Y-tube into bottles of different shapes and capacities. A stopcock above the tube branch is used to control water flow.

1. Before stopcock is opened, the experimenter asks: "Which bottle will fill faster?"

2. After smaller bottle has been filled: "Did water start flowing in both branches at the same time? Stop flowing?"
3. "How long did the water take to rise to A_1? Did it take the same length of time, more time, or less time to reach B_1?"
4. When the child understands that flow is simultaneous in branches, the experimenter asks: "Is there the same amount of water in A as in B?"
5. Given the same set-up using bottles of different shapes but equal capacity, the experimenter asks: If C_1 is filled in the same length of time as C_2 and C_2 is filled in the same length of time as C_3 (a hypothetical bottle), is C_1 filled in the same length of time as C_3 and do they contain equal amounts of water?"

Stages

1 [AR 4–6]: The child fails to grasp simultaneity and synchronization. He is unable to quantify flow of water and conceives time as the course of an action (since one bottle is filled before the other, the flow could not have stopped at the same time). [Intuitive answers]

2 [AR 5–8]: The child recognizes simultaneity and separates time from velocity. He predicts intuitively that the larger bottle will be filled less quickly and in more time, but fails to synchronize durations with simultaneous starting and finishing points or to quantify flow of water (smaller bottle contains more water because it is filled to the brim.) He begins after trial and error to grasp the equality of synchronous durations and to quantify liquid. Having achieved correct results, the child generalizes to analogous situations, but does not coordinate synchronization and equalization of quantities. [Empirical discovery of synchronization]

3 [AR 7–8]: The child immediately grasps synchronization and quantification. At stages 1 and 2, the child fails to understand transitivity; Not until stage 3 does he understand that the equations $C_1 = C_2$, $C_1 = C_3$, and $C_2 = C_3$ are transitive. [Immediate synchronization and quantification]

SERIATION OF DURATIONS

Task   *73 T4*

Given: A set of ten bottles of various shapes and capacities, and a reservoir of water to which a Y-tube is attached. A stopcock above the branch controls the flow of water out of the reservoir. For each trial two of the ten bottles are chosen randomly.

The child is asked which of two bottles will fill more quickly? Why? Will it take more or less time to fill this one?

After these questions have been asked about at least two pairs (or trials), the child is asked to arrange the bottle in increasing order of "filling time," a complex seriation since bottles have been taken two at a time.

Stages

1 [AR 6–8]: The child is unable to seriate three bottles by comparing two at a time. He tends to compare two of three bottles by filling them simultaneously, but then judges the third independently. He cannot construct a unique time scale. [Inability to compare two terms at a time]
2 [AR 7–9]: The child checks all cases by working with pairs, but fails to coordinate several pairs. He increasingly coordinates pairs and successfully orders three bottles by trial and error, but fails to order four. He no longer judges the flow by looking at one bottle in isolation, but the pairs chosen for comparison remain uncoordinated. [Empirical discovery of aspects of the correct sequence]
3 [AR 8–10]: The child uses operational methods to solve problems. Using transitivity, he picks out a middle bottle against which to compare others. [Operational coordination]

ADDITIVE AND ASSOCIATIVE COMPOSITION OF DURATIONS

Task   *74 T5*

Given: One large (I) and one small (II) object to "run a race" by stages and at different speeds. Objects will start from the common point 0 and run at a 90° angle to one another. Times are equal for each interval.

1. Additive composition: equal times, different speeds. The experimenter must discover whether the child realizes that objects start and stop simultaneously and whether he assumes that elapsed time is equal at each interval for the two objects. The experimenter asks whether objects take equal lengths of time to proceed through the entire "race."

2. Associative composition: different times, same relative speeds. After the first distance has been travelled by both objects, the experimenter asks which object ran for the longer time. After the second distance has been travelled, the same question is asked and then whether the total elapsed time of I is equal to that of II.

Stages

1–2a [AR 6–8]: The child fails to grasp the equality of elementary durations even when prompted. [Inability to synchronize elementary durations]

2b [AR 7–9]: The child recognizes that starting and stopping points are the same but denies equality of synchronous elementary durations. With prompting, he accepts equality of partial durations, but denies equality of total durations and associativity. Gradually the child accepts the equality of partial durations but refuses to admit the equality of total durations and their associativity. S is confused by the simultaneous starting and stopping and the different speeds. Increasingly, the child accepts additive and associative composition of durations after trial and error. [Synchronization of elementary durations but failure in additive and associative composition]

3 [AR 8–10]: The child realizes that total durations are equal because they are composed of equal parts. [Immediate grasp of additivity and associativity]

DISSOCIATION OF AGE FROM HEIGHT

Task   *75 T6*

Given: Two drawings of trees on separate sheets. One tree is large and has a thick trunk, the other is thin, twisted, and smaller than the first. Both trees have brown trunks and bright green leaves.

The child is asked: "Are the trees the same kind?" "Look at these drawings and tell me which tree is older." "Can you be sure?"

If the child bases answer on height, the experimenter asks: "Is a larger tree always older than a smaller one?

Stages

1 [AR 4–8]: The child believes that age is proportional to size and is closed to all other arguments. He uses ordinal referents. [Lack of differentiation between age and size]

2 [AR 5–8]: The child shows gradual differentiation between age and size but does not succeed fully in separating time from speed and age from size. [Transitional behaviors]

3 [AR 7–10]: The child completely dissociates age and size. He either refuses to guess the respective ages of trees or is certain that more information is needed to determine age. [Operational thinking]

RELATIONSHIPS BETWEEN AGE AND UNEQUAL
GROWTH RATES

Task   *76 T7*

Given: Eleven drawings on cards measuring 10 × 15 cm, depicting apple and pear trees. The trees are highly schematized (so that the child does not get bogged down in unimportant details): They are drawn in the forms of circles of different sizes resting on a rigid trunk and bearing either small round red apples or small elongated yellow pears, both at equal intervals. The number of fruits is proportional to the size of the trees. There are six apple trees: A_1 (13mm diameter and 4 apples), A_2 (30mm and 7 apples), A_3 (40mm and 13 apples), A_4 (60mm and 27 apples), A_5 (70mm and 36 apples), and A_6 (80mm and 44 apples). Their respective heights are: 1.5, 4.5, 6, 9, 10.5, and 12mm from the base of the trunk.

There are five pear trees: P_1 (12mm diameter and 4 pears), P_2 (28mm and 7 pears), P_3 (60mm and 27 pears), P_4 (87mm and 46 pears), and P_5 (99mm and 74 pears). Their heights are 1.5, 4, 9, 13, and 15 cm respectively.

The child is told that the drawings show the trees at one-year intervals. He is asked to arrange the six drawings of the apple tree by age. He is then told that when the apple tree was two years old the pear tree was planted. He is then asked to seriate drawings of pear tree by placing them above the drawing of the apple tree that was made the same year.

After both sets have been seriated, the child is asked which tree is older during a particular year and by how many years.

Stages

1 [AR 5–8]: The child is able to seriate drawings but does not differentiate between age of trees and their sizes. He views time as heterogenous and duration as independent of order of succession. [Lack of differentiation between size and age]
2 [AR 5–8]: The child oscillates between undifferentiated, heterogeneous time and homogeneous time separated from spatial order. [Intuitive regulations]
3 [AR 7–10]: The child now separates time from space and develops understanding based on a systematic correlation of durations (ages) and succession of events (births and anniversaries). He considers durations and ages independently of space and height. [Operational solutions]

The Development of Movement and Speed

INTRODUCTION

Movement is an integral part of our life. A normal day of work involves many movements from one place to another. When we use a car or a subway, we expect to reach our destination with some speed. We vary our speed according to our internal needs or our external obligations or an intersection of both. In *Remembrance of Things Past,* Marcel Proust writes,

> Even from the point of view of simple quantity, in our life, days are not equal. To go through days, nervous natures as is mine, have at their disposal, as have cars, different "speeds". There are hilly and arduous days that take an infinite time to climb and other days which pass by, at full speed and that one goes through in singing.

Proust's qualifications of movement and speed within our days, reflect an intersection between subjective and objective factors. We have a sense of our own movement. We have a sense of our own speed.

Movement is an ever present component at all levels of our activity. Everybody takes the movement of his body for granted: We move our legs, our hands, our eyes, and our heads in a coordinated fashion. Sensorimotor coordinations are organized movements: Without these coordinations we would never come to differentiate between goals and means. Without movement there would be no goal. Conceptually, we think of development as a movement, as a directed movement with a rate and a speed. What Piaget terms the American Question, "How much could one or should one accelerate

113

the intellectual development?" reflects an educational concern about this concept. Yet, except in physics, movement and speed have never been topics of our school life.

Formally, movement implies a difference in space or a change of place. Erected into a universal principle by Heraclitus, it was denied as a possibility by Parmenidies and Zeno. Our intuition of movement and speed underlies in essence a principle of energy that reflects the power by which things act to change other things. It is a potentiality in the physical. Aristotle saw it as a synonym for actuality or reality.

The concept of movement is firmly rooted in the activity of the child; at the beginning of life, at the sensorimotor level of development, the child's own movements and his actions with objects, simultaneously generate his physical concept of object and his practical group of spatial displacements.

From its inception, movement has a dual polarity that can easily be distinguished: On one hand, one finds what Piaget calls the coordination of actions, which is the root of logicomathematical operations; on the other hand, one has the specific or particular features of the actions (the description and characteristics of the actions themselves), which according to Piaget are at the source of physical operations.

In its most global sense, movement is a change of position. There are many actions in which the child is only interested in the change; the movement in itself (the trajectory of the movement if one prefers) is only considered from the point of view of change. Thus, the child will take an object out of a box to put it in another one. His action consists of "placing" the object in a certain fashion, then "displacing" it and "placing" it at some other location. There are other actions in which the movement is no longer a simple displacement but a more elaborate act that implies an effort during a time interval. The effort in this case represents a speed under the form of an acceleration. Moving one's arm up and down can be done at different speeds.

In the development of movement and speed, it is in reality this second aspect of movement (the action plus the effort it implies) that Piaget studies. His approach consists of an analysis of movement in terms of its physical features.

From this point of view, at the inception of the concept of movement (the concept referring here to its conceptual representation in opposition to its sensorimotor organization), during the preoperational or intuitive period of thought, movement is not differentiated in its physical and geometrical characteristics. It does not mean that one derives from the other. It only means that the two poles of the action (the action itself and its physical features) are still too near to each other for the child to differentiate between them.

For instance, a 6 or 7 year old child will believe that a straight, ascending pathway is longer, independently from time and speed, when going up than coming down. When presented with a strip of paper with which the child can measure the interval, the 6 or 7 year old will be surprised to discover that the two distances are equal and that the slope does not matter. It is only after 7 years of age that the distance becomes symmetrical: Between two points A and B, no matter how one measures it (from A to B or from B to A) the total distance remains the same.

Once this differentiation is done, the crucial physical aspect of movement is constituted by its speed and the problem becomes one of the formation of the concept of speed. From this point of view the first intuition one observes in the child deals with the order of succession and this order is considered only from the point of view of points of arrival: Young children think that the fastest of two objects is the one which passes the other. The concept of overpassing that implies an order of succession is at the root of the concept of speed. In other words, speed has its roots in the spatial order of points of arrival.

Before being able to conceive of speed as a relationship between time and space, the child generalizes the concept of overpassing in prolonging in thought the perceived movements. As such, overpassing implies a physical element derived from the objects themselves and no longer only a general coordination dealing with the spatial order of the points of arrival. The child comes slowly to establish a correspondence between points of departure and points of arrival. This allows a qualitative construction of the concept of speed and it is only once this qualitative construction is done that the child will be able to construct a quantitative measure of speed.

Epistemologically, Piaget comes to the conclusion that there is a real convergence between the data emerging from the history of the concept of space, movement, speed, and time and its development within the child. Furthermore, the examination of the stages of development of movement, speed, and time demonstrates an essential law of evolution: First undifferentiated from each other, logicomathematical and physical concepts become more and more distinguished according to a dual movement of internalization and externalization. It is to the degree of their differentiation that they come to coordinate themselves in an increasingly successful and objective fashion. In becoming more and more objective, mechanical concepts also become more and more subject to the general operatory coordinations that result from the activities of the subject. Lastly, the contact between the subject and the object is always present; it has three distinct phases that correspond to this slow decentralization.

The first phase corresponds to an undifferentiation between external data and the subject's concepts, which remain egocentric: On one hand the real is distorted in relation to the ego, on the other hand, the child's concepts do not deal with a strict dissociation between logicomathematical coordinations and the actions or physical operations. The first phase is thus characterized by an intersection between objective and subjective factors. The second phase corresponds to a parallel between deduction and experience: Physical experience once detached from its egocentric elements finds its tools of coordination in an operatory logic. In the last phase the experience goes beyond our spatio-temporal scale of observation, and looses its intuitive leftovers. The remarkable aspect of Piaget's findings for what concerns these concepts is thus again the parallel one can draw between their development in children and their historical evolution.

ALTERNATING DIRECTIONS OF TRAVEL

Task   *77 M1*

Given: Three beads: A (red), B (black), and C (blue) threaded on a length of wire. The experimenter passes the wire through his half-closed fist so that the beads reappear in ABC order. He then passes the wire back through his half closed fist so that beads reappear in inverse (CBA) order.

Given: The three beads are placed in a cardboard chute in ABC order and are guided through chute to reappear in the same (ABC) order.

Given: Three wooden dolls are strung on a wire. They are passed in ABC order behind a screen.

The child is asked the following questions: "In what order will object emerge from hand, chute, and screen?" "In what order will objects emerge after travelling in opposite direction?" With ABC in the chute, the child is asked to change places with the experimenter and is asked in what order object will emerge on his right hand side. (If the child's starting position showed right-to-left movement, he will now see left-to-right movement.)

Apparatus is rotated 180° and the child is asked again in what order objects will emerge.

The same question is asked for a random number of semi-rotations. Does the child ever believe that the middle object could come out first?

In all cases, the child makes drawings of objects with colored pencils to serve as reminder. In this way, the problem of reasoning is separate from that of memory.

Stages

1 [AR 4–6]: The child is aware of direct order and its conservation during lateral movement. He does not, however, deduce the inverse order of objects on the return journey, yet he can recall and generalize this having once observed it. [Path retraced without inverting the order and displacement of middle object]

2 [AR 5–8]: The child is now able to forecast return order correctly. But these articulations remain intuitive because he can neither generalize nor regulate them. Increasingly, without arriving at correct solution, he manages to anticipate order when he changes places with the experimenter, upon semi-rotation of the apparatus, or even upon two quarter turns. He tends to set up alternating system (one turn, A out first; two turns, C out first; three turns, A out first; etc.) but still does not relate color of bead to number of turns. [Transitional behaviors]

3 [AR 6–8]: The child now forecasts order of objects with any number of semi-rotations and whatever the order of numbers chosen. He abstracts from these the law according to which direct order corresponds to an even number and inverse order to an odd number of rotations. [Operational coordination]

ORDER OF SUCCESSION IN CYCLIC MOVEMENTS

Task   *78 M2*

Given: A four- or six-sided prism revolving around its longitudinal axis. Each side of the prism is a different color. The prism is shown openly and is turned while the child counts the colors. The prism is then placed in a cylindrical box slit by a wide longitudinal gap that reveals one side of the prism at a time. The child is given strips of colored paper and during the first rotation of the prism is asked to line up strips to reproduce order in which colors are observed. This line-up is the model.

1. The first color is shown in the slit. The child is asked to predict the order of colors to follow. He is asked to arrange a second set of colored strips in predicted order and is allowed to refer to his model. He is asked which colors follow the last as the cylinder is turned further.

2. An intermediate color is shown in the slit and the child is asked the same series of questions.

3. The child is shown that the cylinder can be turned in either direction. He is now asked to produce the inverse order of colors and to continue beyond the first color. Then the child is shown an intermediate color and asked to reproduce the inverse color from the intermediate point through the entire cycle.

Stages

1 [AR 4–6]: During the construction of the model the child has difficulty in translating cyclic order to linear order. He cannot yet coordinate relationships of proximity and direction of travel. As he becomes capable

of translating cyclic to linear, he does not succeed in forecasting which color will follow another even by referring to model. When simultaneous perception of the whole is impossible, coordination of these relationships becomes difficult. The child either reconstructs proximity and loses direction of travel or preserves direction of travel and loses proximity. [Lack of understanding of succession]

2 [AR 5–8]: The child succeeds in forecasting cyclic series when he begins with the first unit, but fails when starting from an intermediate unit, or when starting from last unit to find inverse series. Series A through D or A through F forms a rigid block and the child is unable to break it apart. He reproduces proximity intuitively while keeping direction of travel constant. Gradually the child learns to forecast direct and inverse order from end units and to continue beyond them. He is able to forecast direct and inverse series from intermediate unit but only as far as last unit; he cannot continue beyond that point. When asked to extend series from an intermediate unit, he tends to reverse direction of travel (EFABCD becomes EFDCBA and CBAFED becomes CBADEF). [Transitional behaviors, rigid series]

3 [AR 7–8]: The child is now able to solve all tasks. He has attained operational mobility, including reversibility. [Operational behaviors]

THE PATH TRAVERSED

Task   *79 M3*

Given: The child is asked to compare 2 paths taken, one in a straight line, the other an indirect line, but such that the points of arrival and departure of the moving objects can always be visually correlated according to the relationship 'above' or 'below.'

Two pieces of string are stretched out on 2 planks of wood horizontally. On plank A, the first string is straight (A1) the second piece of string describes a kind of Greek frieze where all the segments are equal and at right angle to each other. (A2).

On plank B, one string is again straight (B1) and the second string is stretched out in irregular zigzags with variable angles and unequal segments (B2).

A moving bead on each string on both planks represents a car.

1. The experimenter takes car on A2 and begins with a journey of several segments then asks: "Would you make the other car (in A1) go exactly the same distance" or "go as far as mine."

2. The experimenter returns to the starting point on A2 and moves his car forward one single segment and thus it is left opposite the starting point of the child's car in A1. The experimenter asks the child to do an equal distance on his line A1.

Stages

1 [AR 5–7]: The child declares paths to be equal. The two distances are considered the same length when their finishing points are the same. He uses ordinal referent. Gradually he separates distance from order of arrival at goal for short journeys, but for longer journeys reverts to evaluating according to arrival at goal. The length of the paths traversed is generally evaluated in terms of the intuitive order of the points of arrival. [Intuitive answers]

2 [AR 5–8]: The child begins to see that order of arrivals does not correspond to lengths of paths traversed. He begins to evaluate lengths themselves, either by eye or by measuring with finger. But he continues to view journey as a total movement. He does not break it up into discrete units in order to use cardboard strips to measure. Even as begins to distinguish between length of paths and order of arrivals at goal he fails to divide path into units and cannot accurately transfer a measuring strip through a sequence of positions. Eventually, after trial and error, the child is able to measure distance of equal units (Plank A) but not of unequal units (Plank B). [Separation of path traversed from order of finishing points but failure in measuring]

3 [AR 7–9]: Path traversed is distinguished from points of arrival, and order of successive positions no longer interferes with addition of intervals or distances. The child can now divide total path into distances comprehended as intervals between points of departure and arrival, and measure them by transposition of the unit section [Operational comparison of paths traversed and success in measurement]

ASCENDING AND DESCENDING DISTANCE

Task   *80 M4*

Given: A three-dimensional cardboard mountain with a trail on one slope, a bead to be moved along the trail, and strips of premeasured red and blue cardboard of lengths OA, OB, etc. to be used as unit measures.

The experimenter moves the bead according to the patterns shown above and for each pattern asks, "Is it further going up or coming down?"

Stages

1-2 [AR 4-8]: The child sees distance up the trail as greater than distance down. Initially, measurement with cardboard strips will not change his mind; later he sees distances as equal if he is allowed to measure. [Inadequate compositions]

3 [AR 6-11]: The child answers the question for (a) correctly but is unable to construct the pattern (b) mentally. He recognizes equality in (b) and (c) by spontaneous measurement but does not generalize from (b) to (c). Gradually he learns to transfer and predict. [Complete reversibility of the operations of displacement]

4 [AR 8-12]: The child no longer analyses journey. By formal mechanisms he immediately grasps that partial displacements up and down compensate for each other. [Correct solution through formal anticipatory schemes]

HORIZONTAL MOTION

Task   *81 M5*

Given: A straight line OD with reference points A, B, and C, and strips of premeasured red and blue cardboard.

An object or objects is moved along the line. For each pattern, the child is asked whether OD equals DO and whether the red strips equal the blue strips.

Stages

1-2 [AR 5-8]: The child shows no operational composition; he does not anticipate or deduce results. He estimates randomly or chooses the longest section perceived. Later he manages to guess results but is not able to justify them. [No operational composition]

3 [AR 8-11]: The child shows concrete composition of distances with cardboard strips. He makes correct predictions and understands concept only after reconstruction of operations involved. [Concrete thinking]

4 [AR 9-13]: The child constructs the equalities or disparities deductively from the beginning. He no longer aligns partial journeys in order to understand solution. He uses deduction to anticipate results and realizes that as long as object starts and stops at the same points the distances must be equal. [Immediate solution by formal deduction]

RELATIVE MOVEMENTS

Task 82 M6

Given: A small snail shell is placed on a board or a piece of cardboard between 10 and 15 cms. long and between 3 and 5 cms. wide. The child is told that the snail is going to take a walk on the plank and that because of its slowness we can watch its movement very closely. Only while he is moving along the experimenter shall play tricks on him; by moving the card quite slowly too, without his noticing it: sometimes in the same direction as him, sometimes in the other direction.

The snail is then put down on one end of the cardboard, a clearly visible line of reference being marked on the table at the same time and the snail and board are moved along simultaneously, sometimes in parallel, sometimes in opposite paths.

Paper strips are used to measure paths of both snail and board.
The following 4 four questions are asked:

1. The snail and the card are proceeding at the same time in the same direction with the path of the card either longer or shorter than that of the snail. Locate the point snail has reached after the materials have been removed.
2. Same reconstruction with aid of the paper strips, but the paths are in opposite direction.
3. The experimenter tells the child, without actions, simply by a verbal statement or by sketching the movements in gestures but without the child being able to observe the result, that the snail and the card are going in opposite directions from one another but both travelling the same distance at the same time. The child should therefore foresee that the snail will stay in the same spot.
4. The snail is placed at one end of the card, on the guide line and the S is asked to forecast whether he will arrive on the right or the left of this line according to whether the paths he covers is longer or shorter than the card, while this is moving in the opposite direction.

Stages

1–2 [AR 6–9]: The child does not attend to more than one movement, usually that of snail. He may use paper strips to measure one of the distances. Later, he uses strips to measure both paths but continues to consider only one of these. Increasingly he measures both distances but places the two measuring strips side-by-side at the starting line without combining them by simple addition or subtraction. [No composition of movements]

3 [AR 8–11]: The child is successful in composing movements in one direction or equal movements in opposite directions without experimental observation. But when opposite movements are unequal, he shows no composition. The idea of simultaneity is lost and each distance is measured separately. For unequal movements in opposite directions, he gradually recognizes that the total journey of the snail is shorter than if it had moved by itself (and board underneath it had not moved), but does not know how to perform subtraction or how much to subtract. Attempts at quantification begin. Later, he finds correct solution for two unequal movements in opposite direction by trial and error. [Concrete composition of movements]

4 [AR 9–13]: The child thinks of the two movements as simultaneous. He first measures them in succession and then reconstructs their synchronization operationally. [Immediate solution by formal operations]

SPEED OF 2 MOVEMENTS
(ONLY STARTING AND STOPPING POINTS ARE VISIBLE)

Task   *83 M7*

Given: Two straight tunnels of unequal (55 and 40 cm) length and two dolls with rigid wire rods attached to their backs, to pull them back and forth.

The dolls are placed at the entrances of the tunnels (entrances are aligned and serve as starting points). The dolls start through the tunnels simultaneously and appear together at the far ends. The child is asked whether one doll travelled faster than the other.

Stages

1 [AR 5–7]: The child fails to recognize that one object is moving faster than another (overtaking is closed from observation). He cannot imagine the correlation between lengths and equal duration even within a restricted field of perception and is even less capable of imagining this when movements are hidden. [Failure in comparison of speeds]

2 [AR 6–7]: The child begins by affirming that speeds of movements in tunnels are equal, but soon modifies his original opinion. He begins to succeed in visualizing what is going on in tunnels. Notions of distance,

duration, and order, however remain uncoordinated and intuitive. [Transitional behaviors]

3 [AR 6–8]: The child manages to establish the difference of speeds simply by correlating factors of time and space traversed. [Operational solutions]

SPEED (STARTING AND STOPPING POINTS COINCIDING OR IN ALIGNMENT BUT PATHS OF UNEQUAL LENGTH)

Task   *84 M8*

1a. Given: Angle CAB, the arms forming paths AB and AC. The child is first asked if one path is longer than other. Then he is told that two cars are going to travel along them at same speed and asked whether one will finish before the other. The experiment is performed and he is asked why the car traveling along AC arrives at C after other has reached B. The experimenter moves cars by hand as the cars can be fixed on 2 rigid wire rods that can be pulled back and forth.

1b. Given: Two cars (a and b) traveling at same speed between points A and B. The questions given above are repeated.

2a. Given: Two cars traveling along AC and AB. They start and finish at same time. He is asked if one car must go faster than other. After experiment is performed, he is asked whether speeds are equal.

2b. Given: One straight line and one wavy line AB. Same conditions and questions as above.

Stages

1 [AR 4–7]: The child is unable to structure speed or duration and frequently not even path to be traveled before perceiving movements. [No understanding of differences in speed]

2 [AR 5–8]: The child solves 1a and 1b without difficulty. He judges that time is proportional to distance travelled regardless of order of stopping points but fails in problems of speed (2a and 2b) even after experiment is performed.

The child gradually discovers correct solutions to 2a and 2b, but only after experiment is performed. [Intermediate reactions]

3 [AR 6–8]: The child immediately solves all four questions appropriately grouping and distinguishing the relevant factors of speed and space. [Operational solutions]

SPEED ON CONCENTRIC CIRCLES

Task   *85 M9*

Given: Two concentric circles. Two objects start around simultaneously at guide line, one on each circle. Objects return to guide line at same time.

1. Which object goes faster, one on outer circle or one on inner circle? Which one has to hurry more?

Given: a bar fixed at one end to pivot. Two objects fixed on bar—one near either end. Bar is moved through 45°. (Unification of moving objects makes conditions for intuiting more complex)

2. Does one object move faster than other?

Stages

1 [AR 6–9]: The child considers speeds to be equal in the absence of overtaking. When forced to consider unequal lengths of circles, he judges speed to be greater on smaller circle. [Preoperational behaviors]

2 [AR 7–10]: The child gradually achieves correct result after wavering between 3 points of view: (1) *equal speeds* (simultaneous starting and stopping points); (2) *greater speed on inner circle* (shorter distance, therefore òbject arrives sooner); (3) *greater speed on larger circle* (cyclic movement is translated to parallel linear movement). [Intermediary reactions]

3 [AR 7–11]: The child solves #1 operationally: sees circles as parallel lines and is not misled by cyclic order. However, he is unable to forsee this in the second task because objects are fixed to same bar. [Operational solution]

4 [AR 11–13]: The child decomposes movement of bar and realizes that object that is farther away from pivot goes faster. [Formal reasoning]

SYNCHRONOUS MOVEMENTS AND
UNEQUAL DISTANCES

Task   *86 M10*

Given: Two cars, A and B. A starts from a point some distance behind starting point of B. Cars start simultaneously and finish simultaneously at same point. The child is asked which car has moved faster.

Given: Same apparatus as above, but this time A does not quite catch up with B. S is again asked which car has moved faster.

Given: Same apparatus again, but A now overtakes B. Same question.

Given: The two cars now move toward one another from opposite directions and they meet at same point. Same questions.

Stages

1 [AR 5–6]: The child equates speed with visible overtaking and is at a loss in situations where objects move toward one another from opposite directions or catch up to one another to some extent. He judges speed by finishing point alone, disregarding distance traveled. "More quickly" usually means "finishing in front of" or "before" in a spatial and temporal sense. [Intuitive evaluation of speed]

2 [AR 6–7]: The child gradually corrects answers during course of experiment. Attention is directed to finishing points. A progressive regulation in terms of starting points and distances travelled occurs. Progressive decentration of intuition fixed on the stopping point. [Intermediate reactions]

3 [AR 7–8]: The child composes relations operationally: (1) temporal order is dissociated from succession in space; (2) distances travelled are conceived as lengths occupying interval between given starting and stopping points; and (3) for synchronous movements, speed is defined in terms of lengths covered in equal times. Relations of speed are expressed in terms of distances and no longer with factors of order. [Operational composition of relationship]

PARTLY SYNCHRONOUS TIMES AND EQUAL DISTANCES

Task   *87 M11*

Given: Two cars, A and B. The cars travel equal distances, but A begins a short time before B and they stop simultaneously.

The child is asked if one car goes faster than the other.

A begins a short time before B and they stop simultaneously, but B does not quite catch up to A.

The child is asked if one car has travelled faster than the other.

Stages

1 [AR 5–6]: The child either believes speed to be equal because objects reach same point simultaneously or believes that the speed of the object that left first is greater because it moves ahead of the other. He does not dissociate between succession in space and succession in time. [Intuitive evaluation of speed]

2 [AR 6–7]: Early in this stage, the child wavers between right and wrong answers without being able to justify them. Through successive

manipulation of material, he is able to formulate correct answers; but this is not through a coherence of operations. [Intermediate reactions]
3 [AR 7–8]: The child solves the problem by immediate grouping of relations involved. Correct answers are given spontaneously—relations of speed are expressed only in terms of distances and no longer of order. [Operational composition of relationship]

RELATIVE SPEED

Task   *88 M12*

Given: A movable belt with eight cardboard cyclists fixed to it. Speed of belt can be regulated by a handle. Figures are numbered to prevent confusion. A length of string is stretched parallel to the belt and carries a doll. Movement of doll along string can be regulated by a handle. Duration of action is about fifteen seconds.

1. The belt is given one 15 sec rotation. The experimenter says, "Now the doll is going to travel along *its* path in the same direction for the same length of time. When it was standing still, the doll saw eight cyclists pass in front of it. When it is traveling, how many cyclists will it see pass along beside it, like this (the experimenter gestures to make action clear) – eight again, or more, or fewer?" The child is asked to provide a reason for his opinion.
2. The experiment, including the experimenters' comments and questions, is repeated with the direction of the doll's path reversed.

Younger subjects are helped to understand the task by being asked whether it take more or less time for the doll to reach the cyclist if the doll stands still, if doll and cyclist travel in the same direction, or if doll and cyclist move toward each other from opposite directions.

Stages

1–2 [AR 6–8]: The child shows no understanding of relativity of speed. He does not even understand absolute speeds nor does he dissociate time from spatial successions. He cannot answer the question of time needed for the doll and single cyclist to meet and gives random answers to problems relating to eight cyclists. [Intuitive reasonings]
3 [AR 8–11]: The child considers only one of the movements or one point of view at a time. He therefore does not understand that it is addition or subtraction of movements and their speeds which alone decides result. He

is concerned with absolute length of doll's path and not at all with its length relative to movement of eight cyclists over same time period. The child does however, solve problem of single cyclist by simple intuitive anticipation of displacements. [No relativity of speeds]

The child gradually discovers correct answers by trial and error and a succession of approximations. He does not yet use direct deduction. He might foresee results, but is not able to generalize or explain them. [Concrete operations]

The child predicts results correctly and explains them fully before the experiment is performed. [Formal thinking and use of correct metric operations in the resolution of the problem—general solution of the problem by formal operations]

QUANTIFICATION OF SPEED

Task   *89 M13*

Given: an object that moves perpendicular to a base line, a second object that moves parallel to first. Both distances are timed by S with stop watch. Distances are then represented on paper and times are recorded next to line. Movements of 2 objects follow patterns: (a) times equal, distances unequal; (b) distances equal, times unequal; and (c) times unequal, distances unequal.

The child is asked if both objects traveled at the same speed or if one went faster than the other? Different ratios of speed and distance are used. (2:, etc.)

Stages

3 [AR 7–11]: The child is unable to compare successive movements in (a) or (b). He is also unable to establish proportions in (c). Instead of correlating time and distance, he simply centers his judgement on (a). The child gradually accomplishes the task for (a) and (b) patterns, and comes to (c) more slowly. Increasingly, he no longer experiences difficulty in comparing speeds when either times or distances are equal but are at first unsuccessful, then gradually succeed, when both factors are unequal and usually more easily in the case of larger disproportions. [Concrete reasoning]

4 [AR 9–13]: The child constructs and measures proportional ratios. He understands that proportions are operations, but early in this stage has not developed technique; he makes mistakes and shows some uncertainty. Increasingly the child employs systematic method using correct measurement immediately. [Construction of accurate proportions]

CONSERVATION OF UNIFORM SPEEDS

Task   *90 M14*

Given: Two parallel straight lines drawn on a sheet of paper. The child is told that an object travels along one line a certain distance on the first day. The position achieved is marked on the line. The child is then told that during the same time (simultaneous departure time), a second object travelled only half that distance along the second line. The position of the second object is marked, and the following questions asked:

1. If the objects travel at the same time and speed, will the distance covered on the first day be equal to that achieved on the second day for the first object (car); for the second object (doll)?
2. If the first object travels at the same speed for half as long, where will it be on the second day?
3. If the car departs first, followed by the doll, how long will it take the doll to catch up with the car?

Stages

1 [AR 5–7]: Speed is not conceived of as a relationship between distance and time. The child cannot carry forward distance in order to express conservation of speed. As for the doll's journey, two types of reactions are found: (1) The child simply marks a slight difference in the stopping points of car and doll, as if the doll traveled the same distance but remained slightly in the rear. (2) The child keeps constant the absolute differences between the two moving objects, and does not understand that these distances are in a constant, proportional relationship. Hence, speeds are measured by stopping points. [No conservation of speed]

2 [AR 6–9]: The child still sees the differences between stopping points as absolute, but will accept the correct solution if he compares two series of journeys, and will understand explanations where relative differences are suggested. He can only use one speed at a time. [Progressive discovery of conservation of speed in a single moving object, but no understanding of the relation between dissimilar constant speeds]

3 [AR 6–11]: The child shows operational conservation of speed (equal time and equal speed produce equal distance), but does not understand formal proportionality. He can find the simple 2:1 ratio in (3), but does not succeed in generalization. [Operational conservation of speed without understanding of formal proportionality]

4 [AR 8–12]: The child forsees that the distances between the stopping points of the two objects in all tasks increase continuously, and that there is a

constant ratio between their paths. [Deduction of the ratio of uniform speeds and formal operations of proportionality]

CONSERVATION OF ACCELERATING SPEED

Task   *91 M15*

Given: An inclined plane calibrated into 4 separate, equal intervals. A ball is rolled down the incline.

1. The experimenter asks how the ball comes down. "Is the speed of the ball always the same?"

2. Then the child is shown a drawing of a person on a sled going down a slope divided as in (1), and asked over which interval the sled's speed is greatest.

3. Given as in (1) above. The child is again directed to the inclined plane and asked, "How long does it take the ball to travel the 1st interval? 2nd? 3rd? 4th?"

4. Given as in (2) above. Finally, the child is told that every minute the person on the sled shouts "Hey" and a marker is placed at each point where this happens. The child is asked, "What is the distance between markers?"

Stages

1–2 [AR 5–7]: The child does not understand uniform acceleration. He has experienced such movement but cannot translate his experience. Increasingly, he acquires intuitive understanding of uniform acceleration, but he does not translate it into a relationship of time and distance traveled. [No acceleration as a function of descent; intuitive acceleration]

3 [AR 7–11]: The child knows how to correlate operationally the distance traveled and time taken when comparing 2 simultaneous movements, but has difficulty in considering successive parts of a single journey. He can be helped to more advanced reactions by being reminded of simultaneous movements. Increasingly, he applies this knowledge to acceleration and gives correct answers. He corrects himself spontaneously or as a result of questions asked. He persists in reasoning that the speed of the last interval is reduced because "they put the brake on at the foot of the hill." [Articulated intuition of acceleration but without accurate correlation of times and distances traveled]

4 [AR 7–13]: Acceleration is conceived operationally. The child accepts without hesitation the fact that for each succeeding equal distance traveled, time decreases, and that with each succeeding equal time segment, the distance covered increases. [Immediate solution of the problems by formal operations]

The Development of
Physical Causality

INTRODUCTION

One of the interesting facets of the concept of causality derives from the observation "One can give one's self for a cause." In this case, the abstraction becomes the object of someone's actions, thoughts, interpretations, and dedication. The cause represents a set of principles that determines courses of action, decisions, and commitments. There are great and small causes. There are meaningful and meaningless ones. One can even fight for one's cause. In short, a cause implies assigning a meaning; a cause is a directing force. That the concept of causality is underlied by a notion of interaction, connection and force, that this concept might encompass simultaneously all levels of an individual's or a social group's activities is hardly surprising. What is surprising is that this concept, considered as a principle, is analogous to the dilemma of the "chicken and egg"—that is, which came first, the cause or effect. This relationship has been mostly determined as a relation between events, processes or entities in the same time series such that when one occurs, the other necessarily follows (sufficient condition), that when the latter occurs, the former must have preceded (necessary condition), and when both conditions prevail (necessary and sufficient condition), the concept of causality is complete.

In short the concept of causality implies a time sequence as well as the establishment of necessary and sufficient conditions in the succession of events, processes or entities. In the history of philosophy, numerous interpretations were given to the term cause under the general connotation of anything responsible for change, motion, or action. Aristotle distinguished between the material cause, that out of which something happens, the formal cause, the pattern or essence determining the creation of a thing, the efficient cause, the force producing an effect, and the final cause or purpose. During the Renaissance, with the development of scientific interest in nature, cause was usually conceived as an object. Today it is generally interpreted as energy or action whether or not it is connected with matter. The first clear definition of the principle was formulated by Leukippus: "Nothing happens without a ground but everything through a cause and of necessity."

Thus, how this concept evolves in a child's mind is of great interest because the problem that physical thought poses is to understand the mechanism of the relationship between the mind (which means at the beginning the sensorimotor coordinations and actions) and the experiences of external reality. This interaction is commonly perceived as taking place through perceptions and sensory organs. Yet such a reference is not, as Piaget shows, complete unless one introduces the action as a referent. For instance the perceptions that give an impression of weight or of movement are essentially relative to a context of potential or real actions. Physical thinking is built upon the actions of the subject as are the logico-mathematical operations. The problem is thus to understand how the development of physical knowledge comes to a degree to dissociate subjective and objective elements to promote the establishment of a reality independent from the self.

It is in this context that the problem of physical causality is studied. The evolution of this concept in the child closely follows the stages of the operational development. It proceeds through an egocentric assimilation of the perceived phenomena to the self that brings about modifications of the reality through the actions of the subject. At the preoperational level of development, children are paradoxically nearer and more distant from the reality than adults are: They are nearer because of their egocentrism and more distant because of the fact that their empirical observations are filled with subjective connotations, which are the result of their assimilation through their own schemata of actions. Thus when a 7 year old child believes that the moon follows him, he interprets this apparent movement either in attributing to himself the power of moving the moon or that the moon desires to follow him. At the concrete operational level, causality becomes detached from its egocentric quality to proceed towards the direction of a deduction applied to the real. The overall evolution of the concept of physical causality during the individual development is directed through this dual process of decline of egocentrism and the replacement of the empirical appearance through the discovery of deeper abstractions not directly perceptible but logically deduced. Observe that here again Piaget essentially considers an epistemological concept and attempts to understand its construction in the child's mind.

My presentation involves only the first study of causality done by Piaget in 1927. Recently, Piaget has restudied the concept, but more in terms of the development of forces and compensations. In a sense, this version of the child's development of physical causality is a general overview of the child's changing beliefs and interpretations of a number of diverse natural phenomena. The later study focuses on the physical concept of causality within a more defined context of action, forces, and reaction. The paradigm of equilibration and equilibrium modified Geneva's approach to the problem of physical causality, and from that point of view, the latest study of causality inscribes itself within the context of the problem of equilibration and general mechanisms of development.

AIR PRODUCED BY PRESSURE OF HANDS

Task   *92 C1*

Given: The experimenter clasps his hands together and by repeated pressure of the palms toward each other produces small currents of air. The child is asked to explain where this air comes from.

Stages

1 [AR 4–8]: The child maintains that it is sufficient to squeeze hands together to make air; that there is no air in the room. He adds that as soon as hands are pressed together air comes rushing in from outside the room. The child perceives immediate participation between the air produced by the hands and a reservoir of air out of doors. Causality is conceived as directly analogous with the child activity. [Egocentric causality and genuine participation]

2 [AR 6–11]: The child believes that the air is produced by pressure of the hands which causes air to come out of skin and interior of the body. He believes that there is no air in the room. [Egocentric causality]

3 [AR 7–11]: The child believes that air is produced simply by hands with no additional factors. The hands create the wind. [Transitional period; mixed subjective and objective factors]

4 [AR 8–11]: The child understands phenomenon: the room is full of air and hands simply collect and then send out again the air that surrounds them. [Objective concrete decentered causality]

AIR FROM A PUNCTURED BALL

Task   93 C2

Given: An india-rubber ball filled with air.

The ball is punctured at a point clearly visible to S and deflated. The jet of air is directed so that the child can feel it. When ball is flat and contains no more air, it is refilled and the experiment is begun again. The child is asked to explain how the air emitted from the ball is produced.

Stages

1 [AR 4–8]: The child believes that the air produced comes both from the ball and from outside (even through closed windows). [Dynamic participation]
2 [AR 6–9]: The child thinks that the ball is full of air because it "was filled at the shop where it was bought." This air can go in and out at will. [Egocentric causality]
3 [AR 8–10]: The child realizes that the air in the ball comes from the room, but continues to claim that in an airless room deflating the ball would produce air. [Transitional period; mixed subjective and objective factors]
4 [AR 9–10]: Correct explanation is given: air in the ball comes from the room. When the ball is deflated there is no air in it. [Objective concrete causality]

AIR CURRENTS

Task   94 C3

Given: A box lid attached to a length of string so that the lid can be swung in a circle.

The experimenter swings box in a circle and asks the child to explain where air that is produced is coming from.

Stages

1 [AR 5–8]: The child thinks that lid is making wind (air) which is attracted from outside. [Egocentric causality]
2 [AR 6–9] The lid makes air in a room thought of as airless, or could do so if there were no air in the room. [Transitional period]
3 [AR 8–12]: The child realizes that the lid simply displaces air in the room and does not produce air itself. [Objective concrete causality]

MOVEMENT OF PROJECTILES

Task   95 C4

Given: The experimenter throws a ball across the room. The child is asked to explain why the ball moves along instead of falling immediately to the ground.

Stages

1 [AR 4–7]: The child fails to understand the problem: the ball moves across the room because "it has been thrown." [Egocentric causality]
2 [AR 6–8]: The child believes that the ball moves "because it makes air." He also thinks that air comes into the room from outside to help the ball move. [Transitional answers]
3 [AR 8–11]: The child now thinks that the ball makes air and this air pushes it and that were the room a vacuum the ball could make air. The illusion that movement creates air is stronger in the case of the projectile than it is in that of hands or of punctured ball. [Concrete causality]
4 [AR 9–13]: The ball displaces air in the room. This air, in turn, blows behind the ball and pushes it along. If the room were airless, S feels that the ball would not move and could not produce any air of itself.

Increasingly the child realizes that force of throw is sufficient to explain continued movement of the ball. And, he adds, air hinders rather than helps this movement; in a vacuum the phenomenon would occur more easily. [Objective deductive causality]

CENTRIFUGAL FORCE

Task   96 C5

Given: The lid of a box attached to a length of string, and a penny.
The penny is put into the lid which is then swung round on a vertical plane. The child asked why the penny doesn't drop out.

Stages

1 [AR 5–7]: The child does not attend to the position of the lid during vertical rotation. He believes that the penny does not drop out because the lid has sides to hold it. [Egocentric causality]

2 [AR 6–10]: The child believes that the penny is swinging around very fast and has no time to drop out. [Transitional period]

3 [AR 7–10]: The child believes that as the lid swings round it produces air that flows back into the lid and keeps the penny in position. [Concrete causality]

4 [AR 8–14]: Now the child says that the air around the lid (in the room) keeps the penny in place. Air is not produced by the lid itself. [Objective causality]

NB: In this case there no real relationship between prediction and age was found. Cases of wrong and right predictions might be found at every one of the four stages described. Prediction and explanation are in this case independent of each other. This is exceptional; as a rule one finds a close relationship between the degree of accurate prediction and the validity of the explanation.

FORMATION OF WIND

Task   97 C6

Given: The child is asked a series of questions: Where does wind come from? There is (or is not) a lot of wind today. There was (or was not) a lot of wind yesterday. Why is that? How did wind begin? The first time there was any wind, where did it come from?

Stages

1 [AR 4–7]: The child regards world in terms of human values and experiences: Wind is "made from rain, trees, boats." This idea of being "made from" gives rise to the idea that wind is "made by" people or God. The ways and means of making wind are drawn from daily technical experience (with sticks, fans, airpumps, etc.) or from observations in which wind is connected with movement of trees, clouds, or dust. [Egocentric causality, artificialism, and animistic participation]

2 [AR 6–11]: The child believes that objects in motion cause wind. This belief leads to six types of answers that are not mutually exclusive:

a) Dust moves by itself by means of wind that it has made.

b) Trees are either the sole cause of wind or are partly stirred by a wind of external origin; nevertheless they are capable, in the child's eyes, of producing wind themselves.

c) Waves are partly spontaneous. They "go up high" by themselves, they are the result of a current. This movement produces wind, which in turn accelerates formation of waves.

d) Clouds make winds as they move along. On the other hand, clouds become air (smoke and steam) and in turn make more wind.

e) Heavenly bodies make wind. For example, the child regards sun as a "small cloud, tight and fiery" from which wind comes.

f) Wind is produced by the cold. (Cold is regarded as a substance by the child) [Transitional period of material generation]

3 [AR 8–13]: Wind makes itself from air that is spread out everywhere. Air sets itself in motion by virtue of its own force, with air behind pushing air in front. [Concrete causality]

4 [AR 12–15]: Mechanical explanation of wind is achieved in terms of physical forces and including their properties. (This type of explanation is interfered with by adult and educational factors that tend to minimize their spontaneity.) [Formal thinking]

MECHANISM OF BREATHING

Task   *98 C7*

Given: The child is asked a series of questions: What is breath? Where does this breath come from? Can we make this "air" in a room without air? To be sure that the child understands what "breath" is, the experimenter has him blow on his fingers and then questions him about this air.

Stages

1 [AR 4–9]: The child believes that breath is simply a wind, partly produced by us and partly coming from outside into us. He also believes that the air we breathe is localized in the organism. He confuses it with intestinal gases or with air we swallow in eating. [Egocentric causality and artificialism]

2 [AR 8–14]: This child knows that there is air in the room and admits an interchange between internal air and air of the room, but continues to think that if there were no air in the room he could make some by blowing or breathing. [Transitional period]

Piaget does not give examples or age ranges for stage 3. He simply states that now "the child's ideas conform entirely to ours."[Objective causality]

MOVEMENT OF CLOUDS

Task   *99 C8*

Given: The child is asked to explain what makes clouds move. The experimenter uses an indirect method: He begins by asking vague questions and by taking advantage of every answer by adding, "Why do you say that?" or "How does that happen?"

Stages

1 [AR 4–10]: The child relates his own movement and that of clouds. Because of his egocentric orientation, he concludes immediately that there is a dynamic participation between his own activity and the cloud's. He makes cloud move by walking. Clouds are alive and conscious. [Egocentric causality and magical beliefs]

2 [AR 4–10]: The child believes that clouds move both of themselves (because they are sufficiently alive and conscious to carry out their particular function) and under external influence (God and man). There is no real contradiction; a moral constraint is exercized on the cloud, which then responds with voluntary obedience. [Artificialist and animistic factors]

3 [AR 5–11]: The child still believes that internal and external influences move clouds, but now the external influence is seen as "things"; e.g., sun, moon, night, rain, and cold now condition cloud movement. For the child, rain or night moving clouds is the same as clouds moving along in order to bring rain and night. Both are moral and finalistic. Five types of responses can be distinguished:

a) Heavenly bodies move clouds.

b) Night causes cloud to approach because it is cloud's business to bring about night.

c) Rain is both motor cause and final cause of cloud movement.

d) Wind, cold, and bad weather move clouds, but clouds also move by themselves.

e) Clouds move by themselves, for the benefit of man; "they must come in order to bring us rain." [Artificalism transferred to objects]

4 [AR 8–12]: The child believes that movement of clouds is due to the action of a body external to them (wind). He still believes that clouds themselves make wind that drives them along and that in moving the cloud is directed toward functions that serve man and that make use of wind as their instrument. Finally, he achieves belief that wind pushes clouds and that this wind is not in any way produced by the clouds themselves. [Mechanical explanation]

THE MOVEMENT OF THE HEAVENLY BODIES

Task   *100 C9*

Given: The child is asked a series of questions similar to the following:

"Why does the sun move along?" "How does it do this?" "Is the sun alive?" "Could the sun move by itself?" "How does the moon move along?", etc.

Stages

1 [AR 4–6]: The child believes that movement is magical and animistic: We make heavenly bodies move when we walk, and they obey us consciously. [Egocentric causality; magical beliefs]

2 [AR 5–9]: The sun and moon move of their own free will, but their movement is controlled for moral reasons by God or by man. [Artificialistic and animistic factors]

3 [AR 7–11] Heavenly bodies are still believed to move on their own, but their movement is not seen as controlled by clouds, rain, wind, etc. Rather, moral influence still is believed to exert pressure on the heavenly body by means of the "thing" that causes its movement. Five types of answers can be distinguished:

1. Clouds move the sun along, but the sun can leave them or flee from them and retain in their absence a considerable capacity for self-movement.
2. The night influences the movement of the sun and moon both morally and physically.
3. The movement of heavenly bodies is accounted for by the action of weather, especially rain.
4. Heavenly bodies make use of the wind, sometimes at the risk of being blown away, but more often to guide them so as to keep same direction as before. *But* when there is no wind at all, they can also move by themselves.
5. The sun and moon move along by themselves and do so for our benefit. [Artificialism transferred to the object.]

4 [AR 9–11]: The child believes that the sun and moon by moving or turning around produce a current of air (wind) that flows behind them to drive them ahead. The sun is pushed along by heat or vapor that it emits (vapor, smoke, and air are more or less confused. [Appearance of objective factors and physical determinism]

The child progressively eliminates moral factors, and physical factors—wind and air are conceived as the only true causes of movement. [Mechanical explanation]

WAVES OF WATER

Task   *101 C10*

Given: The child is asked: "What are waves?" "What makes them?"

Stages

1 [AR 4-6]: The child regards waves as alive and conscious. He attributes their movement either to a life of the wave itself or to some human or artificial action, such as the movement of cars. He may also believe that waves are made by nature for man's use (in boating and swimming). [Combined animistic and artificialistic causality]

2 [AR 5-10]: There are 4 types of explanations used during this stage but all of them endow waves with a certain spontaneity, the aim of which is moral:

1. Stones and rocks produce waves. The child views the obstacles to be overcome (stones and rocks) as the sources of energy that cause the movement (waves).
2. Either the current of water produces waves—waves are a manifestation of the spontaneous force of water; or the waves produce wind, which in turn produces waves.
3. Waves result simply from the air which is in the water. Waves of the lake rise and fall like water that has been brought to boil.
4. Wind produces waves. A moral factor is also added to this explanation. Waves are alive, move spontaneously, and are generally endowed with intentions or duties which are useful to man. [Transitional behaviors—internal and external factors are mixed]

3 [AR 8-10]: The child believes that waves are produced by wind. He no longer believes that waves are spontaneous (movement is entirely mechanical). [Concrete objective causality; mechanical explanation]

THE CURRENT IN RIVERS

Task   *102 C11*

Given: The child is asked a series of direct questions: "Why does the water in rivers move along?" "How does it do this?"

Stages

1 [AR 4-8]: The child maintains that water flows for the good of man and because man compels it to do so—dualism of external and internal motor force. [Combined animistic and artificialistic causality]

2 [AR 5-9]: The child gives a pre-causal explanation of the movement of water—moral and physical, finalist and causal. He might maintain that stones are the stimulus of water's activity; or that rivers move because of the waves they make; or that the current of rivers is attributed to the wind, whatever the origin of the wind may be (that is, he is not concerned with the

wind's origin). This last explanation does not exclude the presence of moral factors. [Transitional behaviors, subjective and objective factors are mixed]

3 [AR 6–12]: The child gradually sees the movement of rivers as determined by purely physical causes—the slope explains the current. The child does not yet understand the role of weight——he says that the river goes down the slope simply because it does not have the strength to go up. He explains the current by cumulative drive and thrust. [Concrete causality]

4 [AR 9–12]: The child becomes capable of giving a correct explanation of the movement of rivers. The idea of weight now enters into this explanation: The water does not go up "because it hasn't enough strength to go up. It's too heavy.") [Objective causality; mechanical explanation]

THE SUSPENSION OF CLOUDS

Task   *103 C12*

Given: The child is asked a series of questions similar to the following: "How do clouds stay in the air?" "Why don't they fall down?"

Stages

1 [AR 4–6]: The child attributes the suspension of clouds to both artificial and animistic means—"they stick," because God is there and takes hold of them, "because God wants them to stay." [Artificialism]

2 [AR 6–9]: The child believes that clouds are either stuck on to the sky or tightly wedged into it because everything is organized to be of the greatest benefit to man. [Transitional period]   '
The child views clouds as being large and heavy and, to him, any large and heavy object keeps its place by itself, because it has sufficient resistance and strength.

3 [AR 8–12]: The child begins to bring air and wind into his explanation, but the relation between cloud and air is dynamic in that suspension is related to the forward movement of the cloud. [Concrete causality]

4 [AR 9–13]: The child discovers that clouds remain suspended, not because of their movement, but because of their lightness. [Mechanical explanation]

THE SUSPENSION OF HEAVENLY BODIES

Task   *104 C13*

Given: The child is asked a series of questions similar to the following:

"How does the sun stay up there?" "Why doesn't it fall?" "Why does the moon stay in the sky?"

Stages

1 [AR 5–9]: The child believes that the sun and moon are suspended for both artificial and animistic reasons—"It's God that makes it stay up" or "Because it doesn't want to come down." [Egocentric causality; magical beliefs]

2 [AR 6–9]: The child still uses primitive explanations like those described above, but he also introduces the idea that heavenly bodies do not fall because they are "clothed" in clouds or in sky, that is, the clouds or sky "hold" them. [Artificialistic and animistic factors mixed]

3 [AR 7–13]: The child now believes that the movement of heavenly bodies, are both spontaneous and externally propelled (e.g., by wind), is sufficient to cause suspension. [Artificialism transferred to objects]

4 [AR 9–13]: The child regards the sun and moon as light in weight and he attributes their suspension to their respective weight. [Objective factors; mechanical explanation]

THE FALL OF BODIES TO THE GROUND

Task   105 C14

Given: A book or other object is held by the experimenter at a certain height above the ground. The child is asked to describe what would happen if the experimenter lets go of the object and to explain why.

Stages

1 [AR 5–9]: The child believes that the object falls to the ground because it wants to or because nothing holds it back. [Egocentric causality, finalism]

2 [AR 9–11]: Increasingly, the child is able to bring in the idea of weight as the cause of the fall, but he still connects the effect of weight with other factors of dynamic order, such as the air produced by the actual fall of the body. [Objective causalities]

THE EXPLANATION OF MOVEMENT

Task   106 C15

Given: The child is simply asked to explain movement.

Stages

Piaget does not deal in age ranges in this general discussion of the child's conception of movement. He simply reports the developmental stages involved. These are:

1. Movement for the child is spontaneous. All movement is conceived of by means of pre-notions and pre-relations. Heavenly bodies move or rest as they please, clouds make wind by themselves, trees swing their branches spontaneously to make a breeze. Movements become complex and are conceived of as due to many various accumulated influences. Movements also become bipolar: they are caused by an external will and an internal will, a command from God or man and an acquiescence. [Egocentric causality, artificialism]

2. The child begins to explain movements of nature by nature. The internal factor is always the free will of objects and external force is the sum of bodies morally attracting or repelling moving bodies. Rain and night attract clouds, sun and clouds repel each other, rocks help water to flow, etc. [Transitional answers]

3. The child's explanation of movement becomes more physical. External force is supposed to act more and more by push or pull (contact). Movement remains dynamic and bipolar in the sense that the force is never abolished, the moving body may use external force or may remove itself from its influence. The sun is driven along by clouds but at the same time it follows us and uses wind for its own end. [Artificialism is transferred to objects]

4. The child simplifies his conception of movement and gradually reaches a mechanical causality based on inertia. All signs of artificialism and animism disappear. [Objective causality, mechanical explanation]

FLOTATION

Task   *107 C16*

Given: First, the child is asked, "Why do steamboats stay on water?" "Why do boats lie on water?"

Then the child is allowed to play with bits of wood, stones, nails, etc. He is then asked whether the objects will float and why. The experimenter and child together build small boats to study relationships between form, volume, and capacity for floating.

Stages

1 [AR 4–6]: The child believes that a boat floats because of some moral necessity that is both connected to the will of its maker and to the obedience of the boat itself. [Moral necessity]

2 [AR 5–8]: The child uses a dynamistic approach that appears in several forms. His explanations are often confused and contradictory: A boat floats because it is heavy and heavy boats have the strength to keep themselves up, they are capable of resistance. But water, when it is deep, is sufficiently "heavy" to raise the boat. Also boats have sufficient force to keep themselves up because people row or an engine provides power. He predicts from his explanations whether or not these are false. [Moral necessity dependent on observed, dynamic factors]

3 [AR 6–11]: The child has no notion of specific weight of bodies; what enables a boat to float is its capacity for pressure as compared to that of the total bulk of the water. He believes that heavy objects try to pierce water but if water is sufficiently plentiful and deep, it produces an upward flowing current, which sustains floating objects. When he has difficulty applying this explanation (why does a small pebble, which is light, sink?) he resorts to a second stage explanation: The boat is bigger and water is better able to hold it up, while the pebble slips through waves. [Intermediary answers with mixed dynamic and static factors]

4 [AR 8–14]: The child now believes that all boats float because they are lighter than water. He makes use of the relationship of density and weight to volume in his explanation. The boat floats because it is hollow and contains air that keeps it up—he relates weight to volume but believes that boat floats because air is strong or because air dislikes going in water. Gradually his thinking loses all trace of dynamism. The child believes a body, when it increases in sizes, maintains its quantity of matter but loses some weight. Boats lose absolute weight in proportion as they are increased in size. They are "more hollow." Finally, he reaches a relative notion of weight: He understands that a pellet of plasticine loses relative weight on being brought to bowl-shape although it retains its absolute weight. [Progressive elimination of dynamic factors and progressive establishment of the notions of weight and volume; mechanical explanation]

WATER LEVEL

Task 108 C17

Given: a drinking glass, three-quarters filled, and a pebble.

The child is asked to predict result of dropping the pebble into the water. Once he has answered, the experiment is performed. The experimenter points out that the water level has risen and asks the child to explain the phenomenon. The experiment is repeated using a bulkier and lighter object.

Stages

1 [AR 5-11]: The child thinks that submerged bodies make the water level rise because of their weight: A small, heavy object will cause a greater rise than a larger, lighter object. The child thinks that the submerged object exercises continuous pressure in the water to lift its level, that it sets up a current ("a wind") that runs from the bottom to the top of the water like a wave. When asked if a pebble held by a thread halfway down a column of water would also raise the water level, he answers "No," it no longer "weights" on the water. [Confusion between weight and volume; dynamic explanation]

2 [AR 6-11]: The child now bases his predictions on volume and declares that a bulky but light piece of wood will make water rise higher that a heavy, small pebble. However, he persists in explaining water level rise by appealing only to weight of the submerged object and ignoring any contradictions that may arise. The pebble raises the water level because it lies heavily at the bottom of the glass and wood because it lies heavily on the surface. [Partial dissociation of weight and volume]

3 [AR 10-12]: The child is now able to explain the rise in water level by displacement. Weight accounts only for the immersion of the body in water. [Complete disassociation between weight and volume]

SHADOWS

Task   *109 C18*

Given: The child is asked the following series of questions: "Why is there a shadow here?" (Experimenter makes a shadow using his hands.) "Why is a shadow black?" "What makes a shadow?"

Stages

1 [AR 4-7]: The child believes that a shadow has a dual origin: It comes out of the object itself and it comes from outside (the sky). These two aspects are superimposed but do not mutually exclude one another and there is participation of one in the other. The apparent contradiction does not worry S in any way. [Transductive reasoning; participation]

2 [AR 6-8]: The child now thinks that a shadow is produced entirely by the object itself but has a substance of its own. He is not always able to predict where the shadow will fall in relation to the light source. [Mixture of subjective and objective factors]

3 [AR 7–9]: The child can foresee that the shadow will appear on the side of the object away from the source of light; he has discovered a relationship between shade and light. He persists in his earlier belief that shade emanates from the object itself, ignoring the part played by the light source in generating a shadow. Shadow is still thought of as a substance issuing from an object and occurring even at night. [External origin and qualitative relationship between shade and light]

4 [AR 8–10]: Shadow is no longer thought of a substance that is chased away by light. It becomes synonymous with the absence of light. [Mechanical explanation]

THE MECHANISM OF BICYCLES

Task   *110 C19*

Given: The child is asked to draw a bicycle on a sheet of paper. Care should be taken not to let the drawing be too small. The child is asked, "How does a bicycle go?" and "What happens when a person sits here?" The experimenter points to each of the parts that have been drawn (pedals, wheels, chain, etc.) and asks about each in turn, "What is this for?"

Stages

1 [AR 4–6]: The child confuses the cause of movement: The bicycle is sometimes moved by "the mechanism," sometimes by "the lamp," "the light," or any other particularly striking part which seems sufficiently charged with efficacy to account for the whole movement. The typical drawing consists of two wheels and a pedal. [Transductive reasoning]

2 [AR 5–8]: The child examines each piece in detail; each is thought of as necessary. Movement is still confused; no causal order is attributed to the action of one part on another. His drawing shows a juxtaposition of parts without any real connection between or among them. [Partial relationship; global view]

3 [AR 7–9]: The child gives up synthetic explanation and looks for an irreversible sequence of cause and effect in detailed interaction of pairs of parts. Most of the explanations, however, are rudimentary: He imagines that chains or bars are attached to the tires and is unperturbed by the unlikeliness of such being the case. [Dissociation of actors]

4 [AR 8–11]: The child is able to give a mechanical explanation. [Objective causality]

THE STEAM ENGINE

Task *111 C20*

Given: A toy engine, the workings of which can be seen from the outside. It consists of a vertical boiler with a small spirit lamp beneath it. When the lamp is lit, the water in the boiler is heated and steam escapes through a little pipe that can be seen from outside to run into a cyclinder. The piston contained in the cylinder is not visible, but the connecting-rod at the bottom of the cylinder powers a large wheel on the outside of the engine. A belt can be attached to the wheel to utilize the energy. The fire is lit in front of the child, and he is then asked to explain the mechanism.

Stages

1 [AR 4–7]: The child believes that the fire or heat moves the wheel even though the wheel is external to the cage in which the fire is enclosed. He is unconcerned with the "how" of the process and does not try to find a connection between fire and wheel. Fire and air must be able to direct themselves, to go to the wheel with intention and intelligence. Fire is "good at" making the wheel turn; this goodness has causal value and is sufficient to explain the turning. [Animistic and finalistic explanation]

2 [AR 6–10]: The child believes that fire enters the water and provides the current there for setting the wheel in motion. He discovers that the connecting rods and axle are necessary for the movement of the wheel, and explains the movement of the connecting rod by the impetus of the water, which is in turn pushed along by the wind, smoke, or air produced by the fire. Gradually, he comes to believe that the fire simply heats the water and the water, having come to a boil, acquires impetus through the heat to move the connecting rod. Steam is not yet regarded as useful. [Transitional behaviors; dynamic factors]

3 [AR 8–11]: The child now believes that steam pushes connecting rods and wheel. Neither quantity nor expansion comes into play. Impetus alone is what counts. Gradually, impetus is seen as a pressure due to accumulation. [Objective causality; mechanical explanation]

STEAM ENGINES

Task *112 C21*

Given: The child is asked the following questions in the order given: "How does a train move?" "What makes the wheels turn?" "What makes the engine work?"

Stages

1 [AR 4–8]: The child is not concerned with "how" things happen, but simply takes vaguely conceived forces as being responsible for movement of steam engines or motor boats and does not find intermediaries between origin of this force and the wheels; the fire and smoke work directly on the wheels to make them turn. [Egocentric causality, animistic and finalistic explanations]

2 [AR 7–9]: The child now begins to look for links. The connecting rods take on a function: "The fire makes a bit of iron that's sort of bent go and that makes the wheels turn." [Transitional behaviors; dynamic factors taken into account]

3 [AR 9–12]: The child makes a complete explanation: The engine goes "with steam. That makes the wheels turn. There's a piston that has two little holes. The steam comes out under pressure, it presses on the piston, and makes the wheels turn." [Objective causality; mechanical explanation]

AUTOMOBILES AND AIRPLANES

Task   *113 C22*

Given: The child asked to explain how a motor works.

Stages

1 [AR 4–9]: The child dissociates himself from questions of contacts and intermediaries. He believes that currents of air or fuel ("a force") drive the engine, but that neither need be in contact with the engine to act. Some children explain movement by the turning of the steering wheel or the turning of a crank. [Egocentric causality; animistic and finalistic explanation]

2 [AR 9–13]: The child begins to form a spatial series that connects fuel with the wheels of the automobile. His explanation is crude but he begins to add intermediary parts to the process. Increasingly correct explanations appear that are inspired by adults. [Transitional behaviors, dynamic factors]

The Development of Early Logic

INTRODUCTION

When a person says that a story is logical, he generally means that the story makes sense. The affirmation that a story is logical underlies a judgement, an appreciation of the order of succession and a classification of the events. "Logical" is thus a judgement that one deduces from the real, a judgment that encompasses or is applicable to all levels of our activities. Our actions, thoughts, symbols, and even dreams or fantasies are perceived as being sensible or as being nonsense, as being logical or illogical. In effect, the recognition of the fact that something is logical or not implies a focus on the process, the mechanisms, the unfolding of a set of events, or the entities that one considers in their totality.

Although logic was probably not part of a specific topic in our school years, it was present in many if not all school subject matters and probably came to represent that aspect of thinking that one assimilates with formal reasoning. One may think formally or informally about events, objects, or persons. Yet the definition of this concept also implies a tautology: Logic is what is in conformity with the laws of correct reasoning.

The early growth of logic in the child is a study of the laws of reasoning constructed and used by the child until the concrete operational period of thought, that is, until 9–11 years of age.

The subtitle of the book, classification and seriation, explains Piaget's purpose. His goal is to examine the genesis and construction of these two types of categorization of the real. The psychological and educational significance of coherent classifcations and ordering is undoubtedly important and relevant. Almost all actions and any judgment entail some kind of classification. Explicit classifications are relatively seldom in the reasoning of young children and in everyday adult reasoning. But the type of analogy, sometimes loose, sometimes precise, which directs our thinking is itself a classificatory activity. The main aspect and interest of studying classifications and seriations comes from the fact that they are deeply connected with the ability to abstract criteria of generalization. An activity of classification implies the abstraction of relationships of similarities or differences between objects, persons, events which are grouped into an abstract set which encompasses all possible members of the set. Thus a classification entails two main activities: the first one refers to the ability to abstract and maintain constant a number of similar features under which the set has an existence. This operation Piaget calls the "intension of a set." The "intension of a set" is the set of properties common to the members of that set together with the set of differences which distinguish them from another class. The "extension" of a class is the set of members, or elements or individuals comprising that class as determined by its intension. Thus there is a close relationship between the intension and the extension of a set. The former implies the abstraction of similarities, the latter signifies the number of elements a set contains.

Early logic is the account of how the child comes to solve the problem of coordinating the intension and the extension of a set. For instance, when a 5 year old child is presented with a bunch of flowers made of primulaes (15 of them) and daisies (2 of them) and is asked if the bunch contains more flowers or more primulaes, he fails to understand the logical necessity of the answer until he is capable of coordinating the following: although the number of primulaes that he sees is greater than the number of daisies (extension), the set of flowers (intension) will always be greater than the any particular subset he can imagine. In other words, the numbers (extension) of elements he perceives as part of a subset of a set does not matter. Yet until the acquisition of the concrete operational level of thought, the child will reason that since he sees more primulaes, since he has 15 primulaes there must be more primulaes than flowers. He fails to coordinate the intension of a set with its extension. It is an essential part of Piaget's thesis that logical reasoning in relationship with classification and seriation develops before the formation of systematic hypotheses and their verification by a deduction of their implications. The latter bears on another branch of logic, the logic of propositions and entails the study of the development of the formal level of thought. Yet the study of early logic reveals that children are not unable to make hypothesis about the real and to verify them. On the contrary. Nevertheless there are profound differences between the testing of hypotheses at 8 or 15 years of age. At the concrete operational level of thought the child does not reason upon "abstractions of abstractions." The child can only classify or order the objects or events he has in front of him. In short his activity will be concrete and limited to the testing of one hypothesis at a time. On the other hand, the procedure of formal reasoning implies a systematic "operational" coordination of hypotheses. All of these aspects imply a systematic coordination of actions entailed in grouping or classifying objects according to their attributes. In short, early logic is a necessary prerequisite to the development and the emergence of formal logic. In the latter the constitutive hypotheses are themselves operations which explain why these kind of operations become "second order operations."

In the former, the experiments presented here illustrate the crucial achievement that results from a systematic classification of attributes in a realistic context. The reasoning becomes systematic and therefore logical and the system to which it conforms is a classificatory one. This kind of logical inference together with inferences based on the systematic ordering of differences (seriation) are constructed several years earlier than formal reasoning. It is from this observation that Piaget argues that there is a need for a logic which will codify these systems.

Although partial and incomplete, concrete operations are from Piaget's point of view necessary prerequisites to the construction of a higher formal cognitive organization, which is encompassed by the formal level of thought.

"ALL" AND "SOME" APPLIED TO SHAPES AND COLORS

Task *114 E1*

Given: 2 series of counters (8–21 elements in each): (I) red squares and blue circles; (II) red squares, blue circles, and blue squares. A row of these counters is placed in front of the child who is then asked: "Are all the circles blue?" "Are all the red ones squares?" "Are all the blue ones circles?" "Are all the squares red?" The child may also be asked to answer the same questions from memory (by replicating the series he has just seen).

Stages

1 [AR 5–6]: The child finds even series I too difficult at times. He becomes confused. When presented with the two kinds of elements from both collections (red squares and blue circles) which are alternated irregularly, he tends to confuse the combinations of color and shape when seeing the elements in a heterogeneous group. When collections of red sqaures and blue circles are separated, the combinations of properties are emphasized and the child does not confuse them. When a third collection of elements is

added (blue squares in series II), he cannot dissociate the elements of the collections at all. [Graphic collections]

2 [AR 5–8]: The child's answers are inconsistent—he may give a correct answer to one question but not for another. He can now envisage total collections of "reds" or "squares," but cannot yet reason in terms of a class-inclusion schema. He tends to reduce "Are all the squares red?" to "Are all the squares all the red ones?" Questions tend to be easier when the collections are defined by shape rather than by color—"Are all the squares red?" is easier than "Are all the red one squares?" The child still forms graphic collections in his mind and often it is easier for him to form these collections on the basis of shape rather than color. [Difficulties in coordinating the extension and the intension of a set]

3 [AR 6–8]: The child gives correct answers. He understands class inclusions: total squares = the red squares + the blue squares; and red squares = total answers – the blue squares. [Concrete coordination between the extension and the intension of the set; logical transitivity achieved]

"ALL" AND "SOME" APPLIED TO
TESTS OF EXCLUSION

Task   *115 E2*

Given: an ordinary scale with a counter-weight in the shape of a ball hidden in its base. Boxes of various shapes and colors but of only two weights are put on the scale—one at a time. Under heavier ones the ball appears through side of scale whereas the lighter ones do not.

The child is asked to predict which boxes will make the ball come out of side and to classify them on that basis (weight is determinant while color and size are not). Then he is asked questions of the following type: "Are all the red boxes heavy?" "Do all the red boxes make the ball come out?" "Do all the heavy boxes make the ball come out?"

Stages

1 [AR 4–7]: The child does not disregard size and color as determining factors; he does not use the quantifier "all." The child has difficulty in evolving the notion of "all,"—that is, in abstracting a quality common to all elements of a class. He does not rule out the quantifier "all" in face of experimental exceptions. As a result, he fails to discover that weight is the sole factor. [Inability to isolate determining factor]

2 [AR 4–7]: The child now distinguishes between light and heavy boxes and, therefore, answers the last question correctly. His handling of "all" and "some" is intuitive. He may invert the question or introduce an incorrect quantification of the question. [Difficulty in dissociating "all" and "some"]

3 [AR 7–8]:The child does not choose a quality as constituting the intension of a class unless it applies to "all" its members, and "all" is itself determined by a quality of this kind. [Correct logical coordination]

ABSOLUTE AND RELATIVE USES OF "SOME"

Task   *116 E3*

Absolute

Given: 3 series of objects; I) blue circles and red squares, II) drawings of white and yellow roses, white and yellow tulips, III) drawings to be colored in; fruit, trees, landscapes. Each series is presented to the child one at a time and he is asked in I and II to "hand over *some* objects" and in III to "color *some* elements of each drawing." He is also asked to compare "some" and "all" or to define the word "some."

Relative

Given:The child is seated at table on which are placed 5 white tulips, 4 yellow tulips, 4 white roses, 5 yellow roses.

A) The child is first asked to take "some" tulips, "all" white roses.

B) Are "all" and "some" the same?

1) If John says "All tulips are flowers" and you say "some tulips are flowers," who would be right? Why?

2) You: "Some flowers are tulips." John: "All flowers are tulips." Who would be right? Why?

3) Which is more correct: "All flowers are tulips", "All flowers are yellow tulips"?

4) "All yellow tulips are flowers," or "All flowers are yellow tulips."

C) Are there more tulips of yellow tulips in this bunch?

Stages

1 [AR 5–6]:The child sees no difference between "all" and "some" [Absence of differentiation]

2 [AR 5–8]:The child is now aware that "some" is not "all," but is unable to stabilize their different meanings. The distinction he makes between them is either in the verbal definition or in practice, and practice is not always

coordinated with the definition. Increasingly he can distinguish between "some" and "all" but has difficulty in verbalization; confusion arises in analyzing collections of two or three objects. "Some" has an absolute meaning limited to "the number of elements" rather that "a relationship between part and whole." The child also tends to restrict his meaning of "some" to identical elements: "Some" of a collection of red and blue squares includes only one color. "All," however, takes on a constant meaning here—"the set of elements of a collection, without exception." For the relation of "some," the child fails to understand the inclusion implied in "All the As are Bs" and thinks of this as "All the As are all the Bs." In so far as "all" refers to a property, it represents a collective entity instead of being a quantification of its members. [Functional relationship between all and incorrect quantification]

3 [AR 7–10]: The child realizes that "some" is a part of the whole "all." "Some" tends to have a more quantitative meaning—he no longer restricts his definition to one characteristic of elements (color, type of flower, etc.). [Correct concrete quantification]

CLASSIFICATION (FLOWERS)

Task   *117 E4*

Given: A series of 20 pictures: Four colored objects, 4 yellow primulas, 4 different-colored primulas, and 8 other flowers. The following problems are put to the child:
1. Spontaneous classification: "Group the like objects."
2. Inclusion: "If you make a bunch out of all the primulas, will you use blue primulas?"
3. Quantification of inclusion:
   a. "Which has more flowers, the bunch of yellow primulas or a bunch of all the primulas?"
   b. "Are there more primulas or flowers?"
   c. "If you take all the primulas, will there be any flowers left?"
   d. "If you take all the flowers, will there be any primulas left?"

Stages

1–2 [AR 4–7]: The child's answers to problems of inclusion are confused. He is not able to make a genuine quantitative comparison of part to whole; as soon as he separates the components (classification), he loses track of the whole and is left to compare components. [Difficulty in dissociating the part to whole relationship]

3 [AR 6–10]: The child can classify objects into additive groupings, and also recognize the inclusions implied in the classification. He can retain the concept of the whole separated into its components, but resorts to previous reasoning when asked to apply the relation of inclusion to flowers and primulas "in a wood";—he compares primulas growing in a wood with other flowers (excluding primulas) and increasingly compares the class of primulas with the higher ranking class of flowers that includes it. [Concrete additive groupings]

CLASSIFICATION (ANIMALS)

Task   *118 E 5*

Given: Pictures of animals are presented to the child in the following series:
Series I consists of 3 or 4 ducks, 3 to 5 other birds, and 5 other animals. Primary classes here are: (A) ducks, (B) birds, and (C) other animals.

Series II consists of 3 ducks, 4 other birds, 4 winged animals (not birds), and 3 inanimate objects. Primary classes here are: (A) birds, (B) flying animals, (C) animals, and (D) the universal class. Transparent boxes of sizes which fit inside one another correspond to primary classes A, B, C, etc.

The child is first asked to name the pictures. Then, the following problems are presented:

1. *Spontaneous classification:* "Make piles of pictures that are all alike."
2. Inclusion: "Can a bird be placed in the duck pile?"
3. Quantification of inclusion:
   a. "Is *all* ducks bigger, smaller, or the same as *all* birds?"
   b. "Are there more birds or animals?"
   c. "Take away *all* birds. Will there be any animals left?"
      "Take away all animals. Will there be any birds left?"

Stage

1–2 [AR 7–9]: Preliminary classification is inadequate. The child does not understand relationships in terms of extension. There is not quantification of relations of inclusion. He has difficulty comparing the part with the whole. [Failure in quantification of the inclusion]

3 [AR 9–13]:The child first forms a number of classes that show no coherent structure, *but* when given the boxes, he is able to form proper categories. In answering the questions, he sometimes responds incorrectly; but when prompted by the experimenter, he might be able to answer successfully. Along with the progressive development of hierarchical classification,

there is a correspondingly greater facility with the quantification of the inclusion. [Difficulty in coordinating extension and integration of set]
4 [AR 10-13]: The child gives correct replies immediately. [Correct coordination between the extension and the intension of the set]
Note: Conservation of the whole and quantitative comparison of whole and part are two essential characteristics of genuine class-inclusion. Inclusion, in this sense, has not been acquired merely because the child talks correctly and uses verbal concepts which reflect inclusions implicit in the language of adults. On the contrary, inclusion has an essentially operational character. The child orders classes instead of only differentiating between them.

SINGULAR CLASS IN A PRACTICAL CONTEXT

Task   *119 E6*

Given: Groups of varying geometric figures, with 3 to 6 figures per group. One figure per group is always dissimilar, and that dissimilar figure always has a cross on its reverse side.

The child is asked to guess which figure has a cross on its reverse side. To guage what the child has understood, the experimenter first asks him to explain the reasons behind his choices, and then tells him to make up a similar puzzle of his own without using the same items and arrangement.

Stages

1-2 [AR 5-7]: The child either fails to solve the problem, or succeeds without understanding the system used. Increasingly, he is able to choose the unique element right from the start, but does so without real understanding of the principle. The child provides a description of the configuration rather than uses this principle as a classificatory schema. He is generally unable to replicate the situation. [Intuitive recognition]

3 [AR 5-11]: The child states a rule and generalizes it as "always" being true. He structures the notion of a "unique specimen" by the operations of classification: It therefore assumes the character of a single class. There may take place a sort of regression that has nothing to do with the mechanism of classification: the child tends to expect more complicated "puzzles" than the one actually put before him. He may advance several hypotheses before considering the simplest one to be correct. [Discovery of the logical correct principle]

CLASSIFICATION AND THE RELATIVE
SIZE OF CLASSES

Task 120 *E7*

Given:
(a) Initially:
4 large blue squares (5 cm × 5 cm)
4 small blue squares (2.5 cm × 2.5 cm)
4 large blue circles (5 cm dia.)
4 small blue circles (2.5 cm dia.)
1 large red circle (5 cm dia.)
1 small red circle (2.5 cm dia.)
1 small red square (2.5 cm × 2.5 cm)

(b) Later on:
1 large square (5 cm × 5 cm)

1 small red square (2.5 cm × 2.5 cm)
1 small red circle (2.5 cm dia.)

(a) The child is first asked to classify these objects according to any criteria he likes into two classes. He is then asked to redivide them into two classes using different criteria, and then to reclassify them a third time, using yet other criteria. (b) Three more objects are added to the set, and the child is again asked to classify them.

Stages

1 [AR 5–7]: The child tends to avoid the properties of the unique element (red circle), and to treat it as though it is just like the others. When the other red elements are added, and when it is suggested to him, the child begins to accept a classification based on color. [Failure to dissiciate numerical extension and concept of set]

2 [AR 6–9]: The child spontaneously adopts classification by color when the additional red elements are brought in, but not before. He initially neglects to make the classification by color because he tends to classify objects by constructing collections, and a single red circle cannot form a collection. [Difficulty in coordinating numerical extension from correct quantification]

3 [AR 6–9]: Complementarity (red vs. blue) overrides numerical extension. At times, the child refers to "the red ones," considering that the fact of only one red object is immaterial to the validity of redness as an intensive property. [Correct classification]

"SECONDARY" CLASS IN A FORCED DICHOTOMY

Task   *121 E8*

Given: Two sets of pictures, one representing several primulas of different colors, a pansy, a rose, a tulip, and a lily of the valley, the other representing several apples, 1 or 2 pears, a couple of cherries, a banana, a melon, a bunch of grapes, and an orange.

There are four steps to each part of this experiment: (1) The child is asked to divide the elements into two classes—"Can you put all of these pictures into two piles?" (2) Further elements (either fruits or flowers) are added, or some are removed. (3) A control experiment is performed in which an apple and several pears are presented. (4) After the elements are classified, the child is asked to label both classes using only a word or two.

Stages

1 [AR 5–7]: When forced to construct a dichotomy, the child constructs an arbitrary one in which no rules of classification are observed. Either the classification is not exhaustive or there are similar elements in each of 2 classes. He does not try to define the second class by referring to the first one. [Intuitive classification]

2 [AR 5–8]: The child begins to recognize "otherness": Dichotomies consist of one relatively homogeneous collection and a second collection defined by reference to the first. *But,* he does not yet understand class-inclusion. Complementarity and otherness are still lacking, for they are determined once and for all by initial elements and cannot be extended when new elements are added. [Lack of differentiation between set and subset]

3 [AR 7–11]: The child now structures complementarity by inclusion. He indicates the existence of the whole and the relativity of "secondary class" (fruit other than apples) to "primary class" (apples). [Correct differentiation between the part to whole and set to subset relationship] *Note:* Although subjects of 7 to 8 years succeed in integrating complementarity and inclusion when dealing with such clear-cut and familiar classes as flowers or fruit, they will be less advanced when asked to classify vegetables or coats-of-arms, in this kind of experiment.

LOGICAL SUBTRACTION OR NEGATION (I)

Task   *122 E9*

Given: 18 cardboard geometrical shapes, 3 large and 3 small circles, 3 large and 3 small squares, 3 large and 3 small triangles. Each group of three

elements includes one blue, one red, and one white. The following problems
are put to the child:

1. "Give me all those which are not circles,... which are not blue
   circles,... which are not small blue circles."
2. "Give me all those which are not red and large."
3. "Give me all the objects except the red circles."
4. "Give me all those which are not small white triangles,... which are not
   small triangles,... which are not triangles."
5. "Give me all those objects which are not green."

Either before or after these questions are asked, the child is asked to classify
the elements as he wishes.

Stages

1 [AR 4-5]: The child tends to refer negation to the entire set, and finds it
   difficult to deal with two or three properties at once (e.g., small and blue
   circles). He has difficulty dealing with ordered inclusions, and tends to
   refer negation to a class of intermediate rank (one that is not the whole or
   the next including class). [Intuitive and global perception]
2 [AR 5-7]: The child begins to analyze various shapes, asking himself what
   to include or exclude. As he moves from the global perception of the
   previous stage to this more detailed analysis, his performance seems to
   deteriorate. [Difficulty in logical coordination]
3 [AR 6-8]: There is a lessening of the tendancy to think of negation as
   applying to the whole. The child applies negation with respect to the next
   including class. [Correct coordination and negation achieved]
   Note: For younger children, one can replace the word "triangle" with the
   word "roof."

LOGICAL SUBTRACTION OR NEGATION (II)

Task   *123 E10*

Given: A variety of objects arranged to represent a farm, including people,
animals (domestic quadrupeds and birds), vegetables (including flowers), and
inanimate objects (tools, equipment, etc.). The following questions are asked:

1. "Which are not animals?" Is it funnier to say that a person is an animal
   or that a ladder is an animal, and why?"
2. "Which ones are not birds?" Is it funnier to say that a cat is a bird or that
   a barrel is a bird?"
3. "Show me everything except (the elements of any specific set)."
4. "Show me which ones are not tulips."

5. "Are there more things which are not birds, or more things which are not animals?" "Are there more birds or more animals?"

That the results are delayed when compared with those in experiment 122 E9 is probably because the child must *think* about the problems posed, rather than *perform* simple actions.

Stages

3 [AR 8-10]: The child tends to think of negation in the absolute sense. When asked to indicate "not birds," he refers to the entire set of objects. He tends to believe that the strongest negation is the one that is most meaningful: An orchid is more like a tulip than a cow is, because a cow has less of the *shape* of a flower (tulip). [Difficulty in logical coordination]
4 [AR 10-13]: The child now tends to refer to the next higher class. When asked to indicate "not birds," he limits his answer to "animals." He uses neighboring classes to determine the most useful negations. To say that a rose is not a tulip is more correct than to say that an animal is not a tulip because both the first two belong to the *category* of flowers. [Correct logical coordination]

THE INCLUSION OF COMPLEMENTARY CLASSES
AND THE DUALITY PRINCIPLE

Task   *124 E11*

Given: Pictures of animals, which can be divided into successive dichotomies—birds and other animals, ducks and other birds. The following questions are asked:
1. "Show me all the things which are not ducks, all those which are not birds."
2. "Are there more living things which are not ducks, or more living things which are not birds?" (Similarly with birds and animals.)

Logic If the class of animals (B) includes the class of birds (A), then the class of not-birds ($\bar{A}$) includes the not-animals ($\bar{B}$). Thus, there are more not-birds ($\bar{A}$) than not-animals ($\bar{B}$) because not-birds ($\bar{A}$) include both not-animals ($\bar{B}$) and not-birds ($\bar{A}$).

If the class of birds (A) is smaller than the class of animals (B), then the class of not-birds ($\bar{A}$) is bigger than the class of not-animals ($\bar{B}$). This expresses the duality between the ordering of classes (A and B) and the ordering of their complements ($\bar{A} \cap \bar{B}$). This duality is expressed logically in the following way: [(A) < (B) → ($\bar{A}$) > ($\bar{B}$)]

Stages

1-2 [AR 9-11]: The child fails to answer questions of the form A < B and of the form $\bar{B}$ < $\bar{A}$. He understands concrete inclusions (there are birds that are not ducks, but no ducks that are not birds), but still maintains that there are as many in class A (ducks) as there are in class B (birds), interpreting "All As are Bs," as "All As are all Bs."[Failure in coordinating negation and complementarity]

3-4 [AR 11-14]: Increasingly, the child succeeds with questions of the form A < B, but fails to comprehend questions of the form $\bar{B}$ < $\bar{A}$. After some trial and error the child does succeed with the questions of the latter form. Finally, the child is able to answer all questions without difficulty. In answer to the question, "Are there more living things that aren't birds or that aren't animals?", the child replies, "There are more living things that are animals; there are more that aren't birds. [Increasing success in coordinating both negation and complementarity]

THE NULL CLASS

Task   *125 E12*

Given: A number of square, round, and triangular cards, some of which have pictures of trees, fruit, and animals, while others are blank.

These are presented to the child, who is first asked to classify all of them in any way that he chooses. He is then instructed to make a dichotomy. The question is to determine whether the child will accept that some cards are blank or will limit his classification to positive properties, namely, the one of shape.

Stages

1-3 [AR 5-10]: The child cannot construct a null class. He presents one of 3 types of reactions which represent equal levels of maturity: (*a*) the blank cards may be classified by a different criterion than the others, e.g. by shape rather than by content; (*b*) the blanks may be slipped in with the collections containing pictures; (*c*) the blanks may be ignored while only pictures are classified. There is a systematic resistance to dividing cards into those with pictures and those without, even though there is an explicit instruction to classify *all* elements. [Difficulty in the null class]

4 [AR 10–12]: The child adopts the classification which seems most natural—division into blank cards versus cards with pictures. [Correct dissociation of the null class]

Note: Concrete operations are bound up with objecs to which they apply. This supposes that these objects do exist, and so the notion of an empty class is difficult. Formal thinking, on the other hand, deals with structures independently of their content, and this is true in the realm of classification too.

MULTIPLICATIVE CLASSIFICATION: MATRICES I

Task   *126 E13*

Given: Fourteen matrices, each containing 4 to 6 objects, one of which is to be determined by the child. Variables included in the matrices are shape, color, size, number, and orientation. The following combinations are used:

1. shape/color, 3 items for each attribute
2. shape/size, 2 items for each attribute
3. color/orientation, 2 items for each attribute
4. shape/number, 2 items for each attribute
5. shape/color/orientation, 2 items for each attribute
6. shape/color/orientation, one item for each attribute
7. shape/color/size. 2 items for each attribute

Each item involves 3 questions: (*a*) finding the correct picture, (*b*) justifying the choice, (*c*) and stating whether or not one or 2 of the other pictures might fit.

Stages

1 [AR 4–6]: The child is fairly successful in answering tests involving 3 variables where there are only 3 elements from which to choose. This is the only type of matrix that the child solves. He usually cannot justify his choice, even though he can name the elements accurately. [Graphic solutions by identity or symmetry]

2 [AR 6–7]: The child is less successful in solving three-variable matrices when there are 3 elements from which to choose. Increasingly, he begins to think in terms of objects as such and define them by 2 or 3 attributes. [Difficulty in co-ordinating extension and intension of a set]

3 [AR 7–9]: The child now uses multiplication of properties to answer most of the questions successfully. [Correct coordination]

MULTIPLICATIVE CLASSIFICATION—
STANDARDIZED PROCEDURE:
MATRICES II

Task   127 *E14*

Given: Nine matrices. The first is used as a practice item, the other eight contain the following variables (see Fig. 9):
1. color/shape
2. color/shape
Note: Matrices (1) and (2) form a whole and should be used simultaneously.
3. shape/number
4. color/orientation
5. color/shape/orientation
6. color/shape/orientation

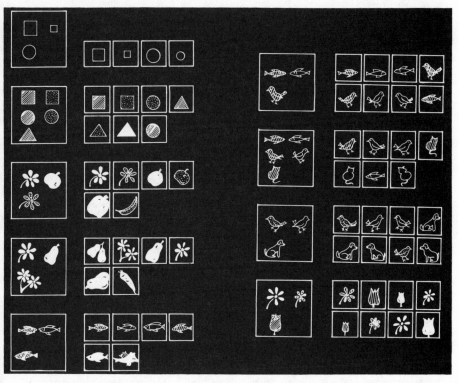

FIG. 9.

7. color/shape/orientation
8. color/shape/size

The choices are presented to the child on small cards one at a time, and the order of presentation is the same for all trials. However, the correct solution varies in random manner form one item to the next. The child is asked to do three things: find the correct picture, justify his choice, and determine whether any other pictures fit as well or better.

Stages

1 [AR 4–6]: From graphic solutions, the child increasingly makes the right choice, although not for the correct reasons, being generally unable to justify his choice. He will accept almost any other picture that is suggested, but seems to prefer one that duplicates the correct picture to the left or above blank space. Once he has to analyze relationships, he generally limits himself to one attribute at a time. [Graphic and intermediary solutions]

2–3 [AR 6–9]: Increasingly, the child's solution becomes operational. He can justify his choice and demonstrate its dependence on 2 or 3 properties; he also resists alternative suggestions provided on cards intended as distractors. [Correct coordination]

SPONTANEOUS CROSS-CLASSIFICATION (I)

Task   *128 E15*

Given: Square boxes that can be divided into 4 compartments by mobile partitions, one horizontal, one vertical. Two classifications are used: (1) One set of elements can be divided into 4 classes each consisting of identical elements, and (2) another set can also be divided into 4 classes in which, however, no two elements are identical. A detailed description of these sets follows:

1a. Sixteen pictures made up of 4 seated black rabbits, 4 seated white rabbits, 4 running black rabbits, and 4 running white rabbits.

1b. Sixteen geometric objects consisting of 4 blue squares, 4 red squares, 4 blue circles, and 4 red circles.

2. Sixteen pictures representing 4 men (policeman, clown, football player, man in morning coat), 4 women (a skier, woman with a hat, woman with a basket, woman with a bucket), 4 boys (two, not identical, with haversakcs, one running, and one playing with a kite), and 4 girls (one with a handbag, one running, one with a dog, and one playing with a doll).

The procedure is as follows: (1) free classification ("Put together the ones that go well together, that are alike."). (2) The child is asked to divide all the pictures into 4 piles, using a box with 4 compartments; (3) The pictures are removed from the box, and one of the partitions is removed to leave 2 large compartments, and the child is asked to now make "only 2 piles," and to justify his division, and is then asked to redivide the pictures into 2 groups again, "but differently"; (4) Finally, the partition is replaced, and the child is told, "You must now make 4 piles again, such that when this partition (vertical) is taken away, these 2 piles (now combined) must go well together, and when the other partition (horizontal) is taken away, these two (combined) piles must also go well together."

Stages

1 [AR 3-4]: The child has no concept of logical arrangement. (See experiment 137 E24) [Graphic collections]

2 [AR 4-7]: Gradual transition from simple or successive classifications, involving the consideration of 2 or more criteria simultaneously. The following types of reaction are seen:

1. Classification of the pictures into two collections, without subclasses, and without change of criteria once the two collections have been constructed.
2. Classification of elements into 4 collections, ignoring the simultaneous relationship.
3. Construction of 2 collections, of which only one is divided into subclasses.
4. Construction of two successive dichotomies. However, the child remains unaware of the symmetry and constructs 4 collections that are similar to those obtained with a simple matrix.
5. Correct classification based on successive criteria. Yet there is still no interaction between the two criteria because the child arranges the subcollection diagonally in the box, instead of following its axes.
6. The correct solution is reached at the end by trial and error. [Nongraphic collection, transitional solutions]

3 [AR 7-9]: Immediate or gradual application of an anticipatory schema of cross-classification with correct results and exhaustion of all possible cases, including correct subclassification. [Immediate cross-classification]

SPONTANEOUS CROSS-CLASSIFICATION II

Task   *129 E16*

Given: A set of 8 pictures (car, truck, motorcycle, motor-scooter, wagon, baby carriage, scooter, and bicycle), and 4 boxes that can be arranged in a square. Each item can be classified as either motorized or nonmotorized, and as two- or four-wheeled. The child is asked to "put together the ones that go well together;" first into 4 boxes, then into 2 and then again into 4. Finally, if he still does not discover the matrix arrangement, he is given the four boxes arranged in a square.

Stages

1 [AR 4–6]: The child does not spontaneously construct the matrix. He aligns the pictures by similarity of single pairs, by functional associations, or simply by the requirement of putting some together. [Graphic solutions; mixture of relationship of similarity and functional associations]
2 [AR 4–8]: The child begins to differentiate the cards on the basis of similarity alone. Subdivisions do not cover all the cards and are governed by a multiplicity of criteria. Increasingly, the child generalizes differentiations to the whole set of elements, and can go from one form of complementarity to another by switching the basis of his classification. These classifications are still applied successively, instead of being combined in a single multiplicative system. [Intermediary solutions]
3 [AR 7–9]: The child uses an anticipatory schema that allows him to combine all dichotomies, which have been established in advance. The child can *cross-classify* objects in terms of two criteria simultaneously. [Operational coordination with correct inclusion and intersection]

SIMPLE MULTIPLICATION (OR INTERSECTION) OF SETS

Task   *130 E17*

Given: A row of green objects (pear, hat, flower, and book), and a row of leaves of various colors (brown, red, yellow, etc.) at right angles to each other, with an empty space left just before the intersection of the two rows (Fig. 10). The child is asked to fill this cell with an object that fits in with everything," either by verbal description, free drawing, or, if necessary, a choice of several alternative pictures. Before the task is posed, the child is asked, "Why have all these objects been placed together?", and, "Are they alike in any way?" If the child has difficulty in solving the problem, more objects may be used to make the similarities more obvious.

Stages

1 [AR 4–6]: The basis for the child's choice is purely perceptual: He fills the empty cell with an element identical in shape or color to one of two objects

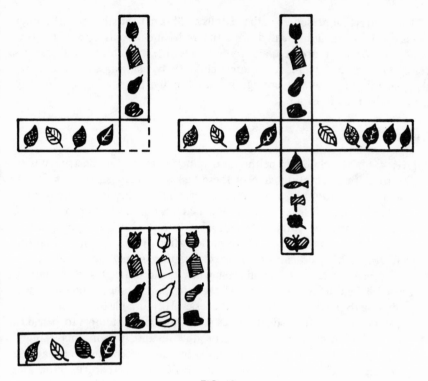

FIG. 10

next to it. Neither the second collection, nor the other objects in the first collection play any role. [Graphic collections]

2 [AR 5–7]: The child looks at the entire row and fills the cell with an element identical to another element in one of the rows. [Partial solution]

3 [AR 6–10]: Increasingly, the child begins to construct logical classes, choosing an element that is not already present. Finally, he arrives at the notion of intersection and makes the correct choice. [Operational coordination]

SERIATION AND THE ANTICIPATION OF SERIAL CONFIGURATION WITH ELEMENTS PERCEIVED VISUALLY: ANTICIPATION AND CONSTRUCTION

Task   *131 E18*

Given: Four dolls of different sizes, 10 rods, .5 cm in diameter, and increasing in length by equal increments (.8 cm) from 9 to 16.2 cm, colored crayons, and ordinary pencils.

The child is first presented with the dolls and asked to arrange them in order of size. He is then presented with the rods and asked to predict their configuration when ordered, and to draw it (either by using colored crayons to represent each stick, or, for younger children, by using a pencil to arrive at the general shape of the configuration.) Finally, he is asked to actually arrange the rods in order.

Stages

1 [AR 4–6]: The child can neither anticipate the series nor construct it with the rods. In attempting each of these tasks, he manages to form small, unconnected groups of two or three elements. Drawing and action seem to be at a comparable level of development at this point. Working with only 2 or 3 elements, the child is usually able to establish correspondence of length between rods and colored representations. [No attempt at seriation]

2 [AR 5–8]: The child can draw correct seriation, sometimes immediately, but not always accurately, and often when it is accurate, it is so by trial and error. The child "semi-anticipates" the series, and is successful only when attending to the global schema of the series. He is unable to account for the color and sizes of the rods. In cases where the child attempts to attend to both, he is confused and unable to produce an anticipation. Increasingly, his graphic anticipation and actual seriation become more equal. He accounts for color and size of the rods in his drawing. He still uses trial and error for the actual seriation. [Success by trial and error]

3 [AR 5–8]: The child now draws a correct, detailed anticipation of the series, using an operational method for seriation. He can bear in mind that a given element is both longer than those already in the series and shorter than the ones to follow. There is a remarkable correspondence between success at anticipation and success at actual seriation. [Operational method]

KINETIC SERIATION AND ITS
ANTICIPATION IN DRAWING

Task   *132 E19*

Given: Two series of rods: (A) 10 rods, 10–19 cm in length varying in increments of 1 cm, with a square cross-section of .5 cm, and (B) 5 rods, 4–16 cm in length, varying in increments of 3 cm, all having a square cross-section of 1 cm. The experiment includes the following steps:

1. Kinetic examination: The child is encouraged to examine the objects until he can "feel" the inequality.

2. Anticipation of seriation: The child is asked to draw the "biggest," then the "next-biggest," and so on, down to the smallest.
3. Actual seriation by touch: The child is asked to state what he is doing, and later is allowed to see whether it is correct.
4. Actual seriation by sight: When the child cannot carry out the seriation by touch, he is asked to do it visually.

Stages

1 [AR 4–7]: The child neither anticipates global schema nor seriates the rods. He simply touches one end of a rod, neglects the other, and never compares two unless directed to do so. The child makes no effort to be sure that he has felt all the elements. However, the child can produce a drawing that is appreciably better than the series he has formed (anticipation is slightly in advance). Further, the child's anticipation becomes increasingly accurate as a result of more thorough examination of the objects: he will examine the line of summits with bases along a straight line; but this schema remains global, and he still fails to seriate. [Failure in anticipation]
2 [AR 5–9]: The child can anticipate global schema correctly, but is still unable to carry out seriation. He forms small subseries and examines the lines of the summits more carefully. Nevertheless, the child still fails to relate each element to a sufficient number of others. He is increasingly able to anticipate and seriate correctly, although successful seriation is the result of successive rearrangements made after checking both ends of the rods. [Success by trial and error]
3 [AR 7–10]: The child uses an operational method to seriate the rods, looking for the longest of all, then for the longest among the remaining ones, and so on. In using this method of seriation, the child makes successive comparisons. [Operational method]

MULTIPLE SERIATION

Task   *133 E20*

Given: Forty-nine drawings of leaves, each of 7 sizes (I–VII) is represented in 7 varying shades of green (1–7). The drawings are presented to the child, who is asked to arrange them as he wishes. If the child is unable to arrange them, the experimenter may arrange one series in a line along one of the dimensions, or two series along both dimensions, leaving the rest of the matrix to be completed by the child as follows:

I1	I2	I3	I4	I5	I6	I7
II1	•	•	•	•	•	II7
III1	•	•	•	•	•	III7
IV1	•	•	•	•	•	IV7
V1	•	•	•	•	•	V7
VI1	•	•	•	•	•	VI7
VII1	•	•	•	•	•	VII7

When the table has been completed (whether spontaneously or with the experimenter's help), the child is asked to pick out a specific element according to two criteria simultaneously. At times, 98 elements (49 identical pairs can be used to test the child's reaction to identical elements. Or, with younger children, a smaller collection of 4 × 4 elements with sharper gradations of size and color may be used.

Stages

1 [AR 5-7]: The child does not spontaneously seriate elements, but simply forms graphic collections based on only one of the two dimensions involved in the problem; or he may vacillate between the properties. He will, however, be able to subdivide the existing collections if reminded of the forgotten second property, and will also be able to fill in the matrix by trial and error when given the upper row and left hand column. [Graphic solution]

2 [AR 6-7]: The child thinks of the seriations on separate levels and has difficulty following both series simultaneously. He is not able to solve the matrix by a multiplicative system: Rather, he finds *either* the correct row *or* the correct column immediately, but then relies on neighboring elements to find the correct intersection. [Intermediary reactions]

3 [AR 6-9]: The child realizes that correct seriation must be made in terms of two homogeneous and equal variables. He, therefore, uses multiplication [Operational method]

CLASSIFICATION OF ELEMENTS PERCEIVED BY TOUCH

Task   *134 E21*

Given: A "house" consisting of a cloth-covered framework, in which the child may manipulate objects without seeing them. A partition may be placed in the house as a divider. Then the following two sets of objects, and two procedures:

Set 1. This set consists of eight identical pairs of elements: 8 curved objects—2 small and 2 large disks, 2 small and 2 large spheres—and 8 rectilinear objects—2 small and 2 large squares, and 2 small and 2 large cubes.

Set 2. This set contains 16 wooden objects, none of which are identical. These are 2 spheres, 2 cubes, 2 cuboids, 2 ellipsoids, 2 squares, 2 disks, 2 rectangles, and 2 ellipses (the same-shape pairs differ in size, hence nonidentical).

The child is asked to put his hands inside the house and to handle the objects that have been placed there (Procedure 1). Later, visual control experiments are carried out (Procedure 2).

Procedure 1. The child is first asked to spontaneously classify the objects. When this is done, he is asked to classify them into successive dichotomies with the help of the partition.

Procedure 2. The cloth is now removed and the child is asked to visually classify the objects into successive dichotomies.

Stages

1 [AR 4–6]: The child tends to focus on the elements recognized during his exploration and to forget about the others. Classification may contain collections, each having a class criterion, but he does not formulate them. The child tends to make graphic collections, and further, tries to reproduce these when asked to classify the elements visually. Gradually, a single criterion may be discovered by trial and error. [Graphic collections]

2 [AR 5–8]: The child constructs his collections on the basis of similarities without recognizing particular spatial configuration. He recognizes his first criterion by anticipation and gradually notes the existence of other criteria by trial and error. The child tends to be more interested in shape (e.g., rectilinear vs. curvilinear) than in any other criterion. [Intermediary solutions]

3 [AR 6–10]: The child is now able to recognize all three criteria: shape, size (large vs. small), and dimensionality, usually anticipating at least two of these. [Operational method]

CLASSIFICATION BY ANTICIPATION

Task   *135 E22*

Given: Eighteen cards: 3 small and 3 large circles, 3 small and 3 large squares, 3 small and 3 large right triangles. Each set of 3 contains one blue, one red, and one yellow element. The cards are arranged randomly on a large sheet of paper. The child is given a set of empty envelopes and is told to *anticipate* the classification of cards in the envelopes: "Try to put everything in order. All the things which are the same will go in one envelope, so that we can write on the envelope whatever will be inside. You must take as few envelopes as possible." He is given some time to examine the elements and then is asked: (1) "How many envelopes are necessary?" (2) "What must be written on these envelopes?" (3) "Point out what will go in each envelope." When the child has completed the anticipation, he is asked to reclassify the elements using a different criterion. Finally, he is asked to actually *do* the classification.

Stages

1 [AR 4–6]: The child has much difficulty in finding any criteria for the projected classification. The actual classification does not necessraily agree with the anticipation. When he is asked to reclassify the elements, he either preserves his first classification or produces a modification of his first classification with no clear criterion. [Difficulty of anticipation and lack of stable criterion]

2 [AR 5–7]: The child shows semi-anticipation: He anticipates "the *actions* involved in *combining* elements and *piling* them together on the basis of their similarities." But his anticipations are usually based on larger collections—red, blue, square, or circle, instead of large red square. When the child actually classifies the elements, he begins with smaller collections (subcollections) and builds from these. He also shows very little flexibility in changing his criterion of classification. Increasingly, he is better able to pass from subcollections to collections, even though the subcollections remain separate instead of giving rise to immediate combinations. He still systematically makes errors in answering questions concerning "all"and "some." [Semi-anticipations with difficulty in shifting criteria]

3 [AR 6–9]: The child's anticipation is based on transformations—the extension of a subcollection is now compared with that of the total collection. The child understands inclusion and is able to shift from one criterion to another. Once he has completed a classification, he can return to a criterion that has been provisionally laid aside and rearrange the classification on the basis of the new criterion. [Correct anticipations and operational criteria]

REARRANGEMENTS CAUSED BY THE ADDITION OF NEW ELEMENTS

Task   *136 E23*

Given: Apparatus I contains two boxes and the following objects: flat green circles and crosses (all smooth and the same size), smooth flat yellow stars, 2 large mauve rombi, mauve semicircles, triangles, and ovals in corrugated cardboard. Apparatus II contains two boxes and the following objects: large and small green circles, large and small yellow circles, large and small green and yellow squares, and large and small squares and circles, both with jagged edges.

1. Using Apparatus I, the child is asked to classify the elements into the two boxes. Each time a new element is added, a change in classification is needed.

2. Using Apparatus II, the child is again asked to classify the elements into the two boxes. This time rearrangement is not necessary.

3. The child is asked to classify the elements in Apparatus II, but this time is given successive partitions which may be arranged inside the boxes as the additions are made.

4. Using either Apparatus I or II, the child is asked to name all of the possible classifications without the use of the boxes. Techniques should emphasize repeated changes in classification, and a retention of the actions performed in that classification.

Stages

1 [AR 3–5]: The child is able to recognize the criterion by which he can establish a dichotomy with the given elements. When new elements are added, he merely continues to classify through the first criterion and fails to recognize any subclassification. If he is able to recognize the second criterion, he will continue to classify by the second criterion, disregarding the first. In these types of classification, the child is trying to find a relationship between 2 elements instead of extending "the properties of 'all' the elements of an existing collection to the added element." [Lack of flexibility of criterion]

2 [AR 5–7]: The child is able to discover other criteria for classification. He can construct different dichotomies, but still prefers to stick to the original division as long as it holds true. He is usually able to deal with 2 criteria but tends to forget them when a third and fourth are added. [Intermediary reactions]

3 [AR 7–10]: The child shows *retroactive integration*. The first set of additional elements results in a 2 × 2 matrix and following additions lead to three-way or four-way matrices *or* he sticks with two-way or three-way classification, but he can change criteria at will. The child does show anticipation of logical multiplication and he shows flexibility when asked to rearrange his pattern. [Operational solutions]

GRAPHIC AND NON-GRAPHIC COLLECTIONS: CLASSIFICATION OF FLAT GEOMETRICAL SHAPES

Task   *137 E24*

Given: Various squares, triangles, rings and half-rings, some in wood and others in plastic. One may include occasionally letters of the alphabet. The child is usually asked to "put together the things that are alike," or to "put them so that they are all the same," or to "put them so that they are just like one another."

Typical Behaviors

Young children do not arrange the elements into collections and subcollections on the basis of similarity alone. They are unable to overlook the spatial configuration of the objects and proceed to unite them in graphic collections that stand midway between a composite spatial object and a set. Types of responses, rather than stages, are described for this experiment, although there is a developmental progression from one type to the next.

1. Small Partial Alignments. Independent arrangements are made, usually with only some of the objects, and most frequently, presented in a linear fashion. The elements are connected by successive similarities: linear sequence by successive by successive one-dimensional vicinities.

2. Continuous Alignments with Fluctuating Criteria. The child generalizes the alignment and arrives at a long line made of subsets, one not constructed on the basis of an anticipatory plan. Reactions are intermediate between alignments and complex objects.

3. Intermediate Reactions Complex Objects As Graphic Collections in More Than One Dimension. Two types of construction occur: (a) several lines that are constructed at angles to one another; and (b) figures that start as alignments but are later elaborated into two dimensions.

4. Collective Objects. This is a two- or three-dimensional collection of similar elements that together form a unified figure.

5. Complex Objects Based on Geometrical or Situational Content. Part-whole relationships are reinforced and the whole becomes a closed set. The child tends to focus upon the shape and properties of the whole. He tends to forget the internal relation of similarity and difference among its elements. There is definitively a geometrical whole form apparent.

The Development of Formal Logic

INTRODUCTION

Formal logic has undoubtedly a great number of connotations in our mind that makes it both abstract and part of our reasoning. Formal logic investigates the structure of propositions and of deductive reasoning by a method that abstracts from the content of propositions and deals only with their logical form. The distinction between form and content will be made precise with the aid of a particular language or symbolism in which propositions are expressed. The formal method, then, can be characterized by the fact that it deals with the objective form of sentences or propositions; it provides, in concrete terms, criteria of meaningfulness and validity of inference.

The acquisition of the formal level of thought consists in a further extension and reorganization of the operations of classification and seriation that come to combine themselves into a new system. It is essential to Piaget's thesis to trace the relationship between early concrete logic and formal logic. Hypothetico-deductive reasoning, which bears on the logic of propositions, represents the final step of the cognitive development. It is the final and highest level of thinking because its structure or system encompasses all possible cases. In effect, formal thinking deals not only with the real but with the possible. The formal level of thought marks the ability to achieve the synthesis between the possible and the necessary. At the level of hypothetico-deductive thinking, the adolescent reasons on the hypotheses themselves in combination, and no longer deals directly with objects that are in front of him that can be either directly or potentially manipulated. The adolescent in his

175

thinking takes objects as pretexts for testing hypotheses, and as the cause for extracting hypotheses, properties or categories. On a verbal level, he will provide exact deduction. He will devise theories. He will construct realities from which he will deduce necessary consequences. Formal thinking thus entails the ability to dissociate the form of a proposition from its content. The most essential feature of the formal level of thought is the constitution of a "logic of the propositions," which is grouped into a new structure that Piaget identifies as the INRC group and lattices. In effect a combinatorial system, the INRC allows all possible combinations, coherently organized. It is not my purpose to detail the logical properties of this new system of thinking. The point is this: There is a profound analogy between the operations and system constructed by the adolescent and their formalization into a logical network. Most logicians are not necessarily concerned with whether the laws and structures of logic have any sort of relationship with psychological structures. The extreme view asserts that the concept of operations is essentially anthropomorphic and that logical operations are, in fact, only formal operations that have no resemblance to psychological operations. Piaget's study of the development of formal thinking in adolescents stands at the opposite end of this point of view. When one tries to discover the entities to which these logical structures correspond, we find four possible solutions to the problem from the point of view of their bearing on psychology. The platonist views logic as corresponding to a system of universals that exist independently from experience and thus are not psychological in their origin. But the problem is precisely to explain how the mind comes to discover such universals and from Piaget's point of view, platonism is in effect a way to deny the problem itself. Secondly, conventionalism holds that logical entities owe their existence and laws to a set of conventions or generally accepted rules. But, according to Piaget, if such is the case why should these conventions be successful and effective in their application, and, in the final analysis, why should there be progress since social agreement is in fact a criteria of conformity and stability. Thridly, the Vienna circle, or the circle otherwise known as that of a "well formed language" distinguishes between empirical truths (non-tautological relationships) and tautologies (syntactical relationships) that, through an appropriate semantics, will be used to express empirical truths. This point of view has psychological significance but entails from a developmental point of view several difficulties. According to Piaget, one cannot speak of empirical truths apart from logical relationships. Experience cannot be interpreted in abstraction from the conceptual apparatus that makes such an interpretation possible. Furthermore, logical relationships never appear as a simple system of symbolic or linguistic expressions but always imply a group of operations whose main tenants are the actions of the subject. Finally, logic is not merely a language and Piaget's studies can be viewed as essentially attempting to refute this assumption.

Logic is a conceptual framework from which language derives. Logic is a system of potential and real actions. Logic is an operational structure. This brings us to the fourth manner in which logical relationships have been interpreted: operationalism, which provides real ground on which logic and psychology can meet. The development of formal logic in adolescents has great significance within this context. To determine the relations between logic and psychology, Piaget constructs a psychological theory of operations in terms of their genesis and structures. He then examines these logical operations as totalities or structured wholes and compares the results of these two kinds of enquiries. To achieve his purpose it is essential that Piaget trace the development of logical operations to its completion. The observation of the development of the formal level of thought lead to the conclusion that the logic of propositions the adolescent comes to achieve is simultaneously a formal structure holding independently of content, and a general structure coordinating the various operations into a single system.

Thus, formal level of thought is simultaneously a psychological entity and a formal one whose relationship clarifies the connections between logic and psychology. What follows is the detailed account of experiments in each of the domains presented.

THE EQUALITY OF ANGLES OF INCIDENCE AND REFLECTION

Task   *138 A1*

Given: A kind of billiard game in which balls are launched with a tubular spring device that can be pivoted and aimed in various directions around a fixed point. A ball is shot against the wall of the game and rebounds to the interior. A target is placed at different points.

The subject is asked to aim at the target. He is then asked to report what he observed and to extract the law that explains it.

Stages

1–2 [AR 5–8]: Subject is more concerned with practical success or failure than with the means by which they are determined. He does not notice the angles formed at the rebound point. Trajectories are not generally conceived of as constituting rectilinear segments but rather as making a sort of curve. [Preoperational behaviors]

3 [AR 7–11]: Subject notes 3 new facts: (a) the plunger can be adjusted to different slopes; (b) the trajectory of the ball is composed of two rectilinear segments; (c) these two segments form an angle whose size varies according

to their slopes. These factors are discovered by the subject through active manipulation of the device. Increasingly, the subject provides a more accurate formulation of the relations between the inclination of the plunger and the inclination of the line of reflection. The subject is not involved in generalizing these discovered relationships. [Concrete operational method without formal generalization]

4 [AR 11-15]: The subject searches for a general hypothesis that can account for the actual correspondence between the angles of incidence and reflection. He searches for a single consistent factor which translates these correspondences. [Formal method]

THE LAW OF FLOATING BODIES

Task   *139 A2*

Given: A number of disparate objects and several buckets of water. The subject is asked to classify these objects according to whether or not they will float on water, and then to explain the basis for his classification. The subject is allowed to experiment, using the objects and the buckets of water, and when satisfied with his experimentation, he is asked to summarize his observations. It is suggested that he look for a physical law to explain his observations.

Stages

1-2 [AR 4-8]: The subject is satisfied with multiple and often contradictory explanations; he does not seem to classify objects into 2 groups (i.e., floating and nonfloating bodies). Once he has determined whether or not a given object floats, he does not generalize his findings to analogous objects. Increasingly, the subject attempts to classify objects into floating and nonfloating categories, but he cannot do it exhaustively. [Preoperational behaviors]

3 [AR 7-10]: The subject acquires the beginnings of the concept of density and begins to use the concept to try to resolve earlier contradictions. He realizes that small objects do not always weigh less than larger ones. Increasingly, the subject is able to order serially the weights of objects of the same volume; but, since volume is not automatically conserved at this stage, he does not yet see operational relationships between volume and density. He begins to compare the weights of specific bodies to the weight of water, but relates the object's weight to that of *all* the water contained in the receptacle rather than to the weight of an equal volume of water. [Concrete behaviors]

4 [AR 9–15]: The subject first relates the weight of the object to its volume and then relates the weight and volume of the object to the corresponding weight and volume of water displaced by that object. Three discoveries are made: (a) the subject finds that to refute a postulated explanation, it is sufficient to invoke verbally or mentally a case where the purported factor is associated with the opposite effect; (b) the subject relates the weight of an object to that of a quantity of water; (c) increasingly, the subject searches for a common metric unity by applying the principle of "all other things being equal." (He introduces necessary links between variables by isolating them from their contextual independence and by deducing relations thus isolated.) In this case weight and volume are not independent since the subject is trying to determine the relation between them and link them. [Formal method]

FLEXIBILITY AND THE OPERATIONS MEDIATING THE SEPARATION OF VARIABLES

Task   *140 A3*

Given: The subject is presented with a large basin of water and a set of rods differing in composition (steel, brass, etc.), length, thickness, and cross-sectional shape (round, square, and rectangular). Three different weights can be screwed to the ends of the rods. The rods can be attached to the edge of the basin in a horizontal position (the weights exert a force perpendicular to the surface of the water).

The subject is asked to determine how a rod can be made flexible enough to reach the water level. The experimenter observes the subject's methods and notes his comments on the variables that he believes influence flexibility. The subject is asked to prove his assertions.

Stages

1–2 [AR 5–7]: The subject simply describes what he sees—the rod does not touch the water because it remains too high, or it does not touch the water because it is attached to the plank (although those that do touch the water are similarly attached). The subject does not perceive contradictions and establishes only global relationships. [Preoperational method]

3 [AR 7–11]: The subject is able to register raw data systematically. He is capable of differentiated classification, serial ordering, or equalization, and correspondences, but is unable to isolate the experimentally relevant variables. [Concrete deductions]

4 [AR 11–15]: The subject isolates successively the different variables and assesses their respective role. He is able to combine them into a "structured whole." He exhibits hypothetico-deductive reasoning and an active attempt at verification. [Formal method]

THE OSCILLATION OF A PENDULUM AND THE OPERATIONS OF EXCLUSION

Task   *141 A4*

Given: A pendulum consisting of objects (weights) suspended on a string. The subject is able to actively vary the length of the string, the weight of the objects suspended, and the amplitude and force of the push. He is asked to find which factors determine the frequency of oscillation.

Stages

1–2 [AR 6–8]: The subject can give neither an objective account of the experiment nor consistent explanations of it because of a lack of serial ordering and exact correspondences. He cannot dissociate the impetus which he gives to the pendulum's motion from motion which is independent of his action. [Preoperational method]

3 [AR 8–12]: The subject is not able to serially order the weights accurately, but he is able to order other factors accurately and does discover inverse relationships between the length of the string and the frequency of oscillation. He is increasingly able to assess the effects of the weights accurately, but still cannot systematically separate the factors. The subject can report inferences based on only some factors, and is limited to simple tables of variation. [Concrete behaviors]

4 [AR 11–15]: The subject is able to isolate factors in combination where one factor varies while the other remains constant, but produces these combinations with help. Finally, his answer becomes a selection among a set of basic combinations of relevant factors. [Formal generalization]

FALLING BODIES ON AN INCLINED PLANE

Task   *142 A5*

Given: A plane adjustable to various angles of incline. Balls of varying weights are rolled down the plane, hit a springboard at the bottom, bound in a parabolic curve, and come to rest in one of the 8 successive compartments (1–8, with the eighth at the farthest point from the springboard).

The subject is asked to determine the factors affecting the length of the bound.

Stages

1-2 [AR 5-8]: The subject intuitively understnads that the steeper the slope, the more quickly an object will fall and the farther it will travel. But the height at which the ball is released is not separated from the angle of the incline. Weight is attributed a systematic role. The specific role of weight, however, remains inconsistent. [Preoperational behaviors]

3 [AR 7-11]: The subject is able to formulate correct correspondences but depending upon the way in which the balls are presented, he often manages to exclude the factor of weight insofar as it is incompatible with serial correspondance. Increasingly, he begins to dissociate the height of release point from the slope. This differentiation is not sufficient for the subject to exclude slope in favor of height alone. He still thinks of slope and distance as independent factors that can compensate for each other. He does not yet see that in order to find correspondence between the length of the bounds or the ball and the determinant causal factor (height), it is sufficient to consider height without regard to slope or distance. [Concrete empirical method]

4 [AR 11-15]: The subject produces hypotheses easily and from the start tries to identify the factors. Initially, he fails to dissociate variables completely for 2 reasons: (a) he does not separate height and distance because with equal slopes they vary concurrently (b) in asserting that distance and slope compensate for each other, the subject actually limits himself to a statement of covariance without looking for the invariant that results from it. Finally, the subject isolates variables by the method of varying each factor in turn while holding all others constant. This allows him to distinguish all 3 factors: slope, distance, and height. [Formal method]

THE ROLE OF INVISIBLE MAGNETISM

Task   *143 A6*

Given: A large circular board divided into 2 concentric circles (A) and (B). (A) is divided along its radius into 8 equal sections of different colors with opposite sections matching in color. Eight boxes with 4 different designs are placed within the sections (again, the same designs are placed opposite each other). One pair of boxes (those with the circles) contains magnets concealed in wax. A metal bar is placed on B attached to a non-metallic rotating disk. This disk always stops with the bar pointing to the boxes with circles. The boxes can be moved to different sections, but they are always placed with one member of a pair opposite the other. The boxes are unequal in weight, providing another variable.

The subject must determine why the disk always stops with the bar pointing to the boxes with the circles.

Stages

1-2 [AR 6-7]: The subject can limit causality to a specific design or to the placement of the boxes on the board. Increasingly, he begins to understand exclusion in the form of the lack of correspondence. He rejects an explanation based on the content of the boxes because all of the boxes are filled with wax; he notes the lack of correspondence but he is unable to organize his observations in a detailed way. [Preoperational behaviors]

3 [AR 7-12]: The subject uses a mixture of concrete disjunctions and exlcusions. He believes that the stopping point can be explained conclusively in terms of weight alone, but he also discovers the diversity of weight when confronted with experimental situation. He uses a type of disjunction that is based on a simple, approximate serial ordering; and he assumes that weight may act in 1 of 3 ways: (a) the effect that results from the heaviest; (b) from the lightest; or (c) from an intermediary value. Because of this correspondence between some of the weights and the disk's stopping points rather than between all of the weights serially ordered, the subject is unable to exclude weight as a factor. Increasingly, he is able to use concrete operations in handling weight. He applies serial ordering to weight to conclude that this factor is ineffective—2 equal weights do not produce the same effect. [Concrete empirical method]

4 [AR 12-15]: The subject uses the formal combinatorial system and views the experiment as a "structured whole." He uses empirical manipulations only for a verification of a stated hypothesis. He isolates the factors one at a time, as so discovers and isolates the determining factors. [Formal method of isolating determining factors]

THE ESTABLISHMENT OF A
COMBINATORIAL SYSTEM:
COMBINATIONS OF COLORED AND
COLORLESS CHEMICAL BODIES

Task   *144 A7*

Given: These chemicals produce the same type of reactions described by Piaget and Inhelder in their experiment. That is, chemicals (a), (c), and (e) produce a blue color, chemical (d) removes the color, and chemical (b)—water—has no effect. The chemicals used are: (a) potassium iodide; (b) water; (c) starch solution; (d) sodium thiosulfate; and (e) ammonium persulfate. Test tubes filled with these chemicals, and a set of empty test tubes are provided. The experimenter places a rack holding the test tubes containing solutions and labeled (a), (b), (c), (d), and (e) on the table in front of the subject. A second rack containing empty test tubes is also placed on the table. The experimenter takes two unlabeled test tubes containing clear solutions (a-c and b), adds a drop of (e) to each and says "See, when I add a drop of (e) to these test tubes, one solution turns dark blue and the other remains clear. I want you to find out how to make a blue color using solutions (a), (b), (c), (d), and (e) in any way you like. You can use these empty test tubes here for working."

Stages

1–2 [AR 5–7]: The subject is limited to randomly associating 2 or several elements at a time, noting simply the result. Color is a sort of active element that emanates from water but may "go away," or "go down to the bottom," or "flatten out" to the point where it becomes invisible. Color can also "come back" but only to certain beakers of "water" and not to others. [Preoperational behaviors]

3 [AR 7–12]: The subject is able to use logical multiplicative operations of one-to-one correspondence, but the concept of constructing combinations of 2-by-2 or 3-by-3 does not occur. His spontaneous reactions are either to associate each one of bottles (a) and (d) in turn to a drop of (e) or to take all four at the same time. He fails to try all possible sequences that combinatorial permutation operations allow. He uses only correspondences and serial ordering, but increasingly, he spontaneously uses n-by-n combinations (each time with e). The subject does not discover any system: The cause of color is still thought to be in the particular elements rather than in their combination. [Empirical method]

4 [AR 12–15]: The subject uses a systematic n-by-n combinatorial system. He does not stop looking for successful combinations once he finds one that brings about color. His main interest is not in achieving a particular combination, but in understanding the role this combination plays among the total number of possible combinations. The subject now searches for the cause of color in combinations of liquids. Increasingly, he arrives at correct solutions by a more direct method, because, from the start, he organizes his experiment with an eye to proof. Combinations and, more particularly, proofs appear in a more systematic fashion; the subject now seeks the solution in organizing proofs and in integrating methods of proof. [Hypothetico-deductive method]

THE CONSERVATION OF MOTION IN
A HORIZONTAL PLANE

Task   *145 A8*

Given: A spring device that launches balls of varying sizes and weights so that they roll on a horizontal plane.

The subject's task is to predict the stopping points of the balls and to explain the observed movements.

Stages

1-2 [AR 5-7]: The subject provides contradictory predictions and explanations—light balls go farther because they are easier to set in motion; larger ones go farther because they are stronger. There is an absence of laws. [Preoperational behaviors]

3 [AR 7-10]: The subject does not always show consistency of motion and bases his predictions on variable factors. Yet, he does show some internal consistency in his assertions as well as in his utilization of experimental results. Some contradictions remain since the subject usually equates the force with which an object is launched with the force of the moving body. [Concrete method]

4 [AR 10-15]: For the subject, the objective of the explanation is reversed— he does not try to understand why the ball moves forward; rather, he tries to understand what limits its movement. The subject touches on two causes of the cessation of movement (friction and air resistance), and he looks for an unified explanation. [Formal method]

COMMUNICATING VESSELS

Task   *146 A9*

Given: Two receptacles of different shapes and volumes joined by a tube running from the bottom of one to the bottom of the other. Both receptacles are placed on stands of equal heights, and contain therefore equal levels of water. To adjust the water levels, the subject can raise or lower the vessels by removing or replacing these stands.

The subject is first asked to observe that both water levels are equal. Then he is asked to experiment with the apparatus and to report what he observes. Through a series of questions, it is suggested that he find a general law describing this phenomenon.

Stages

1-2 [AR 5-7]: The subject fails to dissociate his actions from objective transformations, and he does not see the transitivity between successive actions. He succeeds neither in predicting nor in understanding the symmetry of objective effects in relating both receptacles. [Preoperational behaviors]

3 [AR 7-11]: The subject discovers separately the two inverse relationships between the raising and lowering of the beakers and the change in the water levels. His expectation does not deal with the equilibrium between weight and pressure. Instead, he attributes the change in water levels to impetus, rate of speed, and air; he assumes that water descends from the higher beaker to the lower one simply because the latter is lower. Gradually, the subject discovers laws affecting the water levels in the two receptacles and the conditions of system equilibrium. But he does not discover the cause for the law. [Concrete empirical method]

4 [AR 12-15]: The subject cannot accept that the water levels are equal when the volumes as well as the shapes of the receptacles differ. So he first restricts the scope of the law to those cases in which these factors are equal, thinking that the equality of water levels will no longer hold for unequal forms and volumes. But when experimentation contradicts his expectations, he stops generalizing to other cases. Progressively, the subject does explain equilibrium as a system of actions and reactions whose inversions and reciprocities are stated in mechanical and not merely in spatio-temporal terms. Increasingly, he generalizes the law for cases involving unequal qualities. [Formal method]

EQUILIBRIUM IN THE HYDRAULIC PRESS

Task   *147 A10*

Given: Two communicating vessels, (A) and (B) of different shape and size. Vessel (A) is outfitted with a piston that is dropped into it loaded with various weights to alter the amount of pressure it exerts.

The subject is asked to predict what will happen to the level of the liquid in each vessel as the varied weights are applied.

Stages

1-2 [AR 5-7]: The subject cannot make an unequivocal prediction that the water will rise in (B) as a result of the weight of the piston applied in (A).

Since he shows no conservation of quantities, the tubes may be filled without adequate reason. Increasingly, the subject understands in general terms that the heavier the weight, the more the water rises in (B). Thus, weight is seen as the cause. But the weights are not systematically ordered and equalizations are scarce. [Preoperational behaviors]

3 [AR 7–11]: The subject is able to make the weights and the water levels correspond. In regard to density, he thinks that the heavier the liquid, the higher it will rise, because its weight is added to that of the piston. An equilibrium between the liquid and a piston of variable weight is not conceived of as a reciprocal equilibrium mechanism. Increasingly, the subject realizes that the liquid's resistance is a function of its density, but the volume of the water is always conceived as a function of its weight. [Concrete empirical observations]

4 [AR 11–15]: The system used by the subject to solve the problem is an equilibrium of opposed forces and no longer a one-way process—density (the relationship between weight and volume) is no longer a factor promoting the pressure of the piston, but on the contrary is an obstacle to this pressure and thus a factor whose action is oriented in the opposite direction. The subject is now able to explain equilibrium in terms of direct and inverse factors. [Formal method]

EQUILIBRIUM IN THE BALANCE: PROPORTIONALITY

Task   *148 A11*

Given: A conventional balance scale with varying weights that can be hung at different points along the crossbar.

The subject is presented with 2 equal weights hung at unequal distances, and is asked how he would balance the scale and why he would do it that way.

Stages

1–2 [AR 4–8]: No conservation of weight. The subject cannot balance the scale by distributing the weight and often interferes with the freeworking of the apparatus. He fails to distinguish the effects of his own actions on the scale and those exerted by the weights. The weights are not removed with the intent to equalize. Increasingly, the subject understands that a weight is needed on both sides to achieve balance and that the weights must be approximately equal, but he does not proceed in a systematic way. He makes successive corrections by adding and substracting weights, but does not achieve accurate equalization. [Preoperational behaviors]

3 [AR 7–11]: The subject equalizes the weights and makes the distances symmetrical, but the coordination between weights and distances is still incomplete. By trial and error, the subject realizes that the smaller weight at a greater distance equals the greater weight at a smaller distance, but he does not yet understand it as a general principle. He achieves qualitative correspondences and qualitative proportionality. [Empirical method— Concrete behaviors]

4 [AR 11–15]: The subject uses metrical proportions and explains the system in terms of equal amounts of work, but the schema is taken from notions of compensation. The subject deduces correctly the laws of proportionality:

$$\frac{W}{W'} = \frac{L}{L'}$$

in which W = weight and L = distance form the center. [Formal hypothetico-deductive method]

HAULING A WEIGHT ON AN INCLINED PLANE

Task   *149 A12*

Given: A toy wagon, suspended by a cable, is hauled up an inclined plane by counterweights at the other end of the cable. The counterweights can be varied; the angle of the plane is adjustable; and the weights can be placed in the wagon to provide yet a third variable.

The subject is asked to explain what must be done to make the wagon go up or down.

Stages

1–2 [AR 5–7]: The subject views the total situation as a set of uncoordinated forces that cannot be differentiated from his own actions. [Preoperational behaviors]

3 [AR 7–11]: The subject begins to coordinate the weights in the wagon with the counterweights, and also becomes aware of the fact the the the inclination of the track plays a role, but cannot coordinate these two factors. Ultimately, he cannot coordinate all three factors (weight of wagon, counterweight, and incline) in a coherent united system. [Concrete method]

4 [AR 10–15]: The subject coordinates the three factors in a single law from the start, but thinks first in terms of the degree of the angle rather than in

terms of its sine (height). Later he does discover proportionality of heights and weights:

$$\frac{W}{M} = \frac{h}{H}$$

where W = counterweight, M = weight of the wagon, h = height of angle (sine), and H = total height. [Formal method]

THE PROJECTION OF SHADOWS

Task   *150 A13*

Given: A baseboard with a screen attached to one end, a light source (e.g., a candle), and rings of various diameters. The light source and the rings can be moved along the baseboard.

The subject is asked to produce 2 shadows of the same size using different sized rings.

Stages

1-2 [AR 4-7]: The subject simply manipulates the elements without coordinating any of the factors. [Preoperational behaviors]

3 [AR 7-12]: The subject understands that the size of the shadows depends on the size of the object; he orders serially the sizes of shadows and he formulates accurate correspondences at equal distances. He also understands that the closer the object is to the screen, the smaller its shadow. Two features can be noted: (a) the subject measures the distance from the screen rather than from the light source (larger distances, therefore, make larger shadows—a direct correspondence), and (b) the subject's attempts at metrical quantification are not derived from multiplicative relationships—but from constant additive differences in the serial orders and correspondences. [Concrete empirical operations]

4 [AR 12-15]: The subject assumes proportionality but does not generalize initially to all cases. Increasingly the law is generalized and becomes explicit: The size of the shadow is directly proportional to the distance between rings and light source. [Formal method]

CENTRIFUGAL FORCE AND COMPENSATIONS

Task   *151 A14*

Given: Three metal balls of different weights are placed on a disk at 3 different distances from the center. The disk is rotated faster and faster until the balls roll off under centrifugal force. (The 3 weights are calculated to compensate exactly for the 3 distances, thus, all the balls will roll off the disk at the same time.)

The subject is asked to predict in what order the balls will leave their initial positions and why.

Stages

1-2 [AR 5-7]: The subject tends to believe that everything that occurs *has to be* as it is—no explicit reasons are given. The subject observes the factors of weight and distance, but does not relate them. [Preoperational behaviors]

3 [AR 7-11]: The subject can order the balls serially and can formulate correspondence between weights and distances, but only when the weights or distances are equal respectively. He cannot perform the multiplication of the two relationships when weights and distances are both unequal. He does not see the relationship when the two factors do not vary in the same direction. [Concrete operational method]

4 [AR 10-15]: The subject can organize the experiment without outside help and can anticipate compensations by using a system of proportional operations. Initially, he does not make specific mention of metrical proportions, but later he identifies and uses proportions to which numbers can be assigned. [Formal method]

RANDOM VARIATIONS AND CORRELATIONS

Task   *152 A15*

Given: Two previous experiments are used to examine how the subject reacts to chance and assimilates it to the deductible. (For a description of these 2 experiments see 145 A8, The conservation of motion in a horizontal plane, and 147 A10, Equilibrium in the hydraulic press.) The subject is asked to predict cases and to isolate experimental factors that are logically deductible.

Stages

1-2 [AR 5-7]: The subject's attitude toward chance is paradoxical. He denies chance—he expects the phenomenon to be repeated exactly, or in terms of a definite progression. But, when faced with fluctuations, he believes that anything is possible. He looks for a hidden order or a temporary disorder masked by invisible causes, which may be divine. [Preoperational behaviors]

3 [AR 7-12]: The subject ceases to be surprised by variability, and his predictions often take it into account. However, he is gradually disturbed

by chance ("that which resists his operations"). This generally negative attitude is based on caution and a feeling that it is hard to make predictions. Increasingly, the subject tries to find systematic causes for the fluctuations and also tries to determine their occurence. He sets boundaries for a zone of variation and later understands that deviations comprise a curve with a higher frequency in the median region and a lower frequency at the extremities. He sees variation simply as a multiplicity of causes and makes no effort to isolate respective factors. [Concrete method]

4 [AR 12–15]: The subject tries to find laws by accurately separating out variables in terms of all possible combinations, but he still encounters the fluctuation of results. Progressively, the subject forms a *correlational schema*—this entails a numerical quantification of the difference between confirming and non-confirming cases and its relationship to the total configuration. [Formal method]

The Determination of Cognitive Maps

CRITERIA USED FOR THE DETERMINATION OF EXPECTED BEHAVIORS

The problem of normalization and standardization of principles or areas of cognitive functioning involves a number of issues. Numerous studies have determined at which age a majority of children achieve the understanding of a principle. Such experimental attempts, which in part replicate the results originally obtained in Geneva, entail the delimitation of an experimental population whose background and features are carefully noted as well as a counterbalanced experimental design. Piaget cannot generally be credited for providing these data and we cannot build any form of strong, statistical standardization. From standardized results, criteria of success are determined: For instance, if at a given age, 75% of the children succeed, this age is designated as the mean age of the acquisition of the principle studied. In IQ tests this implies that the questions successfully completed by a majority at a given age will be included as part of the standardized testing procedure. These criteria can vary, ranging from 50% to 75% of the overall population depending upon the rationale used by the experimenters. From this point of view it is difficult to decide in which sense Piaget's experiments could not lead to normative, standardized tests, since there is in each principle an implicit norm. Piaget will sometimes make these criteria explicit, as is the case in Physical Causality where most chapters provide the average age of stage acquisition. Percentages are also given in recent studies; and in the *Child's Development of Early Logic,* Piaget states: "The present volume marks a departure in that it includes detailed statistical tables and gives precise indications of the number of subjects. (p. ix)" Yet these precise indications do not constitute norms. This systematization contains a type of information that involves the determination of hierarchy of behaviors and cognitive structures. Because I have presented a principle, not in order to determine an age of acquisition, but a range of years in which a given stage can occur, it provides information about the overlapping of different substages at a given age.

For instance, one observes that a 7-year-old child is at stage 3 for conservation of matter. Yet, the chart clearly indicates that it is possible for a 7-year-old to be at stage 2. This means that the sequential development observed for this principle involves an overlapping of the two stages at about age seven. This fact is important in that it allows one to establish a bridge between the individual child and the epistemic one.

The underlying thinking is as follows: Let us suppose that at age 4, stage 1 is solely represented whereas at age 5, stages 1 and 2 can both occur. This means that a child at age 5 can conceivably be at either stage. The important developmental and clinical information is that in this case, both stages are likely to be manifested by a 5-year-old. The age-ranges presented allow qualitative measure since they are not derived from a standardized procedure and population. They are also a qualitative measure in the sense that they allow the psychologist to situate a child within a range. Cognitive stages encompass ranges of normality and it is this range which has to be clinically evaluated for a particular child. This leads me to some psychodiagnostic considerations.

In his psychodiagnostic role, the psychologist has at his disposal a battery of tests and measures. Some are projective, some objective, although the criterion differentiating the two is more in terms of the type of information sought by the psychologist to establish a psychological profile. In effect, the psychologist wants to determine the extent of the child's problems, his strengths and weaknesses, his modes of thinking, and, in a global sense, his capacity for change. Thus, the psychologist wishes to determine if the child's problems are more of an emotional, cognitive, or organic nature.

Piagetian cognitive appraisal provides clinical information of a complementary nature compared to projective or classical IQ tests. Since the succession of stages is invariant, the information gathered reflects a progressive cognitive organization. A differential diagnosis leads to the determination of cognitive potentials in the child. The evaluation of delays or advances within or across cognitive areas is crucial in the understanding of detailed analysis of the thought processes and functions of the child. Using Piaget's experiments, the psychologist may qualify and determine the hierarchical cognitive organization within a child. For that purpose, the age-range sequence presented here can be of great help. The qualitative analysis of the state of equilibrium of reasoning from a set of experiments allows an "operatory diagnosis," which gives information about the cognitive gaps and strength, the areas of difficulties, and in general, the child's potential for change and learning. Such a procedure can certainly prove helpful in the determination of the influence of organic factors, neurotic disturbances, or psychotic reactions in a child's symptomatology.

The qualitative measures provided here are consistent with Piaget's own criteria for his stage theory (the concept of age-range within a stage, the invariant sequence of the emergence of cognitive structures), and helpful for a clinical diagnostic evaluation requiring some kind of quantification. I believe that an age range can serve this purpose and is an excellent tool for determining the child's overall cognitive organization in relation to himself and in relation to expected behavior patterns observed in his peers.

Continuity in cognitive development often implies overlapping of stages, and the bridge is conceptualized as a transitional stage. The determination of a cognitive map can reflect cognitive heterogeneity and/or homogeneity depending on the stage of development and the degree of transition observed in the child.

Metaphorically, the child builds parts of cognitive achievements and gradually comes to a total construction, a new structure of thought. This study lays the foundation for a better grasp of the internal hierarchy of such a construction. The problem of hierarchy is important. As long as one considers one cognitive operation (principle) at a time, the problem does not arise. But that approach treats development as isolated, atomistic pieces of behavior, a view in real contrast with that of Piaget.

To stress, as he does, the idea of structure, is also to stress the necessity of establishing the relationship that exists between cognitive principles. The fundamental question is to determine which structures, which come next, and the interrelationships they encompass. Questions concerning the determination of cognitive prerequisites are still open experimental problems and their study is essential for a better understanding of the mechanisms of development and of learning.

On a practical level, the psychologist wants to determine the extent to which the child's cognitive organization is normal, advanced, or delayed, and in which areas. Furthermore the child may display different levels of achievement in problems involving similar mental operations. It refers to the notion of horizontal decalages as they are found for example in the notion of conservation. Here matter precedes weight, which precedes volume. Matter constitutes a necessary prerequisite for the understanding of weight and yet involves the same mental operation of conservation applied to different contents. Conservation is but one domain of cognitive functioning, and the problem of hierarchy goes beyond the situation within a domain. In this respect it is worthwhile noting the remarkable experiments actually carried out in Geneva dealing with learning and using intersecting domains of cognitive functioning. In general, each stage is characterized by an overall structure as well.

It is important to distinguish different types of structures at different levels of organization. For instance, seriation, which is logically defined as an asymmetric, transitive, relationship, has a structure in itself. Yet seriation is part of elementary logic, which has its own structure in which operations such as classification also belong. Both classification and seriation are part of the field of elementary logic.

To take another example, the principle of horizontality, which consists in the understanding of the fact that the level of the water is lined up with an external referent and not a proximate container, has a structure in itself. Yet horizontality is also part of the area of space, which has again its own structure. When one unites with this the concepts of movement, measure, speed, and time, one covers the domain of infra-logical operations, whose structure is different from that of elementary logic.

One can in fact differentiate between the structure of a principle, the structure of an area, and the structure of a domain of cognitive functioning; and it is their simultaneous ascertainment that gives us the cognitive map of a real child. The concrete operational period of thought refers to an underlying logical organization and as such refers to a new structure of thought. It is in this sense that Piaget states that each structure results from the preceding one, that the sequence of stages is invariant, and that each new structure integrates and reorganizes the preceding one. It should be stressed that although each new structure reorganizes the previous one, this does not mean that the previous one disappears. On the contrary, it continues to exist under a reorganized form, and it is this fact that probably leads a normal individual to be normally heterogeneous.

Piaget's statement that intellectual development does not consist in simple linear cumulative changes but in structural changes has yet another consequence: These changes can take place at different moments of a child's life, dependent not only on internal factors of development but also on external circumstances. One of the main aspects of Piaget's theory is his constant stress upon a dialectic between the subject and the object, in terms of assimilation and accommodation, which results in different types of equilibrium at each moment of intellectual life.

If equilibrium refers to the state of the organism at a give time, equilibration relates to the dynamic aspect of cognitive development, a mechanism of change and not a simple descriptive entity. But there is a complex problem here in relationship to the factors of development. For instance, consideration of the formal level of thought entails not only the question of its presence or absence within an individual, but also questions of the intervention of social factors that may permeate change. The resulting change of structure is a realized potential only among some adolescents. For others it is not present but could take place given proper educational conditions. In still other cases, it is beyond the reach of the individual. Such situations must of course be studied with great precaution, and this volume may be of great help in distinguishing among these different situations.

The determination of age-range allows for the construction of what could be referred to as a cognitive map that may be highly useful in examining the determined cognitive organization of a particular child. Use of the chart will thus allow to assess the quality of observed behaviors in terms of abnormality, normality and, to a certain degree, to quantify this qualitfication.

In order to make the determination of age range let me reiterate my line of reasoning. For instance in Experiment 48 N4, Piaget determines three stages. The total age-range for the three stages covers 4–9 years of age. At age 4 most of the children are at stage 1. The age range of stage 1 is from 4–6, whereas stage 2 begins at 5 and ends at 7. Thus some 5 years old subjects can be either at stage 1 or 2. Thus a 5-year-old child can be at either of the two stages. From a theoretical point of view this reflects an overlapping. On another hand there is no real expectation that a 5-year-old child be at stage 3. Therefore a child who is at stage 3 at 5 years is clearly advanced.

At age 6 one observes that a child can be either at stage 1, 2, or 3. We observe a new overlapping this time of three stages (1, 2, and 3) at age 6. Age 7 is marked by the disappearance of stage 1, and the persistence of stage 2. This means that a 7-year-old child is possibly at either stage 2 or stage 3. Should he be at stage 1, this would indicate a real delay, approximately a delay of one year. Similarly, 8- and 9-year-olds are generally at stage 3; hence neither stage 2 nor stage 1 is considered normal development for children after age 7. Naturally, to be at stage 1 at 8 years of age constitutes a more serious delay than to be at stage 2 at that age.

I would like to emphasize again that one of the useful purposes of experimenting with children á la Piaget is to gain understanding of how they solve a given principle. The idea of success is not the emphasis of the experimentation. Success can be achieved through different types of strategy. For example in seriation in stage 2 and 3, the child will construct a correct seriation. Yet both strategies are inherently qualitatively different. For stage 2 the child will use a method of trial and error. In stage 3 he will use a systematic method expressing through behavior rather than success the quality of his cognitive performance.

The problem of achieving a given principle at a given age, further raises the question of determining if the principle can be achieved by using only a concrete logic or if formal operations are necessary for its resolution. For instance, conservation of matter poses no problem since stage 3 which ends at 9 years of age is logically the last possible stage. Experiment 10 G10 on the other hand, is achieved at the level of formal thought, and thus stage 4 is logically required.

For each principle I have indicated if the resolution requires concrete or formal logic. Among all the cases I have examined, few presented serious problems for the theory. Such a consistency suggests the reliability of a structural point of view. To find but few problematical examples within more than 150 experiments is not in itself proof of the validity of stages, but it is a strong indication of their reliability. Furthermore, when one considers that more than 30 years of Geneva's work are covered here (even if in terms of selective cross-sections), one will readily observe that one result of this systematization is to uncover the coherence of Piaget's experiments.

Piaget likes to call himself a revisionist, yet his revisions remain within a consistent paradigm of research. It is worth noticing that this paradigm is in itself flexible enough to sustain changes, modifications and developments without losing that consistency. Evident in this is the real adaptive power of Piaget's theory and structural outlook. While this is a qualification of the results, it is certainly useful information to have.

The determination of an expected occurrence of behavior also presents the possibility of establishing qualitative types of developmental patterns, whose informational value is of interest. There are a number of observations to be made.

The lowest age on the chart is 2 years of age, and generally Piaget's descriptions begin at age 4. The upper limit is 15 years of age and most of the expected behaviors are manifest within these age boundaries. Thus, the total age range is 12 years for all experiments, but most commonly 11 years, since most of the experiments begin with 4-year-olds. Of course, practically speaking, this does not mean that one can begin these experiments only with 2- or 4-year-old children. On the contrary, the limits of practical experimentation should be determined by the child one investigates, not arbitrarily by age. This is again consistent with a stage theory. It is essentially in order to achieve some uniformity in the presentation that these limits are determined. Furthermore, the formal level of thought certainly goes beyond 15 years of age, and this age should be considered as a qualitative limit rather than a norm.

Epilogue

The individual child, in school or undergoing a clinical diagnosis, faces a difficult problem: the tools that educators, teachers, psychologists, psychiatrists, and experimenters have at their disposal can only approximate his real internal organization.

How he emerges today and what potentials he has are continual challenges for anyone involved in studying the growth and the problems of childhood. As I have stressed earlier, the systematization offered here, although incomplete, can serve a profoundly useful purpose: the determination of potentialities of children not only in terms of their actual performances but also in terms of their areas of underlying competence or difficulties. It is my hope that this study will be helpful to children. In a profound sense it has been made by them. It reflects their thinking, their points of view, their intents, their beliefs, and their comprehension. It is my hope that its good use will help us realize and respect the fundamental fact that children are qualitatively different human beings and not adults in reduction.

It is because of this hope that this book is devoted to them. In short, my presentation, which entails the logical principle explored, a description of the task, a brief summary of the behaviors observed at different stages and age-ranges, is mainly meant as a guideline to follow, should one repeat the experiment. In many cases, I have felt that the stages description, or the presentation of the task or the principle explored could have been more fully detailed. Yet I wanted to provide the reader with a spectrum of Piagetian tasks as they are reported by Piaget and his collaborators.

In this respect one of the principles I have followed has been to be as respectful as possible of Piaget's intent in the use of the clinical method and in the elaboration of his theory. The present diversified overview is quite useful in the sense that is allows a better acquaintance, knowledge and understanding of Piaget's implications, in restituting the true observational basis of Piaget's theory. This presentation is thus meant to provide the reader with a "feeling" for Piaget and his method of enquiry. I hope to have reached in some ways this objective.

To complete a study of this type has connotations other than strictly cognitive ones. For me it was simultaneously fascinating, interesting, absorbing, and sometimes frustrating. I have studied in Geneva, and Piaget is someone toward whom I have deep feelings. I know him well and do not think it is possible to interact with him without in many ways being profoundly influenced. I am deeply grateful for the training I received, for the chance I had to observe and comprehend the world of children within this framework. I am very fortunate to have come to know Piaget personally as well as a friend. He is someone toward whom I have respect, admiration and, to use a non-cognitive term, a great deal of liking. These feelings certainly stem equally from the work as well as the person. Piaget has been for me a teacher in the Socratic sense of the word.

As an epilogue I thought it would be of value to include some of my reflections about the Piagetian school, its contributions and developments. An interesting question to ask is how the Geneva School has been able, for more than 40 years, to produce almost invariably original studies and experiments. What makes Piaget's approach, no matter what one thinks of it or how one interprets is, so creative? Where else can one find a place where the child's world has been so thoroughly investigated for such a long, sustained period of time? These questions obviously deal with the very nature of creativity; and, irrespective of individual orientation, almost everyone has come to recognize the enormous impact of the Piagetian School.

A great deal of astonishment arises from this consideration alone, and I am today not sure of the reasons why the Genevan School is so consistently creative. The first explanation that comes to mind is of course Piaget, the scholar. Yet to answer the question in this way is to make creative work the result of one individual. I do not think that such is the case because the Geneva productions have always been the result of a team of people working together.

To use a metaphor, a hero is never alone but is always supported by a crowd. A hero has distinct individual features, but these featuers are fostered and to a great extent supported and enchanced by the people with whom he interacts. In many ways, Piaget has been such a hero.

It is interesting to note the modus operandi of the interaction between Piaget and his team since it certainly contributes to the answer. Let me begin by describing the initial moment at which Piaget has in mind the concept he intends to explore. Usually at the beginning of the academic year he explains the concept, giving no hypotheses, and essentially leaving us with the burden of coming up with some experiments. This then gives birth to a number of preliminary investigations or pilot studies. The team meets once a week to discuss results and step by step the concept under scrutiny comes to have a life of its own, through the children seen. At the end of the year the team is often still unsure of the hypothesis and interpretations. Piaget then packs a bag with protocols and reports and disappears for the summer in the mountains. Usually he comes back in autumn with a completed book.

Piaget's creativity might have something to do with mountains and solitude but this synthesis between cooperation and individual work has always had for me the quality of uniqueness. Probably the most durable message I received from Piaget is the seemingly simple fact that creativity and discipline are necessary complements.

Certainly a careful study should be geared to make this dialectic explicit. The epistemology of Piaget's own creativity has yet to be done. In this respect, there is no a priori contradiction between a psychoanalytic and a cognitive point of view. Rather, I see them as complementary and equally necessary. Yet, that Piaget never studies affectivity is not a relevant criticism from my point of view. In a profound sense, the study of the relationship between intelligence and affectivity as it can be seen today, would not have been possible without the results of the Geneva school. Affectivity has become an open experimental question precisely as a result of the Genevan inquiries, and I would say that if Piaget had extended himself in that direction, his epistemological enterprise might not have been as successful as it was.

I was pondering these considerations when I came to interact with a child in a community college. His mother was working, I was waiting in the hall outside her office, and the child was sitting in an office chair. He was making the chair roll back and forth. I began talking and playing with this 4-year-old, and as I pushed him along the hall in his chair, I asked him what his speed was. He said he was going "fast." Varying the speed, I asked him to tell me what was happening. I noticed that he did not possess the comparative; for him, the terms "slower" and "faster" did not make sense. I made up a game in which he would decide the speed at which he would proceed: fast, slow. At a certain point, I told him that in order to vary his speed, he should say "slower" or "the slowest," or "fast" or "the fastest," and matched my action to his word. Very soon, the child began to comprehend the meaning of the comparative and the absolute, and to use them correctly, as a result of his experience, as a result of his own actions. In short, he got the concept through what could be considered an experimental procedure. It was for me a real source of insight. First, it is highly unusual to witness the spontaneous emergence of a new cognitive concept in a child. In this case, I felt that the child did not know the meaning of the comparative at the beginning of this experience, but used it routinely afterward. How this learning occurred was also very clear to me. It was in effect a beautiful demonstration of Piaget's main hypothesis that abstract concepts are internalized actions. It was through his own actions that the child came to comprehend this new concept.

At this point this experience was properly part of the realm of cognition alone, but the child then began asking me to go faster whenever we passed the open door of his mother's office. He had apparently been waiting for her quite a while, and I suspected that he was using his newly acquired concept to express some underlying feelings he had towards his mother. This hypothesis was verified by turning his chair toward the door just as we approached it. The boy told me not to do so go faster, not to stop. "Go the fastest," he would say each time we would pass in front of the door. He would not establish any contact with his mother. Yet after a while the mother noticed us playing and came out of her office for a second, without saying anything. The very next time that we played our game again, the boy asked me to go slowly when approaching in front of the door and to turn his chair "the slowest." When facing his mother he said: "I see you now."

I do not know how much psychotherapy took place during our interaction or how much of it was cognitive or experimental. In any case, this event came to symbolize very well what I intended to say in this epilogue. Any experinece comes to represent a sort of synthesis between cognitive and emotional aspects in which categorizations vary in terms of label, in which distinction between one ways of looking at the child do or do not make sense for the child. His experience and the content are the important variables. I think that the personality of the child, the nature of our interaction with him, and its outcomes also determine the labels through which we come to know him, and how we might come to understand his thought processes, has been very much a part of this study.

References

Gödel K. (1931) Uber Formal Unentscheibare Sätze der Principia Mathematica und Verwandte Systeme I. Monatshefte für Mathematik und Physik Vol. 38.

Inhelder B. (1970) Initially quoted in Discussion on Child Development Vol. I. Proceedings of the First Meeting of WHO Study Group on the Psychobiological Development of the Child. Geneva (1953) New York IUP.

McCulloch. W. (1965) Embodiments of Mind. The MIT Press, Cambridge, Mass.

Piaget J. (1927) La Causalité Physique chez l'Enfant. Paris, Alcan. Translated as The Child's Conception of Causality. New Jersey, Littlefield Adams Paterson (1960).

Piaget J. (with Szeminska A.) (1941) La Genèse du Nombre chez l'Enfant. Neuchâtel et Paris, Delachaux et Niestlé. Translated as The Child's Conception of Number. London, Routledge and Kegan (1952).

Piaget J. (1946) Le Développement de la Notion de Temps chez l'Enfant Paris, P.U.F. Translated as The Child's Conception of Time. London, Routledge and Kegan (1969).

Piaget J. (1946) Les Notions de Mouvement et de Vitesse chez l'Enfant. Paris, P.U.F. Translated as The Child's Conception of Movement and Speed. London, Routledge and Kegan (1970).

Piaget J. (with Inhelder B. and Szeminska A.) (1948) La Géométrie Spontanée de l'Enfant. Paris, P.U.F. Translated as the Child's Conception of Geometry. London, Routledge and Kegan (1960).

Piaget J. (with Inhelder B.) (1948) La Représentation de l'Espace chez l'Enfant. Paris, P.U.F. Translated as The Child's Conception of Space. London, Routledge and Kegan (1956).

Piaget J. (with Inhelder B.) (1955) De La Logique de l'Enfant à la Logique de l'Adolescent. Paris, P.U.F. Translated as The Growth of Logical Thinking From Childhood to Adolescence. New York, Basic Books (1958).

Piaget J. (with Inhelder B.) (1959) La Genèse des Structures Logiques Elementaires. Classifications et Sériations. Neuchâtel et Paris. Delachaux et Niestlé. Translated as The Early Growth of Logic in the Child. Classification and Seriation. London, Routledge and Kegan (1964).

Piaget J. (1964) Six Etudes de Psychologie. Genève. Ed. Gonthier S. A. Translated as Six Psychological Studies. New York, Random House (1967).

Piaget J. (1970) Seminar Notes. Washington, D.C. Catholic University. June 1970. Mimeograph.

Piaget J. (1972) Seminar Notes. City College and the Graduate Center of the City University of New York. New York, June 1972. Mimeograph.

SUMMARY INDEX OF STAGES

TASKS: INDEX OF BEHAVIORS
(AGE-RANGE/STAGE SPAN)
EXPECTED OCCURENCE OF
BEHAVIORS (EOB)

GEOMETRY

Stages   2   3   4   5   6   7   8   9   10   11   12   13   14   15   Ages

205

2 3 4 5 6 7 8 9 10 11 12 13 14 15 Ages

16 G16 1
        2
        3

17 G17 1
        2
        3

18 G18 1
        2
        3
        4

19 G19 1
        2
        3
        4

SPACE

20 S1   1
        2
        3

21 S2   1
        2
        3

22 S3   1
        2
        3

23 S4   1
        2
        3

24 S5   1
        2
        3

25 S6   1-2
        3
        4

26 S7   1-2
        3
        4

27 S8   1
        2
        3

28 S9   1
        2
        3

29 S10 1
        2
        3
        4

207

NUMBER (cc.)

Ages

208

NUMBER (cc.)   2   3   4   5   6   7   8   9   10   11   12   13   14   15   Ages

Stages

64 N20   1
  2
  3

65 N21   1
  2
  3

66 N22   1
  2
  3

67 N23   1
  2
  3

68 N24   1
  2
  3

69 N25   1
  2
  3

TIME

70 T1   1
  2
  3

71 T2   1
  2
  3

72 T3   1
  2
  3

73 T4   1
  2
  3

74 T5   1-2a
  2b
  3

75 T6   1
  2
  3

76 T7   1
  2
  3

MOVEMENT AND SPEED

PHYSICAL CAUSALITY

212

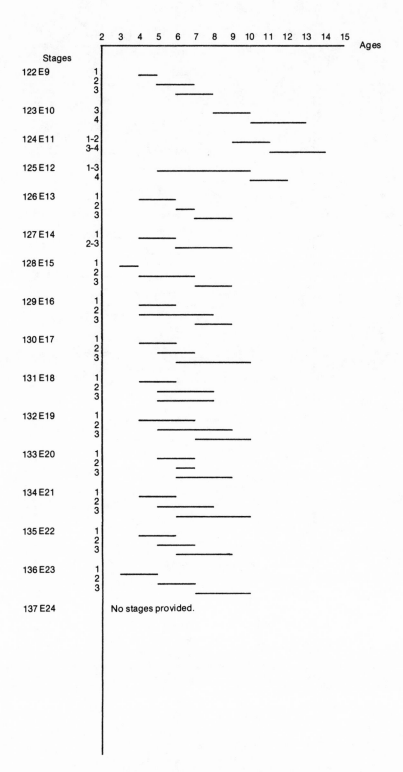

Stages		2 3 4 5 6 7 8 9 10 11 12 13 14 15	Ages

Stages

138 A1 1-2 / 3 / 4

139 A2 1-2 / 3 / 4

140 A3 1-2 / 3 / 4

141 A4 1-2 / 3 / 4

142 A5 1-2 / 3 / 4

143 A6 1-2 / 3 / 4

144 A7 1-2 / 3 / 4

145 A8 1-2 / 3 / 4

146 A9 1-2 / 3 / 4

147 A10 1-2 / 3 / 4

148 A11 1-2 / 3 / 4

149 A12 1-2 / 3 / 4

150 A13 1-2 / 3 / 4

151 A14 1-2 / 3 / 4

152 A15 1-2 / 3 / 4

Ages